The Adventures of ι.

Thornton Wilder's *Our Town* comes to California! This author's debut offering contains perfectly captured scenes and textures from his life growing up in Napa, California. One of the first wave of Baby Boomers (born 1946) he describes poignantly, sometimes painfully, and always joyously the fabric of small town life in the 1950s and 1960s. In describing his coming of age, this author has the gift to see and understand the power of a mother's love, the power of fortitude, the power of forgiveness, and the ability to share all of that intimately with his readers.

This volume provides a rich history of Napa during the post-War years. An offspring of the Greatest Generation, this work by the first of the Baby Boomers is an important chronicle to read now, and for future generations.

Richard A. Bennett
Napa Superior Court Judge (Ret.)

I thoroughly enjoyed this book!! It documents the simple and wholesome lifestyle of a kid growing up in Napa in the '50s and early '60s, while exposing the unspoken side of the community and family interaction during that period. It was a wonderful trip back to my own childhood growing up in Napa. Like the author, I grew up In Alta Heights (Bonita Ave) and visited many of the locations he talks about in the book. Thanks for taking me back to a simpler time in a wonderful community!

Steve Potter
Chief of Napa Police

The perfect gift for the aging Baby Boomer? Try *The Adventures of the Squeezebox Kid* by Ray Guadagni. He may have been a non-reader as a child ... Playing instead with plastic toy soldiers and cowboys, and smelling the glue on the model kits ... But he is a wonderful writer.

His descriptions are spot on, and not specific to his growing up in Napa. I know this because my husband—born in 1948, and raised in a working class Chicago suburb neighborhood—laughed and laughed as he read Ray's book. Jujubes and grandma Nonni and Big Al will be almost too familiar to readers.

Napa today may be different than a lot of other places in the U.S., but in the post-WWII era, the fabulous 50s—Napa was just another sleepy middle-class town. Ray Guadagni brings every Baby Boomer's fond childhood memories to life in his very entertaining memoir. You will not stop laughing. And you will relive your own childhood in a very fun way.

Not unlike Jean Shepherd's now classic *A Christmas Story* and its heartwarming description of a small boy and his family in the 1940s, this memoir brings to life childhood in a typical blue collar 1950s town.

Diane Dillon
Napa County Supervisor

"Get out of the house, it's a nice day!"

And we did.

Ray has captured how the Greatest Generation shaped our own. A nostalgic account for baby boomers and a guide for our children to help them understand where we come from. Ray's openness is touching—I played right field too.

Scott Sedgley
Napa City Councilmember and lifelong Napan

Using this book alone, one could reconstruct with exactness, a lost time and place. Ray Guadagni has a novelist's eye for detail and an honest, humorous, and poignant understanding of what daily life meant. Having been born and raised in Napa (my family going back to the 1870s), Ray touched my sense of nostalgia in an honest and moving way! Great read!

Daniel Lonergan
Retired police officer and lifetime Napa resident

My family, Wagenknecht, moved to Napa in 1960. I was a kindergartener. Napa was known for its state hospital. We were all closer to our heritages; Wagenknechts were German. There were more ethnic neighborhoods. Parents didn't hover. Get out of the house till mom hollers your names from the porch or the streetlights come on. I loved growing up here. Ray has brought us back in time to experience this place through his well-spun story told with head and heart.

Brad Wagenknecht
Napa County Supervisor

This book captures growing up in Napa in the '50s and '60s and brought back a lot of memories of the "good ole days." It is truly a great memoir and brought back a lot of the Italian heritage that was so prominent in Napa at the time.

Ray's description of the people and the places of the time took me back and was a very accurate description of the way it was. A great book that anyone from Napa would enjoy.

Gary Garaventa
Napa native and business owner

My family were weekenders in Napa from San Francisco during the 1950s and 60s. Ray Guadagni's warm, wry, and caring tales of Napa during that period made me feel as if I had lived here instead of just Sunday afternoons at the Wright Spot or a day at the Town and Country Fair. Having been a Napanese full time for almost 50 years and knowing most of the people Ray describes, his poignant portraits of our "still nurturing community" makes me grateful that I chose Napa as our home also.

John Tuteur
Napa County Assessor

As someone who was born and raised in Napa, I enjoyed reading this authentic description of how Napa was growing up in the '50s and '60s...
I felt like I was going down memory lane!

Bill Dodd
California State Assembly Member

THE ADVENTURES OF
THE SQUEEZEBOX KID

Raymond A. Guadagni

Ideas into Books® WESTVIEW
Kingston Springs, Tennessee

Ideas into Books®
W E S T V I E W
P.O. Box 605
Kingston Springs, TN 37082
www.publishedbywestview.com

ISBN 978-1-62880-104-0

First edition, October 2016

Photo credits: The author gratefully acknowledges permission to use the two traffic patrol photos on pages 206 and 211. Photos courtesy of Napa Police Historical Society.

Printed in the United States of America on acid free paper.

Acknowledgments

I have received valuable help from many people. I would like to thank here those who generously gave me their time for interviews—providing me their recollections—or who supplied photographs or other material.

I must first of all thank my dear friend Paul Vallerga. He was so generous in furnishing me his superb recollections, material, and photographs, and was always there for me to talk to about this endeavor.

In no particular order, I want to thank Mary Butler, Sheila Daugherty, Doug Ernst, James Ford, Alexandra Brown, Jerry Davis, Bill Forsythe, Ellwin Jobe, Ken Harbison, Fred Teeters, Mike Kerns, Frank Davidson, Wayne Davidson, Mike Crane, Ken Lloyd, Detective Todd Shulman, Eugene Guadagni, Julia DeNatale, Christopher DeNatale, Angela Carreon, Orlando Carreon, Doug Murray, Bob Benning, Ron Biagi, Don McConnell, Mike McLaughlin, Harriet Martini, Valerie Martini, Jackie Martini, Jonette Pittore Beck, Jeannette Cameron, Scott Sedgley, Larry Hamilton, James Jones, Steve Ceriani, Joe Flax, Joel Tranmer, Terry Simpkins, Bill Jabin, Judge Phillip A. Champlin, (ret.), Kristen Bush McMillan, Bruce Erricson, Len Casanega, Wayne "Blackie" Miller, Judge Michael S. Williams, Larry Fontana, and Randy Snowden.

To those who have also given me help in this effort, but I have neglected to mention, please forgive me. I am old, and with age, memory fails. Indeed, when you bring my lapse to my attention, know that I will thank you profusely at that time.

Mostly, I want to thank my wife, Ann. Since I married Ann on November 2, 1974, I have enjoyed a life of assisted living. That status is usually reserved for the very elderly, but not in my case. Ann has fully supported me in every way imaginable, and no less so in this endeavor. She has given me more help than I can list here.

Prologue

The United States was on top of the world in the 1950s. It was the end of World War II, and our country was experiencing prosperity that it had never known before. Instead of our economy producing weapons and war machines on a large scale, we were manufacturing new cars, affordable suburban homes, television sets, record players, home appliances, gadgets, toys, and more. It was an era of optimism. People could now provide material things for themselves and their children that they could never have afforded before. It was an era of consuming, purchasing, and providing.

On the other hand, the 1950s were also years of great conflict and anxiety. The Korean War, the weapons race, the space race, the battle against communism at home and abroad, the polio scare, and the civil rights movement collectively produced divisions in American society and a painful uneasiness in our state of mind. These, in turn, caused concern about our future both at home and around the world.

As a child of the '50s, I wasn't fully aware of the stressors in our society, but they shaped the context in which I was raised. Of course I was affected by some things more than others. I knew of the polio scare in no uncertain terms. I knew of the civil rights movement only because of television. The divide and prejudice against African Americans didn't touch me in my young life because in my personal experience, there were no African Americans in Napa; of course, the reasons for that never occurred to me in my youth. I was very young, but I knew of the Korean war, although I didn't know anything about Korea (including its location) except that they were our enemy and some of my family's friends' children were fighting over there. I had a vague understanding of atomic bombs, but it was more from watching monster movies featuring creatures that mutated into monsters—as a result of the radioactive fallout caused by explosions of nuclear weapons—than from any scientific or historical understanding. The atomic era was more exciting than worrisome to me (until the Cuban Missile Crisis in the early 1960s, of course—I was old enough to have the wits scared out of me by then).

In those days, Napa was not yet known as a great wine-producing region. It was known even then for its agriculture, although prunes, not grapes were the predominant crop; but it was equally known for the Napa State Hospital that housed the mentally ill. To us kids, however, Napa was a place to pick prunes to earn money and to play with our friends. It was a sleepy little town. For me, growing up in Napa, California in the 1950s was a simple and happy time of life.

I was fortunate to be able to have fun with my friends, go to school, and watch *Hopalong Cassidy* and *Howdy Doody* on television. The stressors affecting our parents must have spilled over to us in some ambiguous manner, making life not as simple, happy, or stress-free as it seemed. Still and all, my recollections, such as they are, are mostly fun-filled childhood memories.

Everything written here actually happened, plus or minus a few details, though some of the names have been changed so as not to embarrass anyone.

As Anais Nin said, "We don't see things as they are; we see things as we are."

Table of Contents

CHAPTER 1

The Girls of Little Italy

I was born into an Italian-American community in East Napa appropriately known as Little Italy.

By the time I made my entrance into the world on October 24, 1946, the geographic footprint of Little Italy was well established. In the 1920s, '30s and '40s, there had been plenty of Italian families living in the eastern part of town known as Alta Heights. By the time I arrived, Little Italy consisted of the eastern portions of First, Third, and Fourth Streets to Silverado Trail, and up the hill into lower Alta Heights.

The families on Third and Fourth Streets in my immediate neighborhood were the Guistos, Marchinis, Buonventuras, Grattones, Martinis, Squicciarinis, Pittores, and of course, my family, the Guadagnis.

Except for my older brother and me, all of the Italian neighborhood kids were girls.

These included the five daughters of Ernest and Gussie Martini: Joyce, Marlene, Harriett, Valerie, and Jacquelyn; Toni Williams (whose mother's maiden name was Squicciarini); Jonette Pittore (the spitting image of Annette Funicello, a beautiful Italian child star on Walt Disney's *Mickey Mouse Club* show from 1955-58); and Jeannette Cameron, whose mother's maiden name was Guisto.

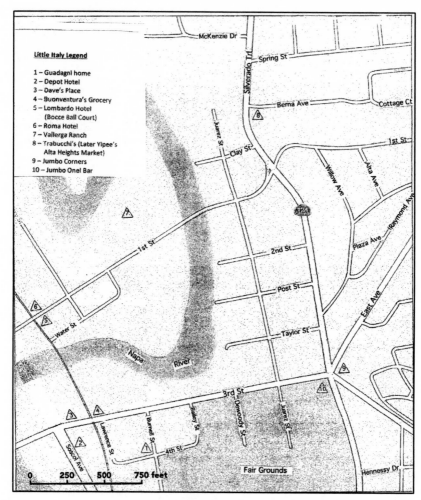

Map of Little Italy.

Expanding the circle beyond my immediate neighborhood, Little Italy included families with names that traced their lineage from Lucca, Genoa, Rome, Milan, Naples, Sicily, and beyond.

It seemed to me that everyone in Napa was Italian. Consider the roster for the Italian Catholic Federation Old Man's Softball Team, taken from the Napa Register's May 9, 1958, issue: F. Sanza, Lou Brazzi, Rome Brazzi, Fred Negri, Leno Negri, Angelo Paoli, Ang

Del Carlo, Bill Cerletti, Oliver Casagranda, John Zanardi, Nick Grimoldi, Lou Avanzino, George Bottari, Larry Zunnino, and Ray Guiducci.

As the Register article stated, "The Old Men's League is now in its 13th year of operation. In that time, the ICF has won the league championship nine times, copping the title in 1945, '48, '49, '51, '52, '53, '55, '56 and '57." By Napa standards, they were as important as the New York Yankees, the dominant team of that same era.

Italians began immigrating to Napa in the 1860s to work on the railroad or in agriculture. More Italians arrived following the 1906 San Francisco earthquake, fleeing from that disaster and relocating to east Napa to start new lives.

My parents moved from San Francisco to Napa after their marriage in 1942. My father's name was Alvin Aspartico Guadagni; his ancestors hailed from Lucca and Rome. My mother's name was Anne Mary Guadagni. Her maiden name was Bianchina, making me full-blooded Italian. Her ancestors were from a tiny village called Rongio, north of Milan, in the Piedmont region of northern Italy. Due to a French influence in her village, she spoke French, Italian, and English.

The Italians I knew were self-sufficient, and knew how to live off the land. No matter how small one's backyard was, everyone had an Italian garden of vegetables and herbs, including plenty of basil, garlic, and rosemary. If space allowed, there were fruit trees as well. My best friend Paul Vallerga's family ranch on First Street produced enough food to feed their large family; they could fish in the Napa River, which flowed behind their ranch; and they raised chickens and cows.

What they couldn't grow or raise on their ranch, they obtained by bartering at small Italian general stores like Trabucchi's or Buonventura's, where credit was given and bartering was accepted. Here the Italians could trade their produce, fish, and meats for sundries. The proprietors would let the Italian children get candy and drinks, keeping tally sheets, and billing the families at the end of the month.

The older Italians only spoke Italian because they did not know English. Everyone took care of each other. They were devoted to family and friends. They were hard workers, but work was a means to an end: what they wanted was to garden, hunt, fish, play music, dance, play cards and bocce ball, take vacations, raise families, enjoy their friends, and help each other. The simple things in life gave them joy.

As children typically do, we played games, but the difference for me was that I was the youngest in the neighborhood, and, except for my brother Eugene, all the other kids were girls. Because of that, we only played games the girls wanted to play. When we played clubhouse, I was the junior member with all the rights that are usually conferred on a junior member—in other words, none. If we played house, I was always the baby. This was good and bad. I was always being cuddled by a cute neighbor girl, but I also had no spoken lines—I just cried when they told me to. I often over-acted my part, crying a lot more than they wanted me to, so they would have to pick me up and cuddle me. As soon as they figured out what I was doing, they shut that down quickly, so most of the time I was quiet except when they wanted noise from me.

If I didn't have a cameo as the baby, I wasn't in the play at all. Instead, I was a designated customer because audience members were hard to come by. I didn't like these plays, but I did get in free. The older girls wrote these plays to target either younger kids or our parents. Either way, attendance was sparse. Good thing, because I can only imagine the reviews had a drama critic attended:

> *This play lacked a plot; there was no character development; the play seemed to self-adjust,*

depending on who was speaking. Corrections were commonly made by the oldest actor during the performance. This play hopefully and mercifully will close after one performance. It is the worst play I have ever seen; a complete waste of time. Its only redeeming value is that it got me out of the office for an hour. Still, I would rather poke my eyes out than ever watch it again.

My brother Eugene and the neighborhood girls.

The older girls had access to trunks of dress-up clothes, which they never failed to pull out for their performances. Sometimes they made their own costumes. To call the costumes crude and simple would take the term understatement to a new level. Pathetic is more accurate. In my few roles as an infant, I was usually wrapped in a smelly, old, moth-eaten wool blanket. I was very believable in the role of a baby, mainly because these plays were usually shown during the summer, and I was so hot and itchy that my whining was genuine.

The plays were usually about a family, with the older girls playing both the father and mother roles and the younger girls, playing children. Some of the plays had themes, depending on the season. Christmas and Halloween plays were put on with far less practice time than the summer plays, because we were in school and had little time to prepare. However, no matter how much time we had, the plays never seemed to improve or evolve. Producers and directors never changed, nor did the actors or their parts. Consistency was the hallmark of all our productions.

Almost every role and every game we played was determined by the queen of the neighborhood kids, Jeepie, whose real name was Marietta. One of the older girls, she was a big girl, physically, and she was not Italian. She seemed to have a lot of material things that the rest of us never had. Consequently, Jeepie ruled the neighborhood.

Jeepie's father, Bill, owned a high-end men's clothing store in Fairfield. One time she wanted to form a Hopalong Cassidy fan club. Her father got T-shirts for all the kids with a cowboy logo. We thought that was super cool and were inspired to make by-laws for the club.

Jeepie had a big raft which the girls spent days cleaning. When one of the girls would get in with dirty feet, Jeepie would make the offender get out and sit for whatever period of time Jeepie arbitrarily determined. After the time out, the girl might be allowed back in the raft, but not always. On occasion, girls would go home and cry to their mothers because of Jeepie's banishment from the raft.

Me in my costume prior to a theatrical production.

This once happened to Valerie and Jackie Martini, and resulted in their mother, Gussie, giving them a lesson on ownership.

"It is her raft and she can do what she wants. Now just stay home and play here, she will get over it soon," Gussie advised in her reassuring, nurturing manner.

Jeepie had a dog called Pepper. We painted bright red lipstick on Pepper's jowls in the shape of human lips. After a couple of days the hair around the dog's mouth turned white. Everyone was afraid we were going to get in trouble, but to our great relief, no one ever said a word about it.

Not all of our time was devoted to plays and lipstick. Sometimes we put on talent shows which consisted of a variety of acts, much like the television variety shows of the era—programs like the *Arthur Godfrey Show* and *The Ed Sullivan Show*. Like these shows, we also offered a variety of acts. Unlike these shows, we were amateurs.

In the acrobatic acts, Jeepie always assigned herself the part requiring the greatest physical strength, and Valerie was usually the one climbing on top of Jeepie, since Valerie was smaller and lighter. Jackie, also known as "Bones" Martini, was by far the smallest, youngest, and lightest of the girls, and therefore the easiest to lift and throw high into the sky. Because Jackie was only a few months older than me, sometimes she was deemed too little to be thrown around.

Also, Jackie and I were considered too young to have gained the crucial knowledge and expertise required to perform these complicated acts.

Although I was sometimes excluded from these acts, I didn't mind being in the audience when I could sit next to Jackie, because she was very cute, always seemed to be clean, and was only about twelve inches taller than I was. She had the same beautiful, long, auburn hair as her mother, which was always exquisitely braided. I didn't realize it at the time, but the difference in Jackie's and my heights was just the beginning of an issue that would plague me with girls for a long time.

The older girls clearly believed they were genuine circus material and would someday be performing on the road under the Big Top. Watching their gyrations and complex acrobatic moves, I bought in completely. They were the real deal to me, and I secretly aspired to one day take Jeepie's place. I had the right build and strength.

The girls would develop names for their acrobatic acts based on the specific moves and their various degrees of difficulty. For example, one was called *The Arm Pitty*. Jeepie would lie on the floor, put her arms under Valerie's arm pits, prop her leg up and suspend Valerie in the air. I used to get chills watching the climax when Valerie spread her arms and legs like she was flying in the air. There should have been a drum roll followed by a crashing cymbal at completion. As a good audience member I clapped as loudly as my chubby little hands could manage.

The girls never had a shortage of costumes, because they were allowed to rummage through their parents' old trunks for clothing from earlier eras. Usually these were hand-me-downs from their parents or grandparents, and included clothes for male roles, although that was never a priority to our group. Valerie once did a soft-shoe routine appropriately called *The Soft Shoe Routine*, in which she wore her grandfather's long johns, a man's big white shirt, tap shoes, a black cane, and a black top hat. Garbed in this attractive outfit she would dance to music from a small 78-speed record player. She was fabulous.

When I was five, I started playing the accordion. It seemed all Italian kids took accordion lessons at some point in their lives, so taking the lessons was not unusual. What *was* unusual was to take lessons at such a young age. My lessons were given in the basement of our landlady, Lilly Cameron (née Guisto)'s house. My teacher, Willie Ferranato, was a kind, older, Italian gentleman with a genuine musical talent.

I started out playing a very small 12-base, but within a few months moved up to a full-sized 120-base accordion. It was too big for me. I couldn't play it standing up, so Mom got me a small stool that I would bring along whenever I performed. The accordion was so huge I could barely be seen behind it. It happened that I only played the accordion once in our neighborhood variety shows, but I consider the performance a success. There was big applause, with Jackie and the other girls clapping long and hard, even though they were at the time themselves performing in the show. I suspect the reason for their applause was less about how well I played, and more about how precious I looked.

Me with the 120 Bass.

pure profit. Mark was reasonable about our food but he was skinny and didn't have my girth or large appetite.

The girls organized other activities in my beginning years besides the talent shows and lemonade stands. We played outdoor games such as Hide and Seek and Kick the Can. We set up clubhouses under someone's front porch. My brother and I set up a fort under my house behind the exterior stairs. In the girls' clubhouses, we played games like school and movie theatre.

The girls staged Halloween haunted houses in Jeepie's basement or Jonette's scarier dark partial basement. I was terrified when they brought me through their haunted house. First, one of the girls tied a blindfold over my face. Then a girl on each side took me by the arms and led me into the basement. One of the girls was the guide, announcing what was coming up.

"And now, Raymee, we are coming to the torture chamber. We have a bowl of eyeballs. Don't worry, these are only eyes."

Then one of the two escorts put my hand in the bowl and I touched what felt like raw eyeballs. It was really creepy. Years later, I learned that it was a bowl of peeled grapes. I couldn't stop squirming, my hands slimy from the "eyeballs." I was urged further along the path through the haunted house. We stopped again, and they made me touch skeleton bones (soup bones).

Next they placed a "spider" on my arm. It had a strong, textured web. This creeped me out more than anything. I was afraid of spiders, having once found a black widow in my basement. Imagining the worst, I decided it was a black widow. The web felt solid and impenetrable. I don't know what the girls used, perhaps cheesecloth, but I believed it was a real venomous spider's web. This was the moment when I understood why the girls used two escorts per customer. When I felt the spider and its web I freaked out. Grasping for the blindfold and struggling toward the exit, I began to cry. It took both girls to hold me. To their credit, they tried to comfort me.

"Raymee, don't worry, the worst part is over. You have been so brave. Now you can have a cookie," Valerie reassured me.

I trusted Valerie. I was crying but Valerie's kindness and the promise of a cookie perked me up considerably. I had just spent five cents to get the holy living heck scared out of me, but I did get a cookie and had learned I was brave because Valerie said I was.

The girls treated my older brother Eugene with kindness. During his early years, Eugene—four years older than me—had tuberculosis, which prevented him from playing outside with the rest of us. He would sit at the bedroom window and we would look up at him from outside. Our house had a ground floor with a basement underneath so it looked like Eugene was up in a tower. All the kids would wave to him. We were all playing together and he was all alone inside on a sunny day. It was a difficult and lonely time for him. The girls always seemed to be especially sad that he was ill.

Sometimes, Mom let the girls in to visit Eugene. He showed them his wonderful Lionel train set-up, which had all the extras. Besides the engine, there was the coal car, transportation cars, a caboose car, a tunnel, a town, stores, and little shopkeepers and townsmen. It came with the chief engineer and his men, plus landscaping, like trees. A train set like Eugene's, with all of the trimmings, must have cost a small fortune. It had been a gift from my mother's brother, our Uncle Jim, who had moved in with us after he was discharged from the Army. My favorite uncle, he had been a captain at the time of the D-Day landing.

My brother Eugene helping me celebrate my first birthday.

My brother made the train blow smoke by putting a small white tablet that looked like an aspirin down its train stack. The girls were impressed. It was a grand setup on a large board and he had it looking just like a real town. Years later, my brother and I put our cat inside the mountainous tunnel and drove the train through, watching the inevitable collision between train and cat. It was cruel, and I regret that we did it—especially, that we did it more than once—but we never put the train at full speed. We rationalized that this showed some humanity.

During the off-season of the Napa Fair, located across the street from our house, the grounds were quiet and still. It was not unusual for the girls and me to go inside the fairgrounds and explore. We would try to recount the food booths and guess which ones were located where on the fairgrounds.

We would stroll over to the big pavilion which had the outdoor stage attached to one side of it. Naturally, the girls would get up on the stage and do some impromptu dance and song. Oddly, their improvised work was not very different than the performances they had strenuously rehearsed with lots of time and effort. Little did I know that within a few years, I would be up on the stage, embarrassing myself with my accordion, while my older Italian neighborhood girls would be in the audience, cheering.

The pavilion was used for big events during the off-season. Dad would sometimes take my brother and me to the wrestling matches held there during the non-fair season.

We would then walk to the other buildings located toward Silverado Trail. Bordering Silverado Trail were the fields where either a rodeo or stock car races were held during fair time. Big attractions or events too big for the pavilion stage were also held in these fields. Portable stands and makeshift stages would be built to accommodate musical groups. Jan and Dean performed there once, but without the Beach Boys backing them up they were not very good, and the Beach Boys had not accompanied them to Napa. It was a serious mistake.

The softball and hardball diamonds near the Burnell Street entrance were fun to visit during the off-season because the backstops, bleachers, and concession stands were still there. We would run the bases and pretend to have a game. This didn't last long because we had no bat or ball, and the girls weren't into it anyway.

One Saturday morning in the summer of '52, the older girls and I went over to the fairgrounds. As we drew near the pavilion, the girls were about to get up on the outdoor stage to do a soft-shoe, when I was spared watching a dance that I had seen a thousand times before because of noise coming from inside the building.

The noise sounded like the buzz of people talking, punctuated by popping sounds. We were all intrigued. We all quieted down in unison without anyone telling us to. Though no one said anything, we were all anxious about being seen where we probably shouldn't be. None of us wanted to be caught or get into trouble. We found a door slightly ajar. To our surprise, we found several men, outnumbered four-to-one by young boys. There was a big boxing ring set up in the middle of the pavilion with two kids boxing and one adult referee. Other boys were pounding heavy bags or jumping rope.

We opened the door completely so we could see, but stood right by the door so we could make a quick exit if necessary. One of the men shouted over to us to come in, while also making a waving motion with his hand.

"Well, ladies, I see you have brought another combatant, huh?" said the man.

I was standing between Jeanette and Jonette. I didn't have a clue what the man was talking about.

"What are you talking about?" Jonette asked. "We were just walking around outside and heard the noise."

"Young lady, this is the Napa Police Athletic League. We are training Napa boys how to box. Does this little guy want to put on the gloves?"

To my surprise and also considerable disappointment, Jonette was much more positive about this proposition than I.

"Yeah, maybe. It might be fun. What do you think, Raymee?"

I wasn't crying yet but I felt like it. I responded to Jonette with a quiet "No." Jonette, however, turned a deaf ear to my negative response.

"Come on Raymee, this will be fun. We will all be rooting for you. You won't get hurt. Isn't that right, sir?" she asked the man.

"Absolutely, we put the kids in with someone their size. Besides, we have them wear 16 oz. gloves. No one gets hurt wearing those pillows."

I was only five years old but I knew enough to know that I didn't know what I was doing.

"I don't know how to box."

"No problem, I'll give you a quick lesson and that is all you will need for today, son."

"See, Raymee, no problem!" chimed Jonette, who had become an unwelcome annoyance. "A lesson first, big pillow gloves, and no one gets hurt. OK?" By now the other girls were also excited and encouraging me.

I relented.

The instructor, as promised, gave me a lesson in keeping my hands up around my face, and how to make a fist inside the big pillow gloves. He put my right hand back near the right side of my face, close to my jaw. My left hand was extended further out from my face. My hands were formed into fists with my thumb overlapping my index finger. He pushed my head down so that my jaw was close to my neck, which in my case created a double chin. As I looked out from this position I was forced to look at people with my eyes pointed toward the top of my head.

After working on my footing for a few minutes, with my right foot back and left foot forward, patterning them after the way I was holding my hands, he concluded that I was ready with a good-enough, if not perfect, stance.

I was ready for my first boxing lesson. It was very rudimentary. He showed me, in a very quick fashion, how to strike with my left. I pushed out my arm and twisted or snapped my fist when my arm was fully extended. He called this my "jab." Then he showed me how to throw a right cross. He said this was what he called my "punch." After about two minutes of this he explained that I should throw these punches in a sequence of "jab, jab, punch." And then repeat, jab, jab, punch or left, left, right.

That was the entire boxing lesson before my first fight. It may have been a record as the shortest-ever training period before an organized fight. I admit it was fun when I was striking an inanimate object like the heavy, stuffed canvas bag that hung from the rafters from a rope. It was also fun to hit the palm of the coach's open hand. I kind of liked it. I was not scared. I was throwing jabs and punches with reckless abandon. And they were powerful punches, too. I felt comfortable until the coach said I was ready to climb into the boxing ring.

As I climbed into the ring, I reminded myself that the morning started out as a peaceful and relaxing adventure with me in the loving and safe custody of my older, kind, and beautiful Italian neighborhood girls who always had my best interests at heart. Now, it was ending up with me sitting on a stool in a boxing ring with big gloves laced on my hands staring across at a bigger serious-looking boy with gloves on who intended to hit me. I was nervous as I wondered how my life had changed so quickly and radically. My stomach didn't feel right. I was not happy, but I didn't know what I could do to escape.

My opponent may have been given some wise words of advice from his adult corner man, but no matter what it was, I am confident it was more useful than the advice I received from my four corner-girls, giggling incomprehensibly and cheering me on.

"You can do this, Raymee! Go get him! Punch him in the face! Win!"

Rather than inspire me, this actually increased my anxiety. I knew that my opponent could hear what the girls were saying. They were yelling. They may as well have been doing a cheerleading routine. They were so obnoxious. What effect would this have on him? I figured it could only motivate him to want to beat me to a pulp. I wanted them to shut up, but I was too nervous to speak. I thought about climbing out of the ring and just leaving. I could say I wasn't ready on such short notice. I also thought about just running, but I didn't do this because I was afraid of looking like a chicken. I was too scared to quit.

These were just fleeting thoughts, because only seconds passed before the instructor who gave me the abbreviated boxing lesson brought us to the center of the ring and announced instructions.

"Remember, boys," he said, "no hitting below the belt; keep your hands up and protect yourselves at all times."

In the center of the ring I stood very close to my opponent. He was taller than me but probably weighed less. This did not surprise me. He was not smiling. I figured he was mean. He couldn't have been less experienced than me, and if he had more than one fight then he probably enjoyed the sport of hurting someone else.

"Do you understand my instructions?" asked our instructor. We both nodded that we did. "Good, then shake hands and come out fighting," he said.

I tried to shake hands with my opponent in the conventional way one shakes hands, but my opponent must have understood the futility of such an approach because he just bumped gloves with me. We each returned to our respective corners—him to his personal adult coach and me to four giggling pre-teen girls devoid of any useful boxing advice.

As I sat on my stool waiting for the bell to ring, Jeanette urged, "Don't be scared, Raymee."

She must have looked at my face. I tried to block out the girls' useless advice. I kept thinking—*jab, jab, punch; jab, jab, punch.* And then the bell rang.

I walked slowly out to the center of the ring and straight at my opponent. Later I learned that this is one of the worst moves you can make. You should always circle your opponent. However, my opponent did the same—he came right at me in a straight line. I kept my guard high and when we met we both threw left jabs, which hit the other guy's jab. I threw another jab, as instructed, and followed that with my punch. This was the only combination of punches that I knew, so that is what happened for the entire round.

I did not feel scared or over-matched. Most of our punches hit the other person's gloves, so neither of us was getting hurt. I was concentrating so hard on "jab, jab, punch" that I had little time for any other thoughts or emotions. I wasn't frightened or angry. I remember that the round lasted forever, or so I thought. Actually, amateur fights are generally three two-minute rounds. This being my first fight, the instructor limited it to only one round of two minutes.

It seemed like a very long two minutes. I was getting bored and tired of hitting the other guy's gloves, and I am sure he was feeling the same. After what seemed like an hour the bell rang and the instructor, who doubled as the referee, brought us both together and raised our hands declaring the match a draw.

I went back to my corner where my corner-girls were all cheering. It was funny because once the fight started, I forgot about my girls. It was like no one was there except my opponent. I sat down on the stool and let out all of my pent-up emotions by crying. I was embarrassed that I cried, because I hadn't been hurt and actually enjoyed the bout. The anxiety, frustration, and anger of being pushed into a fight finally overwhelmed me.

These boxing classes were held every Saturday in the pavilion and were free. I met the minimum age of five so I decided to come back. After all, it was only across the street from where I lived. Besides, after going home that day and thinking about it, I realized I had a lot of fun, even though I didn't want to do it at first and cried when it was over. I enjoyed myself.

I became the coach's most enthusiastic boxer. After a while, I remember him telling some new parent and son that boxing can be fun. He pointed to me as an example.

"This kid was brought to me kicking and screaming. Now I couldn't get rid of him if I wanted to. He loves the sport," he said.

It was true that I was getting something out of it. I was the only one in the ring on my side and I depended completely on myself. When I did well, I was proud of myself. It gave me confidence.

I had a variety of bouts throughout that summer. Several fights stood out to me for the lessons I learned.

In one fight the coach put me in against a taller, stronger, older, and more experienced opponent. I am not sure why the coach did this, but I wasn't scared. This bout was such a mismatch that I was sure the big guy would take it easy on me. The instructor said this fight would only be one round. The big guy was taking it very easy on me, only throwing ponderous jabs. They were long and powerful and hit their mark (my nose) a lot. I am not sure if I ever laid a glove on him.

When the round ended I was happy with my performance. Even though I knew he was toying with me, I believed I had acquitted myself well. I wasn't close to being knocked down or even rocked. He never hurt me. I sat down on my stool, waiting for my trainer to unlace my gloves.

"Well, how does it feel to be bloodied?" he asked.

I didn't know what he was talking about, until he wiped my nose with a white towel. There was a fair amount of blood on the towel and more was gushing out of my nose. It was kind of alarming, because I never had this happen before. It didn't hurt but the towel was really red with my blood. I reacted in my usual stoic manner—I started to cry. The instructor patiently informed me that bleeding was not unusual in this sport.

"Raymond, when you didn't know you were bleeding, you were fine," he said. "You weren't upset at all. Now, his jabs didn't really hurt you and you know it. Nosebleeds are very common when a boxer gets hit on his nose. Don't worry about it. You are okay."

"Yes—Coach," I responded haltingly.

On some level I appreciated his attempt to calm me, but the fact was that while he was comforting me I was still bleeding. I didn't know how long my situation could continue before I might die. Not until the bleeding stopped was I able to completely calm down. My attitude changed 180 degrees once I was no longer near death. I started thinking, *Hey, I survived a round with a true heavyweight boxer. He was not a fat chubby little kid. This guy was older, tall, with a muscular build, and he didn't even hurt me. He was the biggest and best boxer in our camp. Yeah, I got my nose bloodied but that just happens in boxing. I was fine. I even got a few licks in myself!*

All of this bravado was taking place silently, inside my head. Had I actually said this audibly the coach might have put me back in there with the big guy. I was feeling good about myself again. There was no sense pushing a return bout too soon.

Another boxing match that stood out that summer was against an opponent who was actually smaller than me. He was Chinese. He had never been to the camp before but he arrived one Saturday with his father. The coach paired him with the smallest boxer in his stable, me. The boy had a good build (he wasn't fat). In the corner, before the fight, he and his father had expressions of determination.

I should have suspected that the boy's father had been training and teaching him, that the smaller Chinese boy knew how to box, that the boy was motivated to impress his father, and that I would see boxing skills that I had never seen before. I should have suspected all of that, but I didn't. This kid was smaller, and that was all I needed to know. Standing next to him while we were given final instructions, I towered over him by at least two inches and outweighed him by thirty pounds. No way would I lose to him. A couple of inches are no great advantage, but I had never before been taller than any opponent. The only real advantage would be to have a longer reach. My arms were so short that I reminded people of a T-Rex dinosaur, so he probably had me on reach. Still, I was more confident in this fight than any other because of my size advantage.

When the bell rang for the first round, the Chinese boy rushed to the center of the ring and hit me in the stomach with the hardest blow ever inflicted on me in my young life, in or out of the ring. It was more powerful than any punch from my brother, who was four years older than me, and it was a body blow. In our boxing matches no boxer ever hit me with a body blow. In one instant, my opponent taught me, in the most negative way, how effective body blows could be.

I let out an audible groan as air rapidly left my body. I didn't go down and I didn't cry. I realized, however, that I was in for a real war. I believe that the psychological edge I had by being physically bigger kept me in the fight. I was sure that I could not lose to this smaller person.

The fight went the full three rounds. In the end, the instructor raised both of our hands, signifying a draw. My opponent's natural hand speed (a skill that can't be taught) and his superior boxing ability should have carried him to victory. I learned that confidence and a positive state of mind plays a big part in what can be accomplished, even if overmatched.

Years later, we met again in elementary school as classmates. Mike Soon and I became good friends throughout our school years, including middle school and high school.

That summer was one of the best summers of my childhood, and it was all because of the gentle nudge from my Italian girls to climb into a boxing ring.

Other events the neighborhood girls and I attended together during the off-season of the fair included summer-evening softball games. Napa was a great softball town, and there were always games to watch. The girls and I would go to the Burnell Street entrance, adjacent to the softball diamond, complete with covered bleachers, and a wooden concession stand that sold hot cocoa. There was also an official announcer's booth at the top of the bleachers for the scorekeeper and announcer to score and call the game. The announcer's booth was usually manned by Al Adamo, who had a golden voice and a penchant for giving local players nicknames. Al's nickname for my father was "The Little Flower." I have no idea how this nickname evolved, but I suspect that irony had something to do with it.

I had fun at these games sitting in the stands with my girls. One of them almost always brought a blanket so we could all snuggle, with me in the middle. If I retrieved a foul ball I would return it to the concession stand and be paid a dime. I would then quickly turn the dime into hot chocolate and return to my girls, warm blanket, and fresh hot chocolate.

These beginning years of my life evolved when I started school at Alta Heights Elementary. Once I began kindergarten, I acquired a whole new set of friends, and my interactions with the neighborhood Italian-American girls dwindled considerably. They all attended St. John's Catholic School. I was now playing with boys from my public school who would invite me to their houses, or they would be transported to my house by their mothers.

Some of my friends were Italian-Americans like me, such as Paul Vallerga and Steve Ceriani, as well as Raneri, Massa, Pighini, and others. But now I had friends with names like Kerns, Crane, Aguilar, Weien, and Erricson.

I did not find the assimilation difficult at all. There was no language issue, as I only spoke English. Even though both my parents spoke fluent Italian, they chose to speak English in the home so that we would not get teased as they had been. I always enjoyed making people laugh, so I was very popular, according to my teacher's remarks in my first report card. I remember the word "popular" specifically because I didn't know its meaning, and had to ask Mom what it meant. I was relieved to learn that it was a positive comment.

Though my life had changed forever when I began elementary school with a new set of friends and activities, I always retained a warm affection for my Italian-American neighborhood friends.

My lifelong friends from my Alta Heights school days.
Front row from left: Wally Keller, Paul Vallerga, Steve Ceriani, Mike Soon,
Ron Weien, Ray Guadagni. Second row: Mike Kerns, and Shev Aguilar.

CHAPTER 2

My Italian-American Family

I don't know if my family was a typical Italian-American family. I hope not.

I hope that "typical" Italian families were more like the other families around us, who seemed happy. Their fathers were always nice to me though my interactions with them were infrequent. Ernest Martini was super kind to all of the kids, and we watched his television when we didn't have one. He showed home movies of Hopalong Cassidy on Saturday evenings and was very friendly in visiting with us. I felt safe with him. Rico Grattone was also kind and greeted us with a smile when we would see him out in the yard. Pauline Squicciarini's husband Al Williams was a wonderful athlete and would always talk to us about sports. The Guisto family likewise were friendly. From my view they seemed like happy and peaceful families without constant turmoil, hollering, blame, verbal abuse and fear.

In our home, on the other hand, there was usually chaos punctuated with small periods of silence when we were eating, or longer periods when Dad was pissed off and the rest of us were afraid to speak. My dad, Alvin A. Guadagni, wasn't really physically abusive very often, but he was verbally and emotionally abusive every day, which I think can be even worse. Years later, Mom told me that he had instructed her to never praise either my brother or me because it would make us weak. I guess because of that, the negative memories stand out more for me than the positive. When Dad was nice to me I still heard his negative comments in my head and didn't believe the positive ones were genuine. I just thought that on those rare occasions he was in a momentary good mood, and believed his negative comments were how he really felt.

Al and Anne Guadagni in happier days.

Dad was short in stature and in heart. He was hot-tempered and as strong as a bull. He also achieved the trifecta of emotional drawbacks: insecurity, immaturity, and self-centeredness. He yelled a lot when he bullied and he bullied a lot when he yelled. And, he was loud. With his booming voice, there was never a doubt when he walked into a room that Big Al Guadagni had made his entrance. Many Italian people are loud, but they were overpowered and minimized by Dad's voice, which was like a loudspeaker from Hell. After one of his rants, my ears would ring like cathedral bells.

My dad, Alvin.

Big Al is the only person I ever met who was never wrong in his life. Once, when I was a teenager, having stuffed enough anger to choke a horse, I blurted out, "You are never wrong, are you?" to which he responded, "No, you are wrong. I am wrong sometimes and when I am, I am the first to admit it." Thus, I concluded, but did not say out loud, Dad felt he was right even about being wrong. I wanted to tell him this, but my boldness quickly evaporated after that one and only rebellious question.

Everyone blows up now and then, usually out of frustration, fear or stress, and Dad encountered more than his share. He came from a "broken home," as they said, referring to a home with divorced parents. Dad was in the custody of his father, Antonio, who also had custody of his older son, Leo, and his daughter, Inez. This seems very unusual to me that a father in the 1920s, not the mother, had custody of the parents' three children. I never learned the reason why this was the case.

After a short period of time Antonio sent Inez to live with her mother because he didn't believe he could properly raise a daughter. After that, Antonio, Leo, and Alvin (my dad) lived in a small cabin in Healdsburg. Alvin was mistreated by both his father and his brother, causing him to run away to the home of his mother. By then, she had remarried. Her new husband drank a lot and also mistreated Dad, who went from the frying pan into the fire.

Finally, after enough beatings, Dad rejoined his father. Antonio worked in the vineyards all day as a laborer, while his sons Alvin and Leo played in the small cabin. One day in 1927, while playing cops and robbers, Leo shot Alvin, who was ten at the time, with a 12-gauge, double-barreled shotgun. It blew off most of Dad's right thigh. He was lucky to survive the surgery and keep his severely damaged leg. After a while he could walk again, but with a limp.

These surroundings and circumstances may help explain Dad's feelings of inferiority, anger, and frustration, which were his trademarks. He dealt with his feelings of inferiority by bragging and boasting, mostly about things he could not live up to.

Dad and my brother, Eugene.

Overall, at home, Dad was calm except for the five or six times a night that he snapped. During those periods he was unpleasant and scary, and seemed to get bigger when he got angry. When angry, he went from regular size to a blown up hulk.

My beautiful mom, Anne, when she was young.

My mom, Anne, was 4-feet-11 inches tall, although she maintained that she was five feet tall. She was heavy set and weighed as much as 170 pounds. Anne, like Jesus before her, sacrificed her life for the sake of others, specifically my brother and me. She was not nailed to a cross but she had to carry one for every day she was with her husband. She was always there to protect us. She was our safety net. She didn't do this by out-yelling Dad, engaging him in verbal abuse, or getting embroiled with him in a fight—which she would never have been able to win. Instead, even though she didn't intervene on our behalf during Dad's abuse, she more than made up for that failure each and every day, with love, sympathy, understanding, listening, and a whole-hearted caring for our every need.

She loved us unconditionally. Unlike my father, she would never give my brother or me the cold shoulder or stop talking to us for expressing disagreement with her. She could tolerate an opposing viewpoint without vile, vituperative behavior. She welcomed other points of view.

Mom was the opposite of Dad: she was nurturing and kind. She loved to cuddle us when we were young, and hug us as we got older, and she demanded we hug her as well. She was demonstrably loving. She told us she loved us on a regular basis, although she really didn't have to say it. We could feel Mom's love by her actions and by the way she cared for us.

Dad, however, never said that he loved my brother or me. I thought he would have been biologically programmed to love us, yet he never said it to us. Most of the time it felt like he couldn't stand us. And while my dad never said he was wrong (other than the one time he said it just to prove *me* wrong), my mother would instantly apologize and make amends if there was the slightest chance of her being wrong.

I hated it when she would apologize when she wasn't at fault, but if she erred it would always be on the side of making peace. She wanted to make everyone happy. She wanted to make friends with everyone. She rarely raised her voice and was very easy to talk to. She was more than approachable, she was welcoming. She was the parent I could talk with in a meaningful way, and the topic could be about my favorite subject—me.

It didn't work that way with Dad, who vocalized only his needs and his criticisms.

Mom may have been a little over-protective, but even that trait was out of love. I heard "no" a lot as I got older when it came to going out with friends who drove fast in their hot rods, or going to parties at the homes of kids she knew had bad reputations. But this was out of concern for her sons' safety. She also did not speak badly of other people. She was biased toward liking human beings.

Dad, on the other hand, rarely met a person he liked, unless it was a fellow Italian who came from the same part of Italy as he. Otherwise, he could find fault easily.

Everybody loved Mom. My friends loved her, and their parents loved her, with genuine affection. Years later, when I would run into an old friend or one of their parents, they would invariably tell me how much they loved my mom. If Dad was brought up at all, it was usually with a courteous comment like, "Your dad was a real character, Ray, but I got along with him most of the time."

The boyhood name I gave my brother Eugene was Euey. Unfortunately, as the oldest, Euey took the brunt of Dad's anger. He was criticized more and received more verbal, emotional and physical abuse than I did. I think birth order saved me, in part.

Also, my gutless-wimp personality was a big plus in these situations, as well. I was a conniver and charmingly manipulative. I sucked up a lot, didn't talk back often, and stayed out of my father's way. I learned that even "fun" times could go south in a hurry.

Play-wrestling, for instance. Dad would play-wrestle with "his boys," which was fun until an errant elbow would catch him in his mouth or in some other sensitive part of his body. Then the wrestling match, the playful yelling, and the laughing came to a grinding halt as the "hulk" re-emerged in all of his alarming wickedness. Then came the angry yelling and the blame.

My brother Eugene and me.

"Raymond, you are not watching carefully. You don't care what you are doing or who you hurt. You are not thinking. Use your head." This was said with bitter venom. I felt like I was really stupid for not being careful in a wrestling match.

When wrestling matches sometimes turned out the other way, I was often confused by the contradictions in his messages and conduct. If Dad accidently hit *me* with an elbow in the mouth, things would come to a halt with me crying. In those situations, however, Dad would not apologize for not being careful. Instead, his response was radically different.

"Stop your crying. You're eight years old. You are not a baby anymore. You have to shake it off. You weren't hurt. Grow up. You can be a crybaby and quit or you can continue to wrestle. What is it going to be?" I would always continue to wrestle because I didn't want to be labeled a crybaby, but the rest of the match was not fun because my heart wasn't in it anymore.

It was just more pleasant to avoid Dad than to keep interacting with him. Besides, every argument upset Mom so much that it was not worth getting embroiled in an argument or fight. The chances were far too great that any activity, no matter how benign, would end up in an ugly scene.

Even playing cards could turn unpleasant quickly. The four of us would occasionally play Pedro (a card game commonly played by Italian-Americans) and whoever had my dad as partner was under great stress. You did *not* want to let him down. If you made the wrong decision you would hear about it right then and there, no matter who else was present. There would be yelling and throwing cards down on the card table and watching your drink and cards go flying.

"Eugene, why did you bid with that crappy hand? You don't bid with no ace, plus you were holding both Pedros. That doesn't help you, it hurts you. When are you ever going to learn? You really are a stupid idiot. Little kids can play better than you. They are leading and we will likely lose now. I hope you're happy. Jesus

Christ, what the fuck is wrong with you? You are as smart as ice plant."

Our most pleasant family activity was mealtime, especially when my dad wasn't around. Fortunately, due to his work regimen, that was quite often. Eating was something we all loved to do, and in fact, it dominated our household. The word "sacred" does not begin to adequately express the overwhelming importance of these daily events.

When I think back on our time together around the table, the animal world comes to mind. Breakfast, lunch and dinner should really have been called "The Devouring." Those times transformed my otherwise Italian-American family into insatiable hyenas. Everyone immediately fell to chomping, grabbing, snorting, smacking, and swallowing. We were not unlike a pack of wolves attacking their prey.

As the leader of our pack, my father was the fastest eater. He led by example, tearing into red meat like the starved, crazed beast he had become. He did not purposefully eat bones, but I am sure, every now and then, some shards of bone shot down his throat at a high rate of speed. Somehow, though, he avoided puncturing any vital organs.

I always felt that because none of us *intentionally* ate bones, my family was set apart from the animal world. Except for that thin distinction, however, it would be difficult to tell any difference based purely on eating habits. Bones aside, my dad was more like a Viking Norseman plundering the coasts of Europe in the eighth century. He would rip into any meat dish, and, if the meal was of the aquatic world, Dad would swoop and scoop his fish like a pelican, devouring most fish in a single bite.

Over time, my brother evolved (or devolved) into a close second to my father's eating habits, both in terms of speed and quantity.

That left me to be the most measured eater in my family among the males. This fact astounds my friends who compare me, while dining, to a Hoover vacuum cleaner.

Mealtime conversations were almost non-existent. This was because everyone's mouth was otherwise fully occupied. Chaos does not describe our few conversations. We all spoke simultaneously, and since no one ever listened, each spoke ever more loudly, in a vain effort to be heard. Shouting was not caused by anger, but the simple human need to be occasionally acknowledged. But no matter how loud any of us was, there could be no question as to whose opinion was right. There was only one possible, reasonable, certain, well-thought-out position, and if instantaneous assent was not given, the person who disagreed with Dad was, obviously, a fucking idiot.

Shouting was punctuated by long periods of silence because everyone was furious at the other's insane inability to see where the truth lay, and the invariable result was to upset poor Mom, who was bewildered by her inability to achieve peace in the family. Her contrasting opinions and attempts at peacemaking were only expressed in a bout of hives.

Once everyone was weary of being silent, the roars resumed. Of course, when my father became hoarse in his persevering attempts to persuade us what fucking idiots we were, that effect, too, was another example that only added to the undeniable, and unbelievable, level of our imbecility.

As we got older Dad seemed to be absent from all meals. He got up too early to eat breakfast with us, and he didn't come home for lunch. My brother and I did not wait for Dad to come home for dinner because he worked late. We were starved by 5:00 PM, and he would commonly eat at 8:00 PM. Even on weekends Dad was not around for breakfast or lunch because he went to his shop seven days a week.

Sunday evenings, we usually went out to dinner together. That may sound like fun for kids, but Dad usually had a way of embarrassing us. For example, he would bring a transistor radio into the restaurant and listen to the Giants game. He would turn it up so loud that it clearly would be within earshot of many of the surrounding tables. This always embarrassed me. Either Dad was unaware of how loud the radio was or he just didn't care.

There were so many unpleasant times around the table when Dad was around that the rest of us had just as soon skip the togetherness of mealtime altogether. For us, dinner was not a social event. It was not a sharing of our respective day. It was serious eating, fast and quick. Between my brother and me, the subject centered on who was getting a larger portion of food than the other.

Mom would often ask about our day at school or baseball practice or ask other questions about our lives. If there was table talk beyond this it was on the rare occasions when Dad was around, when talk was dominated by our dad's negative pontificating about someone who had wronged him. Or worse, the vitriolic attacks may have been directed to my brother or me. I found these discussions incompatible with a relaxing meal. Sometimes, when Dad went after Euey, I would try to intervene to protect him. A typical complaint by my dad to Euey was about homework.

"I see you didn't bring any work home. Don't you have homework?" Dad would ask.

My brother did not lie and had no ready response so he was just twisting in the wind.

"Yeah, I have some homework, but I forgot to bring it home."

This is all it would take to light Dad's fuse. He'd jump all over Euey, yelling at him. He'd start by making comparisons to me.

"Raymond has homework. Raymond brings it home. You are in a higher grade but you don't bring your work home. Are you a genius? Are you so smart that you don't need to do your homework? Well, let me tell you. You are not a genius, you are a stupid idiot and you will always be a stupid idiot."

If you didn't really know my brother's name and you only watched interactions between my brother and my father, you could easily have concluded my brother's name was Stupid Idiot, for that was what Dad called him constantly. I have to admit that there were times when I called my brother that when I was angry at him. I didn't do this often because I hated it when Dad called him that, and to this day, I regret having ever called him such an abusive name.

"Leave him alone, Dad! Stop yelling at him. It is not helping!" I would plead. That respectful plea was not interpreted as such. It usually evoked a heated response.

"Don't interrupt me. I'm in charge of this family, not you. I know what is best. You keep your mouth shut or I'll shut it for you, you little shit. You are being disrespectful to me and I won't tolerate it." He would then continue his rant by telling me how smart he was and how he knew the future.

"You'll both see that you will amount to nothing if you don't work hard. Neither of you know shit. I learned more from the school of hard knocks and experience than you will ever learn in any book. School won't tell you what you are going to need or face in life. So shut up and listen to me. Do you understand and do you agree?"

This last part bothered me most because it was a requirement that I acknowledge that I understood his point AND that I agreed with him. This made me angry. I felt hypocritical saying I agreed with Dad, because I didn't agree with him and many times I didn't even understand him. It didn't seem very rational and certainly not convincing to me to tell my brother that bringing his books home so he could do his school work was

42

important if you don't really need school Yet that is what I think he was telling us.

There were occasionally times when Dad would make a rational point that I could agree with, however, the manner in which he made his point was awful. His conduct in making his argument was abominable. Dad had zero charisma. In fact, Dad had anti-charisma.

Then, after an argument, for the next few days or weeks, my dad would not acknowledge my presence because I had been disrespectful to him. I was on the "freeze" until I apologized. This was a relief in many ways because he wouldn't talk or yell at me, but it upset Mom so much that I usually sucked it up and apologized for being disrespectful to my father, which, after all, was a commandment.

I had to go to confession to say that I had dishonored my father, though I sometimes wondered if there really was a God, and if he witnessed what transpired, how could he be on my dad's side? My motivation was to get my dad to leave Euey alone before he hit him, plus I thought I was being respectful. Yet I was the one who had to apologize and confess. Things didn't make sense.

The need to confess really wasn't so burdensome, however, because I had to go to confession anyway for gluttony, which was a sin I committed on a daily basis. As a result, there would be no extra trip to the church for my disrespect to my dad. There might be a heavier penance because of multiple sins but another five or ten Hail Marys were no big deal, especially at the speed with which I could say a prayer in my head.

I seemed to pay a higher price than my brother for interceding on his behalf. However, this was the common punitive result. I am sure it discouraged me from intervening on occasion but, as I got older, I couldn't stand by and silently observe this cruel treatment of my brother. He had no chance against Dad. I was his only hope of getting the "warden's spotlight" off of him. Truthfully,

I didn't think I was violating one of the commandments. I thought I was doing the right thing.

Unlike dinner with only the immediate family, mealtimes with cousins and aunts and uncles were almost always fun and pleasant because Dad was usually cooking if the event was at our house, or entertaining adult relatives if we were at one of their homes.

I loved playing with my cousins, especially those who were my age. We always ate at the children's foldable card tables, and the children's table was great. The adults, for the most part, paid us no attention except for the occasional check by one of my aunties. Aunt Carmela was very heavy. No one ever told me her weight but I always assumed that she would have to be weighed at the commercial scale at the livery stable. She must have reached in excess of 400 pounds.

Aunt Carmela was sweet, jolly, and kind, and she loved it if you ate lots of her cooking. Cleaning your plate was a good start, but she wasn't happy unless you had seconds. Clearly, she loved my brother and me. Most of my other cousins were like normal kids—skinny. My brother was built well despite eating like a hog. I was the only cousin who was fat. But none of this mattered. We loved each other and played well together. My older cousin, Judy Guadagni, was my brother's age. She was beautiful, sweet, and very nurturing to me.

My cousin Linda Bianchina, on my mother's side, was my favorite cousin. She was my age, very intelligent, with a terrific sense of humor. She also loved to eat, and though she wasn't fat, she was not skinny. My cousins on my father's side besides Judy were Loren, Wayne, and Pamela. I was closest to Loren as he was my age. We got along great, except his favorite cowboy was Roy Rogers and mine was Hopalong Cassidy.

The few times we kids ate at the big table mostly consisted of one of our parents telling us to quiet down or to not be so sloppy with our food. When it was Dad's turn to intervene he had to show what a strong disciplinarian he was. I am sure he probably believed he was impressing the rest of the adults at the dinner table.

I recall two specific events where I was the subject matter of his keen intervention skills. One incident, I have to admit, was caused solely by me and my penchant for gluttony. We were once more at Auntie Carmela's house. She had a very large dining table, which is probably why all of the kids were at the table. I sat at the very end on one side of the table with my brother sitting next to me. Auntie Carmela had made her rich Bolognese. All of the vegetables she put in her sauce were fresh from her Italian garden. Tomatoes, onions, celery, and carrots were key ingredients. Of course, she added pancetta, ground veal, and fresh Italian parsley. She also added a suggestion of cream. The end result was mouth-watering.

I just couldn't get enough of her Bolognese. We had what we kids called grated parmesan cheese but what our adult family members called parmeggiano. No matter what you called it, we all sprinkled this delicious cheese liberally onto our Bolognese. Some, like me, were more liberal with the parmesan than others. Mine covered my pasta so completely that it looked like snow covering a mountain. Left to my own devices, I ate plate after plate of her delicious culinary magic. Much like a dachshund that will eat itself to death, I couldn't stop and didn't.

Fortunately, alarm bells went off in my chubby but supple body and instead of dying, I simply threw up. Unfortunately, the built-in safety-valve of my system did not give me notice. I just erupted, covering my end of the table. I wish some of my nearby cousins would have been so sickened by what I had done, that they too would have vomited. Then, maybe it would have been difficult to discern the root cause of the puking. But no such luck. It was clear that there was only one culprit—me.

Dad seized the moment to tell me and everyone else within earshot (which included Auntie Carmela's entire neighborhood) that I was, by all objective standards, a gluttonous pig and that I should be ashamed of myself. Then he demanded that I apologize to Auntie Carmela. As I started to express my apology, with chunks of puke clad to my cheeks, I threw up a second time.

Dad then ordered me to go to Auntie Carmela's bathroom. In fact, he even assisted my exit by yanking me out of my chair and dragging me to the bathroom. Mom joined us and took over the chore of cleaning me up. She cleaned my face and washed out my shirt and most, importantly, consoled me.

"It is okay, Raymond, the food was delicious and I know you loved it. Your Auntie Carmela was thrilled that you loved her food and ate so much of it. Don't worry, everything is okay. You know your dad is just that way. He'll get over it."

A host of my aunts bolted to my end of the table and commenced clearing and cleaning. Within a few minutes, there was a return to normalcy for everyone but me. I was still embarrassed.

Later, I apologized to Auntie Carmela, who hugged me.

"Raymond, honey, I know you must love my food if you ate too much. Don't worry about it. I am just glad you really enjoyed my cooking."

I assured her that I did love it. She was so sweet and kind. It was truly embarrassing but I felt a lot better with the kindness of my aunt and mom.

The worst thing of all about this incident was that neither of my parents would allow me to have dessert. I had to sit around and watch all my cousins eat cake and ice cream. My plea that I wasn't full anymore fell on deaf ears, even to Mom.

"I have plenty of room for dessert and I feel great now."

When this request was denied, I modified my position.

"How about a little piece of cake and a small scoop of ice cream? Please, Mom?" This attempt, too, was denied. Having lost those arguments, I had little choice now but to resort to my last line of defense.

"Mom, this isn't fair. Everyone else is getting dessert except me and that is not fair." Mom stayed strong on her position.

"Raymond, you got sick already and having sweets right now may make you sick again."

"But I am not sick now and I am not too full," I responded.

"Raymond, no dessert. No more discussion about it. Now go play with your cousins." I knew better than to push it with Mom. I realized that Mom listened to me and considered it. Also, I knew that it was only a matter of time before Dad would hear me arguing with Mom and intervene on her behalf. And, if he heard the nature of my request, things may have erupted one more time into a scene. No one wanted that. I didn't get dessert that day.

Any extended family dinner hosted by my parents could not be held at one table because our dining room table, even with its extensions, could not accommodate large groups. I was always at one of the card tables with my cousins. Once, when I was having a great time and I didn't overeat to the point of throwing up, a problem occurred when my father came around and noticed that I had not eaten any of my asparagus.

"Raymond, I see you ate all of your rabbit and all of your risotto but none of your asparagus. You must eat all of your vegetables."

"But, Dad, I hate asparagus," I said in a whiny, begging tone. "I can't eat them or I will get sick."

To no one's surprise, my expressed reason was not convincing enough to Dad for him to allow me to skip my asparagus.

"You eat them or I will not allow you to leave this table," he bellowed.

Being eleven and having so many of my cousins to show off to, I ignored my dad and directed my response to my cousins.

"Well, guys, it looks like I will be at this table for a long, long time. Please do come and visit me when you can."

Dad exploded and expanded all at the same time. Looking like he doubled in size and yelling, he demanded that I eat the asparagus immediately.

"Eat them now or you will see what happens next!"

All of my bravado had left me witless. I could see my cousins scattering and I could plainly hear my heart pounding. Wanting to desperately extricate myself from my predicament as quickly as possible, I picked up all four asparagus spears and stuffed the front ends into my mouth. I started chomping them bit-by-bit, hoping to cut them down to size and devour them completely.

I got about three-to-four chomps in before I started to choke. I spit them out on my plate and Dad was not amused. He started yelling that I would have to put them back into my mouth and swallow them. I didn't think Dad's plan would work, but I wasn't about to try to have a civil conversation with him. I picked up the partly chewed asparagus and shoveled them back into my mouth. Not more than two chomps into this second round, I threw it all up, and more. Suddenly a colorful plate of yellow risotto, accented by bits of brown rabbit, all engulfed in green mushy asparagus, appeared before me on my plate.

Emboldened by anger now, and not thinking clearly, I declared, "I told you I get sick when I eat asparagus, and there, sadly, lies the proof." This was not the appropriate response when discussing my situation with Dad. Of course, I was embarrassed in front of my cousins and aunts and uncles, and angry as well, but against a volatile person much bigger and stronger than me, it would have been wise to have measured my words.

Dad exploded in a fit of rage, yanking me out of my chair and sending me to my room, my head and limbs flopping around like a rag doll. Again, I missed out on dessert, even though I had plenty of room in my tummy for it.

Cousin Linda told me later that I might try cutting up my vegetables and spreading them around in my other food so that it would look like I had eaten most of them. I never wanted to have any of my good food touch my bad food, because that was a sacrifice of good food. If it touched the vegetables then I could no longer enjoy the good stuff. However, I did start to rethink my approach after the asparagus incident. Linda was smart and I thought I would give her advice a try.

My problem with her suggestion, however, was that there was rarely any of the good food left to mix with the vegetables. I solved this by taking some of the good food, before I even started eating. Then I would mix them with the vegetables so that it looked like I had eaten a fair amount of all my food. While it was clearly a waste of good food, by following this approach, I could then sit back and enjoy the food I so dearly loved.

I also tried putting some of the veggies in a desk drawer, an approach I thought of all by myself. Often, however, I would forget to retrieve them later. The result was not disastrous because only Mom would find the spoiled, slimy veggies stuffed into the wooden drawer. Mom really did not like this approach. She wanted me to eat my vegetables. However, she clearly understood my desire to avoid a confrontation with Dad. It was a desire she whole-heartedly shared.

Another approach I tried came after our family acquired a fox terrier named Trixie. I subtly took the veggies off my plate when neither Mom nor Dad were looking and inconspicuously dropped them on the floor, where Trixie dutifully sat by my side. This approach, however, was also not a foolproof solution. Trixie wasn't fond of vegetables. She would almost always take them initially but after chewing on them for a couple of seconds she would reject them much the way a vending machine returns your dollar bill when it is too crumpled. Only Trixie had an odd way of rejecting. She used her tongue in a shoveling manner to toss out the bad vegetables. When she ultimately spit them out on the floor I had to pick them up myself. This only caused me more work. Ultimately, I settled on Linda's remedy as the most effective.

Another odd thing about our family, which I hope did not apply to all Italian-American families in general, was the constant flow of old wives' tales, rituals, and superstitions. Actually, to call us superstitious would be to insult the witch-burners of Salem. Compared to us, they were simply levelheaded intellectuals following the evidence.

Mainly, these ancient beliefs influenced my mother, who was only too willing to share them with us, of course for our own good. Her intentions were benign, but some of the superstitions were pretty farfetched. For example, she believed that a pregnant woman could not raise her arms above her head, lest the umbilical cord choke the baby.

"Isn't this obvious?" she would ask.

My brother and I never questioned it as youngsters. We believed it. Mom was clearly the most intelligent and knowledgeable member of our family. But as I got older I questioned her beliefs.

"Mom, you mean you never raised your arms above your head while you were pregnant with Euey or me? For a total of eighteen months you never once raised your arms above your head?" I asked.

"I made it a habit of not doing so, to protect you. You should be thanking me," she responded.

"But Mom, I have seen pregnant ladies reach for things on a high shelf at grocery stores. Do you think their babies were all born dead?"

"Raymond, I am not saying raising your arms above your head during pregnancy always results in the death of the unborn child. What I am saying is that the more a pregnant woman raises her arms above her head the more likely the umbilical cord will eventually wrap around the baby's neck and most of the time the baby will die. That is why I was so careful."

Mom's more detailed explanation added some clarity but it wasn't backed up with any evidence. So, I asked for proof.

"Mom, how do you know this? Did you read it in a book or was it some scientific study?"

Not quite being responsive to my question, mom cited her authority with the use of another wives' tale.

"Basketball players have heart troubles because they have their hands over their heads a lot as they shoot the basketball up toward the ten-foot-high basket." Without waiting for another question from me asking for her sources or the foundation of her premise, she proudly stated, "This, too, cannot be questioned, because a moment's reflection would show that the blood has to be pumped uphill!"

I was prepared to make further inquiry when Mom started in on what a strong advocate she was for a two-foot-high basket. That way, you would shoot downward which would be good for the heart and especially for my relatives.

"Conventional basketball, Raymond, leads to heart attacks and needlessly kills players. Certainly any caring person would not condemn all basketball players to an early death! Since this is true of basketball, and its inevitably fatal consequences, it must also be true of any activity that requires one to lift their hands over their head."

When I saw how deeply her convictions ran, I gave up on my cross-examination. I believed these tales when I was young, but not as a kid in his teens. Whenever I lifted my arms over my head for many years as an adult I would always think about Mom's warnings before ignoring them.

Mom said there were similar, equally obvious truths in other areas of life. The very important need to "break" a fever was done by sweltering the sufferer (me or my brother) beneath mounds of blankets. If she didn't do this, the fever would spread and grow worse. If we broke a sweat, the fever would be defeated.

Another fixation in our family was the concept of the Grim Reaper. Mr. Reaper took two forms. One was The Bloodless Ghoul, who tapped you on the shoulder from behind when your number was up.

The other was framed in a dream I called The Death Dream, in which you fall asleep, perfectly content and ready for a pleasant slumber. Instead, a vision arises of a casket lying on a slab and in it, a corpse. As you approach this ghastly scene, you first see the feet and then coming even closer the head comes into view, and OH MY GOD, it is your face in the bloodless, grim countenance of DEATH. This scared the shit out of me and still does, just thinking that it may come to me tonight, or any night. I dreaded sleep for fear of having The Dream. I vainly fought the onset of sleep after learning about The Dream, but, like in the movie, *The Body Snatchers,* I couldn't help it and drifted off to slumber. When I awoke and realized I was alive I assumed I didn't have The Dream because it wasn't my time.

The Death Dream really caused me some anxiety. I was so afraid of getting The Dream that I tried to push the subject out of my head at night so I could get to sleep. I asked Mom if there was a way to prevent ever having The Dream. Sadly, she said that there was not. If it was your time, you had The Dream.

"How do you know such a thing exists? Did someone have The Dream yet lived to tell about it?" I asked. Mom said that some of her relatives in the old country did have The Dream but didn't die.

"Then getting The Dream doesn't mean you are going to die, right, Mom?"

Mom said that the only ones who got The Dream and lived were ones in which mistakes had been made. For example, a cousin's mother, in the old country, had her daughter in Italy call her son in America to come over to Italy right away because she had The Dream.

"What happened?" I asked.

"Well, Guido did come over to Italy and when he got there a miracle occurred. Suddenly, the joy of Guido's presence sparked new life into his mother and she was up and around like nothing had ever been the matter. You would have never known that she had been ill, let alone on Death's doormat. However, she described The Dream in vivid detail and it was horrifying."

I couldn't help but ask if Guido's mom lived many years afterward, hoping, that if she did, it would prove to myself that this was just a dream and not an accurate prediction of the bleak future of one's life.

"Raymond, Guido's mother died two weeks after Guido returned to America. She must have gotten The Dream a second time but never lived to tell about it. Who knows why she didn't die the first time. Maybe it was Guido's visit that temporarily kept The Dream away. These things are mysteries and cannot be questioned."

That word "mystery" was starting to bug me by the time I had reached the age of twelve. It seemed as if I heard that a lot in my Catechism classes and from Mom. Every time I asked a question about anything I didn't understand (which was plenty,) I was told it was a mystery.

"Who or what is the holy spirit, Sister?"

"It is a mystery, Raymond," said Sister Teresa.

"Who or What is the holy trinity, Sister?"

"It is a mystery, Raymond."

"What is purgatory, Sister?"

"It is another mystery, Raymond."

"Then maybe these things are not true or don't exist, Sister?"

"Oh, they exist, Raymond. They exist. They are mysteries and that is why you must have faith in God," replied Sister Teresa. "Now do you have any more questions, Raymond?" she asked, somewhat sternly.

My First Communion.
Just look for the most devout, seriously pious person in the entire group, and that is me (hint: the third boy from the left in the front row).

"Only two, Sister: It is 110 degrees outside, aren't you hot in that full habit? And, do you have any hair?" I didn't have the guts to ask these last two questions, but I so wanted to. I don't know if Mom talked to the nuns about what to say regarding questions for which there were no answers but, like the nuns, my mom frequently said, "It's a mystery, Raymond," a lot. Eventually, if I was asked a religious question in class, I would answer their question with my own question, "Is this another mystery, Sister?" Many times I was correct.

The second form, in which the bloodless ghoul taps you on the shoulder, only seemed to happen to my ancient relatives, who hadn't been playing with a full deck, anyway. I am not sure if this was a delusion or if a bloodless ghoul really existed, but it certainly explained things. Since—like the Catholic religion—every Italian believed the ghoul to be true, there could be no reason to doubt it.

When I was a youngster, I believed every tale or superstition told to me. As I got older, I wasn't sure of the veracity of these dogmatic truths, but I thought of it like taking vitamins. You don't know if it works, but why not cover yourself? Then, in my late teens I just couldn't accept these weird tales or unverified theories by Mom or other relatives.

By the time I was seventeen and was more educated by my friends who were not Italian, I became enlightened about death. However, no matter how much effort I put into explaining why death occurs, none of my relatives believed me. Why would they? Their explanation was much more likely to be true, and this view was reinforced by mine being a minority opinion, and constantly hearing that, according to my dad, I was a fucking idiot anyway. After all, as he explained, *ad nauseam*, he learned from the school of hard work and hard knocks and not from stupid books written by people who live in ivory towers and don't really know about life (or, apparently, death).

Nevertheless, I painstakingly tried to explain that death is an inevitable outcome of life. All of us may expect either massive physical injury or progressive bodily deterioration to end our existence. Either we expire from some disaster (car accident, avalanche, etc.) or we die of disease or old age. That is what will happen to us. It is a fact of life. This was so obvious to me that I was sure some if not most of my relatives would understand and be persuaded that I was correct.

I took both the Italian theories of death head-on and told any of my relatives who would listen that these theories were meritless. Dad never listened because he was too busy filling the room with impenetrable noise, and my aunts and uncles thought the younger generation was going to Hell in a hand basket because of theories like mine.

Nevertheless, to those whose ears I could reach, I explained that there was as little validity in a supposed "Death Dream" as there was in the clichéd image of Death itself as a grim, bloodless ghoul whose bony finger reaches out to tap you on the shoulder when your number is up. Still, no one listened. In the end, I guess they were right. After all, they went through it, and no one ever came back to admit they were wrong.

Another self-evident truth was passed down from my family to me: If I hugged my Mom it transferred love to her.

To this day, I believe this is certainly true.

CHAPTER 3

A Kid's-Eye View of Downtown

How the town appeared to a kid like me evolved largely from my experiences in downtown Napa growing up in the 1950s, but Napa's socio-economic evolution started 100 years earlier.

According to a chronology of the city's history, outlined in a document titled "Napa City," and displayed in an exhibit commissioned by Judge Thomas Kongsgaard on the first floor of the old historic courthouse:

The California Legislature in 1850 determined that the original boundaries of Napa County included what is now Lake County, and the county seat was designated "Napa City."

Two years earlier, Nathan Coombs laid out the original town site. It included a narrow strip between Brown Street and the Napa River and extended approximately 600 yards from Third Street northward to the Napa River. By 1850, a common method of travel between San Francisco and Napa was by steamship.

"Napa City" was officially incorporated on March 23, 1872. However, in 1874 the city was reincorporated under the name "City of Napa." The boundaries at the time of incorporation in 1872 were approximately Lincoln Avenue on the North, Soscol Avenue and the Napa River on the east, the tannery and Spruce Street on the south and Jefferson and York Streets on the west. The population of the town at the time of incorporation was 2,500.

The town grew over the years, and with it came electricity and telephones by 1889. Industrial jobs revolved around leather processing and shoe manufacturing along the Napa River. These industries were followed by wineries and fruit processing plants that reflected the agricultural environment of the Napa area.

Napa's population growth continued from incorporation at a fairly slow pace until World War II. With the war, a shipyard was built south of the city along the Napa River. This wartime industry brought a large influx of people into the Napa area. The shipyard became the Kaiser Steel fabricating plant after the war, and continued to provide many workers with gainful employment and decent living wages. These industries, together with the jobs created by the Napa State Hospital and the Basalt Rock Company, resulted in substantial population growth.

Adding to these job-producing industries was Mare Island Naval Shipyard, located in nearby Vallejo, Solano County. Many Napans established careers at Mare Island, building vessels that helped win the war. After the war, Napa Valley's budding wine industry, coupled with the desirability of country living, spurred growth in the Napa County area.

This is the context regarding the variety of jobs, size of population, and racial makeup of Napa as the decade of the '50s began.

According to the Bay Area Census the following information pertained to Napa City:

1950 Census:

Total population	13,579	100.00%
In households	13,210	98.00%

Race:

Native white	12,569	92.60%
Foreign-born white	935	6.90%
Negro	5	0.00%
Japanese	4	0.00%
Chinese	58	0.40%
White persons of Spanish Surname	305	2.20%

Median income in 1949: $3,791

1960 Census:

Total population	22,991	100.00%
In households	22,017	99.30%

Race:

White	21,991	99.20%
Negro	14	.10%
Other races	14	.10%
Indian	42	.20%
Japanese	20	.19%
Chinese	76	.30%
Filipino	13	.10%

Median income in 1959: $6,629

DOWNTOWN NAPA

Napa didn't have a notably seedy part of town, even though in 1950 the City of Napa, with a population of 13,579, had eight bars between 800 and 930 Main Street. Starting with Terry's Corral Tavern, located in the Conner Hotel/Terry's Waffle Shop building at 800 Main Street and proceeding north, they included Cronin's Tavern, Fagiani's Cocktail Lounge, the Mite As Well Tavern, the Talk of the Town Tavern, the Oberon Tavern, the Gilt Edge Tavern, and the Log Cabin Tavern.

These were not beer and wine tasting rooms, but bars that sold hard liquor. Some, like Fagiani's, also had off-sale liquor licenses to sell alcohol to go.

I don't know why Napa residents drank enough to support that many bars, but it may have had something to do with the times. It was just after the end of World War II, and places to gather and talk and have drinks may have been in demand. Maybe there just wasn't much else to do.

Downtown Napa on First Street.

Also, around the corner from Main Street at Second and Brown, there was the Plaza Hotel Cocktail Lounge, Bill's Café Tavern (later Napa Swiss Café) and Dave Cavagnaro's bar, Dave's Place, which made a total of eleven bars around one block.

Between these bars were places I thought would be interesting to visit as a kid. The Oasis Cigar Shop was one of these. I could tell from peering through the window that there were more exciting things available, including provocative magazines. Inside, in Lou Payne's snooker room, I could look at the pictures of beautiful, scantily dressed women until they kicked me out. In the back was a dark and dingy area that I knew to stay away from. It reminded me of the Westerns on television where they gambled and drank whiskey. Why not? Everyone else did on Main Street.

Next to the Oberon bar was a little hole-in-the-wall shoeshine shop that had two seats for customers. The proprietor just stood outside his shop and waited for customers as he leaned against the wall of the Oberon.

Above many bars and businesses were private rooms. I didn't know if the owners lived there or if they rented them to small businesses. I never heard or saw anything going on in these rooms above the ground-floor businesses, and when I looked up at their windows, they seemed quiet and deserted. I was always intrigued by the possibility that something scandalous went on behind those windows.

Among the many bars on Main Street were interesting places like Sampson & Rossi Hardware Store (which had a big poster that contained a large picture of a fully stocked refrigerator with the slogan—"You can be SURE ...if it's Westinghouse!") There were also several barbershops, a camera shop, an auto parts store, and a shoe store.

That little block-and-a-half was as seedy as it got for Napa, from the view of a young kid. I am sure there were worse places (May Howard's brothel a few blocks away comes to mind) but they were not within the realm of a pre-teen.

Very close to this seedy part of town was the nice part of town—very respectable, full of businesses, retail stores, and cafés. This heart of downtown Napa in terms of retail and professional offices was a fairly small grid, three or four blocks wide and five blocks long. For example, one block from Main Street was Brown Street, where the courthouse was located.

Brown Street had professional offices that I could not have cared less about, but they show the short distance between seedy and professional. The street had professional offices such as Riggins, Rossi, and Kongsgaard, Attorneys-at-Law; Mayfield Insurance Company; Oscar Tandy Insurance (his ads always said

"Mr. Insurance"); Ernie Mann, Jr., Physiotherapist; Byron Heckard, Chiropractor; Silverado Title Company; and Theodore F. Werner, Dentist.

The fun places on Brown Street for me consisted of the rear entrance to Napa Music Store (which had its front entrance on Main Street), Barwick and Dutton's Stationery Store (also with a front entrance on Main Street), Bettencourt's Motorcycle and Bicycle Shop, Murdock Hardware Store, Bun's Barber Shop, and DeLuxe Do-Nuts Restaurant.

Also on Brown Street was Carithers Department Store. They had apparel for men, women, infants, and children. What attracted me the most about Carithers, however, was their amazing pneumatic tube system. It was, to me, a remarkable invention, whereby the sales lady would put the money Mom gave her for the purchase of an item into a cylindrical container, and it would then travel through a network of tubes by compressed air or by vacuum (this possibly inaccurate explanation was from Mom) to the cashier sitting upstairs in an office. The cashier would then complete the transaction and put Mom's change along with a receipt in the cylindrical container for the return trip to the sales lady. Mom told me that the cashier upstairs was probably the boss who wanted to handle the money personally to ensure accuracy in the transaction. I didn't care about the reason, I just thought it was magic.

Further north on Main Street were fun places like Napa City Bakery. I loved cutting through the music store on Main Street and exiting on Brown Street because I could check out who was there. Napa Music Store usually had young guys and gals hanging out, trying out records. Upstairs, you could get a record and bring it into a booth to play it, listen to it, and see if you wanted to purchase it. I loved it. In this way, I could hear the latest releases without having to purchase any of them. I usually pushed it by playing a lot of records and then not buying any. Of course, I made it a point to purchase one every once in a while when I had money, which was not too often.

Partrick's Candy Store was heaven for a kid like me. I wanted Mom to buy me everything. I never understood why everyone didn't aspire to be a candy store proprietor. What was the downside? Partrick's moved to First Street in later years and became Annette's Candy Store, which also acquired my loyalty.

Further north on Main was another slice of heaven for kids, Brewster's Army-Navy Surplus Store. One of my greatest pleasures as a youngster came on Sundays after Mass, on the walk back home, when I stopped at Brewster's. There, I could talk to a sweet man who worked there named Harry Greco, the brother of Napa's mayor, Joe Greco. I could browse through all the World War II surplus equipment, including gas masks, machetes, knives, bayonets, Army coats, Navy pea jackets, and so much more. It was wonderful. Any kid who had the money could buy this stuff. I still have my U.S. Marine Corps machete and bayonet. There was no better place than Brewster's Army-Navy store to get outfitted to play war games with friends.

A block over on Coombs Street was Adamo Music Center—another cool music store with all the latest releases, as well as sheet music. My big trick here was to study the sheet music of a song I wanted to learn. If it was a simple song (and there were lots of those floating around in the '50s), I could memorize it, run home, play it on my accordion, and commit it to memory. By doing this I saved fifty cents. This was foolproof, as long as I didn't get caught taking notes.

Also on Coombs (near the courthouse) was Napa Billiards. This place reminded me of trouble with a capital "T"—straight out of *The Music Man*. It was a real old-time pool hall that seemed like it was from the '20s or '30s. It felt as if something illicit was going on there—maybe there were bootleggers and gamblers in the back. Something didn't seem right.

Mom would not have approved of me being there. However, there was almost zero chance of being caught by Mom. Being five-feet nothing, she couldn't see over the steering wheel, even if she was driving by. There was a great soda fountain in there and usually some guys from my shop classes—even during school hours.

Hagstrom's Grocery Store, at Coombs and Third, was where Mom shopped, very close to our house on Fourth Street. At age five, I told Mom that I was going to walk home. I was always kidding and my mom knew it, so she would say, "Okay, Raymond, see you at home." Mom didn't realize that I was secretly memorizing the way, which was basically a straight shot.

One day, when I told Mom I was going home, I actually did leave the store and walked home. Once home, I went onto our porch, but was too short to reach the key to let myself in the house. When Mom finally got home, I thought she would be proud that I did what I told her I would do. She was not happy. She had never laid a glove on me before, but this time she beat me like a piñata, with a wooden clothes hanger.

Also on Coombs was Wigger Brothers Men's Clothing Store. I loved this place, except when Mom took me in to purchase Husky jeans. Men could purchase trousers that were full and cuffed (Turn-Ups). For coats, men wore a wide shoulder, with broad lapels and coordinated accessories. Sportswear for men meant plaids and khaki-colored pants, known as chinos. Casuals also included Bermuda shorts, which some men wore with knee socks.

Coombs also had a bar (yes, another one) called the Gem Tavern, a barbershop, a furniture store and the Green Frog Super Market. Further South on Coombs Street was George's Gun and Sport Shop and the CalNap Tanning Company.

As a teen, I visited a friend of mine, Sal Garcia, who worked at CalNap. It seemed so dangerous to me. Sal's job was to put hides into a vat of horribly toxic stuff and stir it. He had to wear rubber gloves that went up to his shoulders and an apron and goggles, but there were still parts of his face and neck that were exposed to this acid should a splash occur from stirring too vigorously. It didn't seem to me that the job was worth the $1.25 per hour they were paying him, pre-OSHA.

On Franklin Street was Community Projects, Inc., a thrift shop. I loved this store, where there was neat stuff I could afford, like shells, rocks, grab bags, toys and, as I got older, used clothes, records and phonographs.

FIRST STREET

To me, First Street *was* Downtown Napa. My favorite fountain—Burrell's Fountain and Café—was where Mom would treat me to vanilla milkshakes and egg salad sandwiches (no wonder I was a little chubby).

Very near Burrell's was the Gordon Building, which contained professional offices but also featured Napa's only elevator. Mom would allow me to take the elevator up to the second floor. I thought this was the most modern convenience ever. It was an old elevator with an iron gate that gave me a feeling that I was in a cage. I didn't mind, however, because of the noise of the motor that started and the feeling I got when the elevator rose without me using a muscle. This was my kind of machine. Never mind that I could have climbed stairs to the second floor before the iron gate closed on the first floor. This was magic to a five-year-old.

First Street also had the beautiful Migliavacca Building. Inside were professional offices with wooden doors and beveled glass windows with the title of the office etched on it—just like "Sam Spade, Detective" from a film noir movie. It was a neat building.

At 1116 First Street was Albert's Department Store (succeeded by Mervyn's Department Store and then Kohl's). First Street also had Watson's Jewelry Store, Archer's Restaurant & Fountain, and yet another bar, Corsetti's Tavern. Woolworth Co.

Department Store also had a luncheonette featuring lunch and sodas.

Further west on First Street were Nielsen's Pharmacy, Stark's Women's Clothes, and Karl's Shoe Store, where Coombs intersected First. Across Coombs was one of my all-time favorites, Miller's Drug Store. It had a mirrored post outside the store under an overhang, where I used to read some of the sports magazines, and the store manager, Larry Fontana's father, never got mad or told me to leave.

Larry was a friend, and later a deputy sheriff and court bailiff. He is a great guy and his father was a very kind and wonderful man. Everyone loved Mr. Fontana. Even my father, who was not known to be a pleasant sort of person and could find a way to dislike almost everyone, absolutely loved Larry's father. They used to stand across the counter, talking about everything and anything, in Italian.

Across the street at Coombs was the Napa Register, an old structure that was the typical representation of what a newspaper building should have looked like. You could see the presses printing the paper. When I became a wise-ass teen I wanted to run into the Register and yell, "Stop the presses!" at the top of my lungs over the noise and buzz of the exciting activities inside, but I didn't quite have that much rebel in me.

Farther west on First were businesses such as Short's Flower Shop, J.C. Penny Department Store and the beautiful Goodman Library across the street.

At Rosee Women's Clothes and Jay Vee Women's Clothes, female customers could purchase the fashions of the day, such as dresses with a length below the middle calf that had a small fitted waist, pointed bust, and a smooth rounded shoulder line. Tailored suits often had fitted jackets, while day dresses had full skirts and fitted bodices. Sundresses, shirtdresses, and poodle skirts also were common. Cocktail dresses also became popular for evening parties. Bolero jackets and short shrugs often were matched with low-cut dresses. Women's accessories in the '50s included hats, gloves, and pearls. As for sportswear, women wore pants or trousers that were narrow and dropped to ankle length. Pants that went to mid-calf became known as houseboy pants. Pants that dropped just below the knee were called pedal pushers. Bikinis were found only in Europe. They were not worn in America until the 1960s.

West of these women's clothing stores was another one of my all-time favorites, Schalow's Shoe Store. It had one of the most technologically advanced machines in Napa, the almost magical Foot Machine. To me, it was the most modern machine ever, and using it was just like being Superman with X-Ray vision.

It was a large podium-shaped wooden and metal structure with a viewing glass atop the structure. We would stand on a platform upon which two feet had been painted. Then when the shoe salesman administered the instructions, after getting the machine warmed up and ready to go, we would slide our feet into the bottom of the machine. With our feet comfortably inside, the sales clerk would turn on the X-Ray and the skeleton of our feet became visible. My feet seemed almost like some science fiction version of the monster's feet from *Creature From The Black Lagoon* (only much smaller). We could see the bones inside our feet.

While my feet were in the machine, the salesman talked to me about what he noticed about my feet. Then Mom had to look at my feet and I absolutely had to look at them again. All the time we were gawking at my feet, the salesman was explaining in technical terms how my arches were flat as pancakes. My feet weren't so flat that I would someday be able to avoid military service, but they were flat enough to require mom to purchase the ugliest pair of black Florsheim shoes, with strong arch supports.

A pair of businessman's Florsheim shoes were fine if you were a forty-year-old businessman—but if you were a nine-year-old, it was not cool. For a shoe salesman, there could be nothing better than to sell a kid an expensive pair of shoes. However, for a kid the only cool footwear were canvas sneakers, white buck shoes, or coffee-and-cream shoes. Anything but black Florsheims.

Even though the machine said I needed these ugly shoes, I still loved the machine and wanted to get my feet checked on a regular basis. I was not the only kid who loved the machine. Schalow's was the most popular shoe store in Napa among my friends. If the owner knew your parents shopped there, he would let us come in and check our feet whenever we wanted. How great was this? This was the atomic age and nothing said modern, atomic gadget better than the most technologically advanced machine in the town. This machine was a legend.

I have no idea how many kids throughout the '50s are now having trouble with their feet or how many cases of foot cancer were caused by the overuse of this incredible atomic-age machine. Maybe it wasn't worth the experience, but we all loved that machine. We were beginning to see the advances of modern science right here in our own town and not just at the movies.

Further west on First was Jack & Jill's Children's Clothes and Sun Lite Bakery. This bakery had the healthiest cake in town, the famous Fruit Basket Cake with different fruits and gooey filling between each layer.

Next door was Napa Toy Shop, which had all the latest toys, including plastic Army men, coonskin caps (a la Davy Crockett), cap guns, electric football, erector sets, Frisbees, Mr. Potato Head, jacks, Lincoln Logs, Lionel train sets, Magic 8-ball, marbles, silly putty, skateboards, slingshots, Slinky, Pez, Play-Doh, Pogo Sticks, Radio Flyer Wagons, Robert the Robot, Tinker Toys, Tonka Trucks, View-Masters and Yo-Yos. I loved this store and so did all my friends. There were toys for girls too, like Barbie Dolls (which came out in 1959); Crayola crayons, Hula Hoops, Raggedy Ann, roller skates, Trolls, and teddy bears.

Napa Toy Store also had games such as Candy Land, Checkers, Chutes and Ladders, Mad Libs, Monopoly, Parcheesi, Pick Up Sticks, Scrabble, Clue, Risk, Chinese Checkers, Tiddlywinks and Yahtzee.

Further West on First Street was Marlene's Women's Clothes, Massey & Franchi Gas Station, Sprouse-Reitz Company Variety Store, Pay Less Drug Store, Senate Coffee Shop, Whitman & Bailey Jewelers, Argo Jewelers, Jenkel Davidson Optometry, Napa Prescription Pharmacy, and Fireside Thrift Corporation.

There was Moffitt Motors (used cars) at Franklin Street, the Napa Police Department, and Safeway Store where Seminary Street intersects with First Street, and Bank of America. At 1750 First Street were the Napa School District offices. Past Jefferson Street was Storcks' Garage and further west was Fairlawn Miniature Golf and Bruno Passini Beer Distributor.

On First Street east of Main Street, on the other side of the train tracks, were my stomping grounds. On Saturdays for Catechism and on Sundays for Mass, I walked to St. John's Catholic Church (the beautiful old church with the pinnacles reaching to the heavens) by walking from my house at 708 Fourth Street to Third Street near Dave Cavagnaro's Tavern and the Napa Bottle Shop, onto the train tracks and the beginning of the train trestle, along the Napa River.

Here was the Roma Hotel with the Roma Tavern and Lombardo's Rooming House and Tavern, where all the old Italians gathered to drink and play bocce ball. I always looked down from the trestle and could clearly see all these old Italian men (really old, like 130 years old) playing bocce and smoking those old Toscana Cigars, which were black, crooked cigars that were lethal to most humans unless you had built up immunity from chain smoking them for decades. They were also taking a nip now and then of wine that was stored in gallon jugs off to the side of the court. These old guys had very wrinkled, liver-spotted skin. They were all very short and, from what I could tell, none of them weighed more than thirty pounds. In fact, from the bridge they looked like miniature Italian action figures with tiny cigars and little toy bocce balls.

Most of them wore wool suits with vests and chained pocket watches. They had gray stubble on their leathery faces from not shaving for days. They were intensely focused on their game. It was common to hear them commenting loudly in Italian on each other's shots, and everyone's Italian sentence ended, in angry broken English, with the phrase, "Son of a bitch!" I was fascinated by these guys, and envious as well. They were just enjoying each other's company, playing a fiercely competitive game. None of them worked (except in their Italian gardens) because they were way too old to be employed. To me, it seemed like a great life.

Heading further east on First Street also on the other side of the tracks was the Napa Tire Shop, at McKinstry Street. McKinstry was also where my father's auto wrecking business was located. At First and McKinstry was a wonderful Italian restaurant called Ruffino's. Stan Vallerga, the father of my best buddy Paul, had his hardware store next door, and Paul's uncle Joe had his original Vallerga's Market grocery store down the street on First. There was also the Club Silver Leaf (yes, another bar) and finally, where Silverado Trail intersects, was Food Fair Grocery.

In terms of marketing, Food Fair Grocery was a great name because kids would nag their mothers and wear them down until they took them there. It was the word "fair" that did it to me. It sounded like there was more than food, like maybe there were games and rides like at a real fair. It sounded like a fun place. I soon figured out that it was just a grocery store.

SECOND STREET

West from Main, Second Street was home to Cervone & Sons, Tailors. Nick Cervone still operates his tailor shop. He emigrated from Naples, Italy, and has been a fixture as a Napa tailor for decades. He plays the mandolin, and when I was a little boy, my parents would take me to his house where Nick would play his mandolin and I would play my accordion. He was always so kind and nice to me, and still is to this day, as I stop by to see him from time to time. He is my calendar for Sons of Italy events and still sells me tickets on their behalf.

Nick Cervone, long time Napa tailor and fellow Italian.

Next on Second was a building that is still there today, a place where my friends and I used to play at night because it was open with no one in the building (except maybe in the back, but they never disturbed us). That building was the United States Post Office. The 1930's-era structure was flanked by majestic-looking lamps on each end of the building. The building seemed immense to me as a kid and was a big building by Napa standards back then.

The doors were always open so that people could bring in letters at any hour. The ceilings were very high and had an echo attractive to kids yelling in the evening. Sadly, the post office building was badly damaged by an earthquake in August 2014. The postal service planned to demolish the building, but due to public outcry, decided to put it up for sale instead. Its future remains unclear.

The majestic Napa Post Office, damaged in the earthquake of 2014.

The post office was not a favorite place of kids to play, but it was an alternative when we got kicked out of the Uptown Theater for loudly goofing off. The Uptown had ushers whose job it was to ensure that patrons would be able to watch and hear movies.

THIRD STREET

The corner of Silverado Trail and Third Street was my stomping grounds because the route from my house at 708 Fourth Street, proceeding east on Third Street, was also the way to Alta Heights Elementary School, and later, the first part of the trip to Silverado Junior High School.

Silverado Trail and Third was known as Jumbo Corners because five streets intersected there. There was the Jumbo Corners Tavern and Grossi's Garage Repair Shop, which I passed every day heading to school. Across the street was the weekly Napa County Record newspaper and the Nemes Printing Company.

Next came the Angelo Buonventura Grocery Store, from a different era. This was a completely wooden structure and looked like it came out of central casting in Hollywood for an Old West general store. It was a very old building that must have been built in the nineteenth century or the early 1900s. There were rooms above the store where Mr. Buonventura and his family lived.

I thought it was a wise way to save money—living and working in one commercial building/residence—but it must have been really mentally challenging to work and live day and night with your immediate family, without some alone time. But that is how many immigrant families lived so that they could survive. I loved that store. My father bought a 1923 Jewett automobile from Mr. Buonventura, restored it as best he could and treasured it as his prized possession.

Next to Buonventura's, on the other side of the railroad tracks, was the Cavagnaro Bottle Shop and Dave's Place Tavern. In the back of Dave's Place was a very large patio for parties and family gatherings. I played my accordion with my dance band at Jackie Martini's wedding in that patio. Our dance combo was good because it included Bill Forsythe, an exceptionally talented musician who played trumpet.

At 983 Third was the Napa Valley Old Book & Antique Shop. I also loved this shop because it contained old items that even I could purchase if I saved my money from returning empties to Cavagnaro's Bottle Shop. I still have a biography of Benjamin Franklin that I purchased there more than fifty years ago.

Then came one of the great joys of my life.

The Uptown Theater was located at 1350 Third. I loved this theater, where in 1953 I saw *War of the Worlds* twice, with my brother and Jonette Pittore; where I had several of my early birthday parties with my friends (Mom allowed this as my special birthday request); where I threw Jujubes from the balcony, under cover of darkness, at people down below, hoping to get a rise out of them and praying not to be discovered; and where Bill Forsythe walked across the stage with Bill Murray just to get laughs.

It is where I single-handedly and proudly had two rows of peers thrown out of the theatre for laughing. The movie (*Come September*, starring Rock Hudson, Gina Lollabrigida, Bobby Darin and Sandra Dee) had not even started yet when we got thrown out. The first row of guys (which included me) were tossed when I made some joke in front of a nearby usher. I remember Frank Davidson saying, "Damn it, Guadagni, I haven't even opened my Junior Mints!" The second row of girls were thrown out while the usher was leading the boys down the stairs with her flashlight to my back. I raised my hands up in the air, in a surrendering fashion, as if the usher's flashlight was a gun. The girls all started laughing and the usher turned to them and kicked them out too. We did not even get our money back. We all went to the post office building and danced and screamed to make loud echoes. We thought we were cool, but we were just stupid kids.

The Uptown Theater, restored to its glory days.
No longer a movie theater, it is now used as a performance venue.

I loved the Uptown for its size (it was enormous to me in my youth), for its magnificent ceiling (I thought I was in a palace), for the ushers (some of whom were so pretty, like Jan Norton), and for all the movie candy.

I became a veritable expert on movie candy. I knew which candy was quality and which candy gave you the biggest bang for your buck. Depending on your budget and personal needs, I could give you the best candy advice on the market.

My counsel depended on whether you preferred to eat the candy or throw it in the dark. If ammunition was what you desired, Jujubes were by far the best buy. They only cost ten cents; there were lots of them in the box, and they were hard as rocks. They made the best and longest-lasting ammunition in the house. However, I did give one caveat. If your target were a long distance away (say from balcony to downstairs front row) then it would require a multitude of Jujubes glued together by your own saliva. If you were willing to use an entire box of Jujubes for one bomb you could kill someone. You had to be very careful with the size of the cannon ball you wished to use. On the other hand, if your adversary were only a couple of rows in front, you could use just one little Jujube at a time and force the person to move. If you had friends to assist you, you could hit your target from one side of the row and your friend could pepper him from the other side. This was very effective against detection and psychologically demoralizing to your opponent, as he felt outgunned by unknown perpetrators.

Except for the desire to make larger ammunition by briefly chewing several Jujubes together in your mouth while they got wet and stuck together, I warned many a friend NOT to eat them because they were also the most efficient candy at removing fillings which, of course, meant another trip to Dr. Nazi, the dentist who did not use novocaine.

Big Hunks had nothing on Jujubes. Jujubes were not to be eaten. Atomic Fireballs, Necco Wafers (especially the all chocolate wafers), and Tootsie Rolls were all reasonably priced, delicious candy. Flicks chocolate candy that came in a shiny foil-wrapped cardboard tube (like a smaller, thinner toilet paper roll) were outstanding but were a little pricey (then, again, they were all-chocolate). Junior Mints were, as advertised, very minty chocolate and were one of my favorites. There were lots of them and very reasonably priced. Milk Duds were another good buy, because, like Junior Mints, you received a fair portion per box and they were chocolate-covered caramel. They were so chewy that they lasted longer than most candy because they slowed me down to a moderately fast gobbling pace.

Old Fashioned Salt Water Taffy was great and chewy—but not so chewy that I might lose a filling. Candy Necklaces were not my favorite, though you did get an ample supply of them in the cellophane-wrapped package. They had several problems in my book. First, they had a name that sounded like they should be purchased by a girl, which was a turn off. They were very plain. Moreover, they contained NO chocolate.

Abba Zabba, Turkish Taffy and Bit-O-Honey were all favorites, too. Clark's Candy Bars were good, but no match for Heath Bars, which had that delicious toffee brittle under the chocolate. Toffee was also the popular ingredient with Almond Roca Bars—just heavenly. It was difficult to beat the pure milk chocolate in a Hershey's Bar.

There also were the Oh Henry! candy bars and the Mounds and Almond Joy bars, which I personally adored with all that coconut. I wasn't as fond of Payday, Baby Ruth, or Butterfinger bars. But, if you were willing to waste a candy bar for laughs you could always put a Butterfinger in your friend's toilet and let him think there was a turd floating around. However, I was way too cheap and gluttonous to ever waste a candy bar.

I did like Mars, Milky Way, and Rocky Road bars. Of all of the candy bars, however, Snickers was my favorite. The chocolate, caramel, and the peanuts all mixed together were just a heavenly delight and very pleasing to the senses. After playing in a hard-fought sporting activity like baseball or basketball I always loved to have a Snickers and wash it down with the citrus flavor of Squirt. That was my signature lunch, if left to my own devices.

There were also non-candy treats that were good sustenance and should be mentioned in any discussion of movie food staples. For example, there were the standard trilogy of peanuts, popcorn, and Cracker Jacks (which contained a toy as a bonus), as well as Spudettes (which were salty, shoe string potato chips, but in stick form like dried French fries), and of course, Bon Bons (chocolate covered ice cream). I loved these as well, but they were usually out of my price range and didn't give me the quantity I most desired in my purchases. My tribute to food at the movie theater mainly is to candy, chocolate, and chocolate candy.

Located at 1436 Third was Thelma's Fountain Restaurant, a small hole-in-the-wall café with three employees: the proprietor who doubled as a waitress, a short-order cook and a young, under-aged, illegally employed dishwasher.

Thelma Borreo was the proprietor and could out-cuss a sailor. Many times she did just that. If you patronized her place you had to have masochistic tendencies. I always thought a person would have to be obligated to take the kind of crap that Thelma verbally dished out. If your employer mistreated his employees, you might put up with it to keep your job. If one spouse verbally harangued the other spouse, you might put up with it to keep your family together. But Thelma's Café was not the only place in town. One was free to eat anywhere in town. Maybe her prices were the lowest. For all I know, that may have been the case, based on what she paid the very young, under-aged, illegally employed dishwasher.

That was me.

I got fifty cents an hour (minimum wage was $1.25 hourly, had I been legally employable). However, I also received one big perk. I got to take home all the stale donuts I wanted. Thelma was so lucky that she hired the one kid who loved donuts so much that he thought the pay was great. I always took the stale donuts home with me, carrying them in the basket attached to my bicycle.

I was twelve, going into the seventh grade at Silverado Junior High School in the summer between Alta Heights and Silverado, when I was employed by Thelma Borreo to work in her café. My transportation was my bicycle or my feet. My job was to wash dishes during her noon lunch business, which went from 11:45 AM to 2:00 PM. She had a great business during the noon lunchtime.

This job was not loading a dishwashing machine but actually washing the dishes in a sink with water the temperature of volcanic lava. It was non-stop labor. My nose was to the grindstone. I relentlessly washed dishes without a break. I remember the sweat pouring from my armpits down the side of my torso, and the same with my forehead, with sweat dripping down onto my chubby, albeit cute, cheeks.

I reflected on the *Flash Gordon* movie serials, the reruns of which I watched faithfully on television. I figured this is what it must have felt like to Flash Gordon after he was taken prisoner by Emperor Ming the Merciless of the planet Mongo. Ming banished Flash to the dungeon, where he was made to shovel coal into the raging hot furnaces of the palaces while he was regularly whipped by Ming's guards. I am pretty sure that the water temperature required by Thelma would have liquefied metal because it was at least 1,000 degrees.

Being dishwasher at Thelma's could have been a beneficial learning experience. Thelma could have taken me under her wing and taught me that humble beginnings come from knowing the drudgery of hot, dirty work. She could have explained that I should value this experience and aspire to obtain a college education so I wouldn't be limited to a life of hard labor. But she didn't. Instead, she came into the kitchen on a regular basis, yelling that I was too slow.

"Jesus Christ, Raymond, you are slower than your brother and he was slow as an ox!" she said shortly after I started working for her. "I am not sure I can keep you around here if that is as fast as you can wash, clean, and dry my dishes!"

I didn't like Thelma yelling at me but her verbal abuse was much less intense than Big Al's, so it wasn't like I hadn't ever heard the profanity or the criticisms of my self-worth. What did bother me, however, was learning for the first time that my brother had worked there before me. I was upset that Eugene did not tip me off as to what a terrible place this was to work and what a wretched employer Thelma Borreo was. Thanks a lot, brother.

After one particularly colorful and nasty scolding regarding how slow I was at dishwashing, I did something I never had done before. I had not even practiced this in my room. It just happened naturally. I turned around and flipped her off behind her back. I was so surprised at myself that I immediately turned back around and started washing again. I was overcome by guilt for having done such a reprehensible thing to another person, and especially an adult. I had been taught to honor my elders. This really bothered me because I knew that I would have to admit this conduct in confession, or not take communion.

The other thing that bothered me was that Thelma's behavior justified my conduct, in my humble view. As a result, I was very conflicted. I apologized in my mind, promised myself to confess it on Saturday, and took my dish of day-old donuts home for my afternoon snack, the evening's dessert, and my after-dinner snack while watching television. Another day, another plate of day-old donuts.

JEFFERSON STREET

Jefferson Street runs north and south through the town. North of downtown were apartment buildings, gas stations, real estate offices, insurance businesses, and dental practices. Many medical offices were located here because Napa's only hospital, Parks Victory, was on this stretch of Jefferson.

Kenny's was a real '50s drive-in restaurant, *American Graffiti* style. Neighboring Kenny's was Lawler's Liquor and Delicatessen Store, owned by Ray Lawler, whose son Michael was a friend and classmate of mine. The deli part of Lawler's had ravioli and malfatti, homemade by Ray's Italian wife. They were delicious. Almost in front of Lawler's was Bill's Burgers, a shack that had great burgers and the best fries ever made anywhere. You could see the bags of potatoes in the back when you were ordering. The fries were so oily rich that I think if you drained them you could have run your car on it.

If the ravioli at Lawler's and the fries at Bill's Burgers weren't enough heavenly cuisine for one's palate, all you had to do was go across the street to Buttercream Bakery, still the best coffee shop/café/bakery in the world. It was so good that later, when I was a student at Hastings School of Law, my roommates would request that I bring them back ham salad sandwiches from Buttercream on my weekend visits home.

I also loved Buttercream because of the down-to-earth waitresses. I once ordered a ham salad sandwich and the waitress whispered in my ear that I might want to re-think my choice because it was day-old ham salad that day. I appreciate and love that kind of candor from waitresses. That probably only happens in a small town where the waitress knows you. That's just how it was back then.

Continuing north were Lyerla Brothers Grocery Store and Robert Lyerla Meats. I loved this grocery store near Napa High, where my friend and classmate Andy Lyerla sometimes worked. Andy was a brilliant student and a great guy.

At the northwest corner of Jefferson Street and Lincoln Avenue were Napa Senior High School and Napa College. Napa High was the only high school in town in those days, so everyone went there. Napa College was the only college in Napa, and if you didn't go away to college, you went to Napa College. The high school building was beautiful. Today, it is used as the administration building.

Napa High looked like a high school ought to look. It had big columns in the front and a majestic-looking staircase leading to the great doors of the school which opened up to the large Indian Head portrait, perfectly laid out in the center of the hallway floor as you entered. If a student stepped on the Indian Head, senior classmates had a right to punch you. One usually didn't have to be punched more than once to remember to avoid stepping on the sacred Indian Head.

Chic's Burgers, where one dollar bought you five hamburgers plus a nickel back in change.

North of the high school were more businesses but, for me, the one that stands out in this area was Chic's 19-Cent Burger restaurant. As a boy who loved to eat and adored burgers, I adored even more the fact that I could get five of them for a dollar. This was never allowed by mom, but if I had the money I could purchase that many when I was by myself. Mom always took me to Chic's after my American Red Cross swimming lessons at the high school. Having graduated from beginning swimmer, intermediate swimmer, and advanced swimmer over the years, that meant that I consumed a lot of burgers. Chic's was also the place to frequent on Friday nights after football games—at least for young kids who couldn't drive. That is because of the convenient location near Memorial Stadium as well as the attraction of fine culinary dining that awaited.

Unfortunately, football was on Friday nights, and in those days, Catholics were not allowed to eat meat on Fridays. I could get a tuna burger then, but that was a far cry from a Chic's burger. I strictly adhered to the no-meat rule on Friday evenings for years, until one day I started blessing the burgers and turning them into fish. This newfound miraculous ability I discovered caught on, because it allowed all of us to consume Chic's burgers and not sin while enjoying them. I don't know why or how I acquired this power, but most of the guys accepted this simple dispensation from the no-meat rule by my simple blessing of the burger with the sign of the cross.

Further north, across the street from Napa High School, was Carl's Hobby Shop, a business that appealed to kids and adults alike—but mostly to kids, who could get so many different things to add to, or begin, a hobby, such as model cars, airplanes, and ships of all sorts. From Model T Fords and Stanley Steamers to the Corvettes and Thunderbirds of the '50s; from the Wright Brothers' airplanes to the fighter jets of WWII; and, from old battleships of yesteryear to the modern WWII aircraft carriers, destroyers, submarines, and battleships, each kit would provide hours of fun putting them together—unless you were impatient like I was.

OTHER HANGOUTS

Kids with cars could go to such fine dining places as The Wright Spot, not too far from the Old Adobe Restaurant (formally known as the Cayetano Juarez Adobe, Napa's oldest building, dating from 1845, and the city's lone surviving structure from the Mexican era). The Wright Spot was on Soscol Avenue next to Wright's Trailer Court and near the Rough Ryders Factory. This was a true '50s drive-in restaurant.

You could venture to American Canyon or Vallejo, but we never did as pre-teens, and rarely did as teenagers, unless word was out about a party going down. Up-valley (meaning Yountville, St. Helena, or Calistoga) was the same. We didn't travel there as pre-teens, unless it was for a sporting event like a baseball game at Carpy Field in St. Helena, or Borman Field at the Veterans Home in Yountville.

The town shut down at night, except for a period of time when the stores were open on Thursday evenings when you could go downtown after dark and the place was alive with people.

I was always happy with the many things to do in Napa as a young boy. Baseball and swimming at Mount George Resort, Oak Park Lake Resort, or especially Vichy Springs Resort, were enough for me, besides the movies, skating, and bowling.

As for roller-skating, there was one roller rink in the '50s, located in a building on Juarez Street, east of the original Vallerga's Grocery Store on First Street. I didn't skate very often, but it was fun to do with your buddies and girls. For some reason, junior high girls enjoyed skating and that was enough reason for me to want to partake. Girls even had birthday skating parties at the rink.

I wonder, if only I had had some proficiency in skating, I might have impressed one of the girls enough to like me. I will never know, because I was one of those skaters who fell down every few seconds, who eventually graduated to being able to skate around the rink, but only at a snail's pace. Though skating was an activity that could be done with girls, it was hard to show off to them when they were generally so much better than me at the sport.

As for bowling, the Napa Bowl on Soscol Avenue had pinball machines and pool tables, as well as a multitude of bowling lanes. We only went there if we were in a bowling league or accompanied by an adult. We had bowling birthday parties there at times, which were really fun. Later on for a while, there was the Downtown Bowl on Second Street and the Bel Aire Bowl on Trancas Street.

Napa also had a second movie theater in the '50s called the Fox Theater, at 1242 First Street. The Fox Theater was just down and across the street from Schalow's Shoe Store. I never went to the Fox Theater. It was always closed.

The KVON Drive-in Movie Theater was located south of town off Foster Road. As a kid in the back seat of my parents' 1950 Ford four-door sedan, I would watch the movie comfortably in my footie-pajamas with my brother and parents. Later, I would go there with my buddies on dollar night, squeezing in as many guys as possible.

One night in 1962 (not a dollar night) at the drive-in with Mike Kerns and Frank Davidson, we saw Paul Vallerga drive in with his parents' new Pontiac Grand Prix. Paul appeared to be the only person in this big car. He parked in the row in front of us and before our very eyes he alighted from the vehicle and walked back to the trunk. Looking both ways to see if anyone was watching, he opened the trunk, and the subterfuge was apparent.

It looked like a hundred kids exploded from the trunk. The number of kids in that trunk was actually four, but that is still a lot of kids to be crammed into a trunk. It appeared to be a scene from a cartoon. The money saved was used for gas, Cokes, and fries. That scene was worth the price of admission. It was a visual image I will never forget.

Between swimming, baseball, bowling, and movies, there was plenty for kids to do. But as typical teenagers, there always seemed to be a deficiency of things to do. There was only one movie theatre by the time I was a teenager (plus the drive-in) and if you weren't into bowling or shooting pool, there was not much to do except hang out at the Kenny's Pancake House on Soscol or the Wright Spot. But these establishments were not Starbucks-type places that cater to people hanging out and sitting around with their computers, sipping coffee. Kenny wanted his tables vacated to sell more pancakes to new customers, and the same applied to burgers at the Wright Spot. One could loiter at these places for only so long before having to move on. So the most common activity was to bomb around in your car or your friend's car, sharing gas money, always in search of parties.

Driving around endlessly some nights did get boring. The town virtually ceased to exist after the stores closed. I am sure I was one of the countless teens everywhere who said, "There is nothing to do in this place for young people." I was not as adamant as some who pledged to "get out of this town as soon as I graduate."

The truth is, I still live here and feel privileged to do so.

CHAPTER 4

This Kid's Food Memories

We all need food to exist, but with me, food is a real joy in life. Everything for me, in each stage of life, revolved around meals and in-between snacks. It became my reason for living. My childhood is where my passion began.

In elementary school, I would trade parts of my lunch to upgrade. All I had one day was an unimpressive peanut butter and jam sandwich. I loved it, but not nearly as much as I loved a meat sandwich. Dorothy Glaros, a nice Greek-American classmate of mine, had a whopping meat sandwich. I could see the pile of meat in the sandwich, topped with tomato and lettuce. It was more meat than I ever got in my sandwiches from home. There was enough there to feed a village. I coveted her sandwich, and quickly, yet carefully, planned my sales pitch. If I could get her to trade, it would be the greatest con job of my brief career.

"Hi, Dorothy," I said. "Nice dress."

"Thank you, Ray," Dorothy responded, looking pleased that someone noticed. Dorothy was too trusting to ever suspect I had some ulterior motive.

"You know, I sure love peanut butter and jam sandwiches, but this is the third day in a row my mom has given me one. I'm getting tired of it, even though I like PB&J. Know what I mean?"

"Absolutely, Ray. It gets monotonous. Say, I have an idea. Why don't we trade, if you want?"

"That sounds like a great idea, Dorothy. What kind of sandwich do you have?"

"It's one of my mother's big meat sandwiches, Greek style," Dorothy responded. The operative words in Dorothy's answer were "Greek style," but I didn't hear anything after the word "meat." I wanted to close the deal. Dorothy made the offer, so I simply said, "Deal." I felt a measure of guilt for my manipulation, but the feeling was short-lived.

We exchanged sandwiches. I remember seeing a small grin on Dorothy's face, which I interpreted as her victory smile—as if she got the better of the deal. I took a quick bite before she could change her mind. Imagine my state of mind when the white stuff I thought was mayonnaise was, instead, a mixture of cottage cheese and Greek feta cheese! There was no mayo, mustard or ketchup, the trifecta of condiments by my standards. I hated the sandwich, but didn't want to hurt Dorothy's feelings or insult her wonderful mother.

Fearful of retching, I rose to my feet and immediately excused myself. I went around the corner and spit out what was still in my mouth, along with dumping what was left of the abomination into a nearby trash can. I didn't dare try pawning the sandwich off on a friend, out of concern that I would lose a buddy forever. I had to go without a sandwich. I was starving.

Later, back in class after the lunch period, it finally dawned on me that the real con artist was Dorothy. I was sure she must have had a good chuckle, knowing she had stuck me with the crappy sandwich, as she chewed my peanut butter and jam sandwich with its rich, creamy, and salty peanut butter deliciousness, accented by the natural sweetness of strawberry.

Sometimes my desire for food left me with irrational thoughts. For example, Ronald Hodges, a friend of mine at Alta Heights, always came to school with a two-pack of Hostess Twinkies. Two Twinkies! Ronald was tall and thin. In the third grade, he must have weighed thirty pounds, tops. He was so skinny that if he turned sideways, our teacher would have marked him absent.

Every day I watched Ronald eat his Twinkies. He ate as slowly as a slug. His bites were like a hamster nibbling on the Twinkie, except in slow motion. It would take more than the lunch hour for him to eat both Twinkies. I hated him, because I don't think he even liked to eat except for sweets. Even then, he didn't rip into these Twinkies and devour both of them within seconds of his first bite. Oh no, he just gnawed at them as if he could take them or leave them.

My problem with Ronald was I couldn't persuade (con) him to trade a Twinkie for anything I had in my lunch. He only liked sweets, and I didn't have any candy, cookies, or cakes to trade for his beautiful treats. I wouldn't trade a sandwich for a Twinkie. Even if I could bring myself to trade a sandwich, Ronald would not go for that because he was a sugar-freak. I finally had to stop eating lunch with Ronald, because I would have lost gallons of saliva watching him slowly eat his two-pack of Twinkies. It was too much for me. I feared ripping them out of his hands, sitting on him, to keep him still, and gulping the Twinkies while moaning in ecstasy.

I had, on rare occasions when Mom allowed, known the exquisite heavenly delight of a Twinkie: a golden outer cake layer that was yielding to an unctuous yet light middle layer, filled with a soft, sweet, creamy filling. I trembled at the thought of each bite. When I thought of the treasures that lay behind every bite my thoughts turned almost homicidal. What was I going to do? Ruin my life? Kill for a Twinkie? No, I had to learn restraint. I had to put distance between Ronald Hodges and me. It was the only solution.

When we were in middle school, around the eighth or ninth grade, a group of us guys would go to the Koffee Kup on Main Street, where we would get the only things we could afford: French fries and a Coke. Sometimes we even split the order of fries. Only Mike Lawler could afford more. He would commonly order the businessman's lunch, which consisted of several hot slices of roast beef on white bread with gravy and mashed potatoes (also with gravy). We considered Mike rich, because he lived in a house with a pool and a pool house, which we used as our clubhouse and where we would listen to Shelley Berman and Redd Foxx records.

Two of my parents' favorite restaurants were the Depot and the Napa Valley Inn. They both served Italian food family style, with all the courses: soup, salad, pasta, and the main course. Following that, you could get spumoni or vanilla ice cream for dessert. I favored the vanilla ice cream over the spumoni ice cream, because spumoni had dried fruit in it like Jujubes. I didn't like the taste, plus they almost pulled the fillings from my teeth.

We frequented the Depot more than Napa Valley Inn, because the Depot was so close to our house on Fourth Street. It was not uncommon for mother to send me with a pot to the back door of the restaurant to pick up an order of ravioli and malfatti. The Italian cooks all greeted me in a friendly manner, like I was family. In a greater sense, I guess I was.

The food at both places was similar, as well as delicious. That may be because it came from the same family. My father told me that Italian sisters were responsible for the two establishments. He said that Theresa Tamburelli ran the Depot, and her sister Rosie Martini ran the Napa Valley Inn. Dad also told me that the malfatti was an invention of Theresa Tamburelli at the Depot. I never knew if this was true, but I have only seen malfatti in Napa at either the Depot or Lawler's Liquors. In **_Roots of the Present_** *(page 196)*, Napa author and historian Lin Weber writes:

> The Depot was a favorite hangout not only for East Napans, but for the whole city. One evening around this time, after she had cooked up her special veal and cheese stuffing for the ravioli, Theresa was startled to find that she had run out of

flour for the pasta. Diners were beginning to arrive. Unperturbed, she boiled small dollops of the stuffing without their cases and served it up as malfatti, an original culinary invention that quickly became a favorite. The Depot prospered.

Dad, who spoke fluent Italian, said "malfatti" meant poorly made or badly made. He said it was definitely a mistake, but we all loved them. I believe that this creation was invented in the 1930s, but it was well established by the '50s when we ate there with frequency. Later, Clemente Cittone came over from Italy and was groomed to replace Theresa as the cook. He later became an institution himself at the Depot. I can still hear him scream from the kitchen over all the noise when an order was ready: "Betty, PICK UP!!!!" he would yell to a waitress.

Clemente always treated me so nicely. He would see me at the back door of the restaurant with my pot and greet me with a booming, *"Hey Bello, come stai? Voletequalche ravioli? Entrare, entrare,"* meaning, "Hey handsome, how are you? Do you want some ravioli? Come in, come in."

I would walk in with mom's big pot, and Clemente would kiss me on the cheek (I remember he was all sweaty and his sweat rubbed off on my face,) and say in English, "How's mama? How's papa?" I would always say fine, and he would take the pot and my order which was always a 50/50 split of ravioli and malfatti; then, although we hadn't placed an order for gnocchi, he would put a couple of servings of those in our pot as well. That always made me feel special, because gnocchi were not even on the regular menu. Gnocchi are an Italian dumpling made from potato dough. With sauce or with butter only, they were out-of-this-world delicious.

I do understand why I was a fat kid. I loved to eat and I was helpless when this food was put in front of me. It was like heroin to an addict.

Clemente Cittone, renowned chef of the Depot Hotel.
He is still going strong today.

We ate at the Napa Valley Inn less frequently, because it was on the north end of town at the corner of Jefferson Street and Trancas Street. Because it was Rosie Martini's place, it was family-style Italian as well. It was a bigger and fancier restaurant than The Depot.

Lin Weber gives the background of how the Napa Valley Inn came to be:

Theresa's sister, Rosie Martini, also had a way with money. Her husband ran the Genoa hotel/restaurant. At Rosie's insistence, the Martinis used whatever cash came their way to purchase land in the northern part of town. A big piece at the corner of Trancas and the newly paved and upgraded Jefferson Street, for example, was among her holdings, and on that location she and her husband eventually started the Napa Valley Inn, which also became a favorite local gathering place and a rival to her sister's. (***Roots of* the *Present***, page 196.)

The Napa Valley Inn remained at the corner of Jefferson and Trancas until sometime in the 1970s, when the restaurant moved to a location on Solano Avenue. The building on the corner of Jefferson and Trancas was replaced by a Lyon's restaurant. The Lyon's location eventually became a medical building.

Ruffino's Restaurant was another popular Italian restaurant, located on the corner of First Street and McKinstry Street. Filippi's Restaurant is now in that location. Ruffino's was run by Ben and Lou Ruffino. It was also Italian style, with great food and a full bar. It was just down the street from Al's Auto Wreckers, my father's wrecking yard at 1274 McKinstry. More than once, at the end of the day, Dad could be found at Ruffino's bar. It was a favorite of our family.

Another very popular restaurant for Napans in the '50s and '60s was Jonesy's Steak House at the Napa County Airport. Jim Ford, Napa historian, chronicles Jonesy's in this way:

Long before Napa Valley became famous for wines, Jonesy's was one of Napa's favorite eateries. It was also a favorite of the general aviation community. From the beginning, in 1946, pilots from around the state flew to the airport to not only log cross-country flying time but to be able to eat at Jonesy's. Today, within the pilot community, the restaurant is known worldwide.

According to Ford, the restaurant was a favorite from the time Hugh Jones Sr. opened a hamburger grill at the airport right after World War II, until it closed in 2010. Said Ford:

> The restaurant prospered and expanded under Jonesy and then the Tuthill family expanded and improved it even more. After about sixty years at its airport location, Jonesy's was sold and the successor restaurant lasted just a few months.

Besides great steaks, the restaurant was known for their special potatoes and Jonesy's salad. The special potatoes were so popular with kids that I remember some kids who stayed home sick from school were able to manipulate their mothers into going to the airport to pick up an order of special potatoes to pamper them because they didn't feel well. I assure you this was not any guy I know, but some girls were able to pull this off with their sympathetic mommies. This specialty looked like a shredded potato mat, fried in plenty of oil, and topped with strips of melted American cheese, chopped scallions, and a large grilled onion ring in the middle. I loved Jonesy's special potatoes.

The special Jonesy's salad was made with chopped romaine lettuce, garbanzo beans, and Jonesy's famous blue cheese dressing. A large scoop of cottage cheese and one black olive topped off the salad. I did not like blue cheese dressing, but Jonesy's blue cheese dressing was like no blue cheese dressing I ever tasted. It was magnificent. I salivate thinking about it. My favorite order was Jonesy's hamburger steak with Jonesy's special potatoes and Jonesy's special salad. Wow! I sometimes had a steak sandwich or a filet mignon, but only when I got older and could afford it. Mom, who would only occasionally have a cocktail, always ordered an Old Fashioned from Jonesy's bar. I tried one once and it was all booze. My little mom had no trouble putting away a Jonesy's Old Fashioned.

When I think of all the popular restaurants of the '50s and '60s, I believe that Jonesy's was the oldest continuously run restaurant in Napa County. It didn't close until around 2010, much later than the Depot, Ruffino's, and Napa Valley Inn.

I may very well be more knowledgeable about the food in these restaurants, than friends in my age group. My dad loved to eat out, and as expensive as that could be, he was willing to spend the money to enjoy himself. Though I am sure it made more sense to stay home and save the expense of eating out, he didn't see it that way. So you might call my mother, brother, and myself, third-party beneficiaries. I knew the menus of the top four restaurants pretty well.

Another favorite haunt of my dad's, and therefore of my family, was Larry's Hickory Pit. It was located in the Food City Shopping Center bordering Jefferson Street and Old Sonoma Road. I loved Larry's. He had toasted buttered hamburger buns with barbeque beef or pork laid out on the buns with barbeque sauce along with great baked beans. Larry's whole family worked there, and when his daughters grew up I speculated that his overhead grew and he had to close. All I know is that it was a sad day for the Guadagni family when Larry's Hickory Pit closed.

The best bang for your buck was found at Palby's Restaurant, located on the Napa/Vallejo Highway 29 in American Canyon. I very rarely ate there, but after Mom and Dad divorced when I was an adult, it was a favorite of Mom's. She was on a very limited budget, and Palby's gave her a chance to eat at a nice establishment that she could afford. As I recall, Mom and her girlfriends could each get a steak, made from mystery meat, baked potato, and dinner salad for $3.98. And the baked potato was the size of a gunboat capable of sailing down the Nile. My mom could eat for a week on that meal and enjoy a night out with her friends. Palby's served its purpose for senior citizens and people of modest income. When I ate there, I enjoyed it. I remember there being large birds chirping in the back in cages, which seemed exotic to me.

In the May 20, 1964 issue of the Napa High School newspaper, THE INJUN-EER, there was a full-page ad for Palby's, inviting kids to eat prom dinner there. We probably should have gone there on prom night and stayed in town, but the foursome I was part of decided to go to some French restaurant in San Francisco. So we went in my 1955 Chevrolet and tried to order from a menu that was written in French, with prices the size of Palby's gunboat baked potatoes. I kind of felt grown-up, although based on the looks I received from both the French waiter and the valet guy who parked my Chevy, my tips were inadequate.

If my dad desired Asian cuisine, then our family would go to the Asia Café on Main Street. The Vallerga family went to the A-1 Chinese Café further north on Main Street. The Vallerga brothers, John and Paul, would always order what would be considered top ramen today, plus fried shrimp and fried rice. One time, Stan Vallerga unknowingly dropped a paper bag full of money and checks from his hardware store business on the sidewalk outside the A-1 Café, after the family had dined there. Fortunately, the restaurant owner found the bag outside the front door and called Stan. I like to think that would still happen today.

A few doors down, at the Asia Café, my brother and I would order mostly the same stuff that Paul and John were ordering up the street. The food at the Asia Café was excellent, but what stood out to me was that it seemed like we were the only people in the restaurant most of the time we went there. Even though it was almost never busy, our orders took forever to be prepared. Maybe the owners waited for a customer to come in and place an order before they even turned on the stoves. I wondered how they stayed in business with so few customers. The Asia Café was a family-owned operation, and the family treated us well. I figured we might have been their best (and perhaps only) customers. It is possible my views about their customer base were skewed, because the Asia Café is still open, and as far as I know, is still family-run.

There may have been fish restaurants around, but I don't remember them. We ate plenty of fish weekly at home on Friday evenings, because Catholics couldn't have meat on Fridays. I have compared Friday dinners with my Catholic friends like Paul Vallerga, and it seems our mothers must have talked to each other, because they all had the same limited menu. Friday's dinner rotation consisted of creamed tuna on toast, fish sticks, or grilled cheese with tomato soup.

By my junior year, there was always someone old enough to drive. We cruised around town, dropping into Kenny's Pancake House, grabbing a bite at the Dairy Queen, Alfredo's Pizza, or Catania's Pizza. We hung out a lot at the Napa Bowl, which had a great burger and potato salad. There was also the pool hall across from the courthouse, which had great milkshakes, featuring the stainless steel container left on the counter with more milkshake in it and condensation dripping down the outside.

There was a fair amount of drag racing, but I never partook. Being the gutless wimp that I was, I would wait at a favorite food place like Vern's Foster Freeze, while Paul would peel out of the parking lot in his parents' Grand Prix. Then he would race with Bill Murray and his '62 Chevy Impala. Quite often, Bill would beat Paul off the line, but Paul would pass him at about eighty. Then Paul would come back and pick me up so we could continue cruising. He would tell me the results of the racing contest, and I would just be happy he was safe and sound.

Hanging out in Vern's Foster Freeze parking lot was fun. It was very close to the high school on Lincoln Avenue, near Napa Electric. It was a convenient spot to meet friends. Also, it had a delicious array of ice cream, shakes, freezes, and Cokes. It was where I first had a Coke freeze, which became my favorite—when I could afford it. There were also some fights in the parking lot, like when John Killebrew cold-cocked Doug Murray, with Doug parked behind the wheel of his car, window down, having no way to defend himself. But these were the exceptions. Most of the time, it was just fun hanging out.

My favorite haunts during daylight hours or noon breaks were Vern's Foster Freeze for a vanilla Coke, and then Bill's Burgers for an order of fries. Bill's was a little shack in front of Lawler's Liquors, within easy walking distance from Vern's Foster Freeze. I consumed untold quantities of the French fries that were cooked in forty-weight non-detergent oil. The burgers were great too, but were too expensive for me to have on a regular basis.

Amid these wonderful eateries was the incomparable Buttercream Bakery, that wasn't just a bakery, but a great diner with superb breakfasts. I liked to start my breakfast with a cinnamon roll heated with butter. This would be followed by eggs, sausage, and hash browns.

Buttercream Bakery: An all time Napa favorite.

In the eighth grade, I worked as a paper inserter with my pal Bill Forsythe for the San Francisco Examiner. Instead of delivering papers, I worked Sunday mornings from 3:30 AM to 5:30 AM.

Poor Mom had to get up in the middle of the night to drive me to the warehouse. I inserted the guts of the Sunday paper into the funny papers and then loaded them onto a truck for distribution to the paperboys to pick up and deliver. Working one night a week, I earned a flat $30 per month, which exceeded what any paperboy could earn working six days a week, and there was no fee collecting. We did our work in an old warehouse near Napa Electric, very near Buttercream Bakery. We would get off work about 5:30 AM on Sunday mornings. We would walk over to the bakery, just in time to get a cake doughnut fresh from the oven. I still have the sensory memory of the most buttery, soft, creamy cake doughnuts I have ever had. Only cash flow limited the amount of doughnuts I would purchase. Of course, I had to eat them at their optimum moment, which was as soon as I got my hands on them, because that is when they were the freshest and warmest and most delicious. They would never be better than right out of the oven.

Unfortunately, the paper inserter job was not a long term one. I was the senior paper inserter and Bill was my assistant (I got $30.00 a month and Bill got $25.00). He got the job based on my recommendation. The boss told me that he would hire Bill, but I would be responsible for him. I didn't exactly know what that meant, but I agreed without hesitation. Bill was fun and I was so happy to work with him. However, shortly after Bill came on board, we experienced a very cold Sunday morning. Bill, without my knowledge or consent, started a fire outside the warehouse to keep us warm. Before long, the fire got out of control and a large portion of the side of the building was charred before he could put the fire out. The boss called me and fired us both. I told him that I didn't start the fire. The boss said that didn't matter because I told him that I would be responsible for Bill. I couldn't argue with that. Lesson learned. So much for those right-out-of-the-oven, melt-in your-mouth Buttercream donuts.

The Wright Spot was a '50s drive-in restaurant that was a real favorite among the teens, located on the south end of town on

Soscol Avenue, where auto row is now. Jim Ford, Napa historian, told me of other local drive-ins in Napa that were here in the '50s, but were around too early in the decade for me to patronize. To the north, across Jefferson Street from Napa High, was the Knotty Pine Drive-in (later to become Chic's Burgers). In between was Kenny's Drive-in on the corner of Jefferson and H Street (it became a cleaners and then a printing business.) Then, there was Lily's Drive-in on First Street, at Silverado Trail. All of the drive-ins had carhop waitresses.

The Wright Spot: A Napa drive-in restaurant from the past.

Going to dinner at the Wright Spot with my buddy Mike Kerns and his father was a treat. Mike was one of the kids who came from a divorced home (which were then called "broken homes"). Mike's father lived in Wright's Trailer Court, and when Mike was in his father's custody, they would go to dinner on a nightly basis at the Wright Spot. Every night Mike would have a greasy cheeseburger with French fries and a strawberry shake. I thought he was the luckiest person in the world.

Mr. Ford gave me a 1954 reproduction of a 1934 "Wright Spot" menu printed to celebrate their twenty years in business. As part of the celebration, prices for one day in 1954 were to be the same as the prices in 1934.

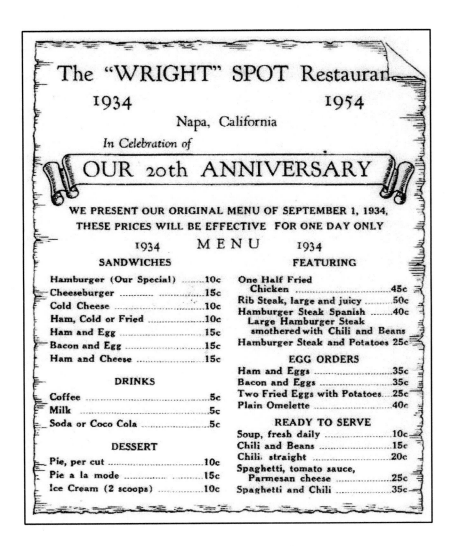

The twentieth anniversary menu of the Wright Spot.

"On that day, hamburgers were a dime, a rib steak was fifty cents and a dime would buy you a piece of pie or two scoops of ice cream," said Ford. "Those really low prices reflect the fact that, in 1934, the country was almost five years into what would become a twelve-year depression."

Mom read to me from the Napa Register about the price reductions reverting back to 1934 prices. I was amazed at how low the prices were in 1934 compared to the very expensive prices twenty years later.

The restaurant operated as a drive-in well into the 1960s.

I was a happy and willing customer in the '50s and '60s at all of these eateries. Some of the old Italian establishments were very sentimental to me and the food was my favorite. Some of the other non-Italian restaurants were also among my top picks. All of them seemed to be more than a place with good food. They were more intimate. The proprietors knew their regular customers by name. To this day, I still bring a pot over to Clemente for his mouth-watering malfatti and a sweaty kiss on the cheek.

CHAPTER 5

Time Was On Our Side

One of the axioms of life is that childhood waits for no one. Kids grow up in the blink of an eye. This particular axiom is true for adults only, because when you are a kid, time goes by slowly.

Summer vacations lasted so long that I actually started thinking that going back to school would not be a completely outrageously terrible idea. I would at least be able to see my friends.

The school year was even worse for dragging on, seemingly never-ending. I couldn't wait for summer to begin. I enjoyed school, but after a while it began to feel like life imprisonment. The hope of the arrival of summer was always a very faint light at the end of the tunnel.

Time moved slowly for kids of the 1950s—at least for my buddies and me.

Car trips took longer than most experiences of my life. A trip to my Nonni's house in Healdsburg was excruciatingly long, for various reasons.

First, it was a car trip in our 1950 Ford, a four-door sedan, which came in a beautiful Hawaiian bronze color and a V-8 engine. I had to sit in the back seat, behind Dad.

Second, the road was curvy, especially with Big Al driving at the speed of sound; carsickness was always a concern. Big Al's speed paradoxically didn't speed up the trip, but somehow made it last longer.

Third, if it was a hot day, all of our windows were down, which meant I would have to duck the spewing of bunched up phlegm that Dad would spit out the driver's side window. The greenish-yellowish phlegm-ball must have had sensors, as it invariably headed in the same peculiar route every time. It started off straight out Dad's window, but then took an immediate boomerang-curve back through my window and into my face. This could happen at any time, depending on when Dad needed to expectorate. I always had to be on guard.

The only warning I had was that before he could deliver his phlegm-bomb, he had to inhale and suck up his mucus from the bowels of his lungs. To accomplish this, he had to use all of his might, which caused a loud sound that is very difficult to describe unless you have heard it. The closest thing to the sound Dad made is the sound a big dog makes when his master pulls on the dog's choker-chain collar to bring the dog to an abrupt stop.

Dad's sound was fair warning, but even with this hideous warning-sound, it was very difficult for me to duck from all of the mucus shrapnel, because with manual windows (not electric like most cars today) I could not roll up the windows fast enough to avoid at least part of my face from being hit.

I could possibly have moved to the other end of the backseat, because there were no seat belts to restrain me from movement. However, if my brother was with me, I couldn't move from my seat. Eugene (four years older and much stronger than me) always made sure I sat in the driver's side back seat (the suicide seat), and when we heard Dad's loud and powerful mucus-inhaling and sucking sound (or as I came to call it—"The German Shepherd hair-ball sound"), Eugene would push me toward my open window preventing me from sliding to the middle of the back seat and forcing me to stay in direct line for the atomic blast. This produced much anxiety in me.

If it had been during a time of war, and instead of phlegm-balls they were enemy bullets, the heck with Purple Hearts, I would be receiving the Silver Star, as I was in the direct line of enemy fire. The Silver Star would have been awarded posthumously, due to the fact that my "bullet" riddled head would not have survived the assault. To this day, I can still see no redeeming value in this experience, other than perhaps it built up my immune system. It did contribute to making time move slowly, because anything you hated (and I hated this nasty experience!) seemed to move at a sluggish pace.

Finally, we would arrive at Nonni's house, where time really dragged. Nonni was always so glad to see me that she would give me a bear hug. She was incredibly strong (think of Big Al, with tits).

I loved the part of the Nonni visits that dealt with eating. The most important thing to Nonni was that I ate her cooking. She was a great cook, and I loved to eat; we were a match made in heaven. Everything was homemade, especially her marvelous ravioli.

I had two major concerns with visits with Nonni after we arrived: one was the knowledge that I would have to make the return trip home on the same winding road at breakneck speed, dodging Big Al's phlegm-bombs. This caused me stress and dread.

However, I had a much more immediate second concern before ever facing the ride home. This concern, which caused acid to drip in my stomach (or "agita," as my Nonni would have said) was that Nonni was going to kiss me at least twice on the lips— once when we arrived, and once when we left. Her kisses were both powerful and painful. They were not pecks on the cheek. They were full kisses on the mouth (she would have probably gone for open mouth but I kept my trap shut tighter than a drum). The problem with the kisses on the lips was that because of her strength, they were long and hard kisses. They were painful kisses as well, because she had started to not look like a female.

She had a well-established mustache that any man would have been proud of. Nonni must have shaved or hedge trimmed this mustache periodically, because her stubble was as sharp as knife blades—and dangerous. Every kiss produced some blood—*my* blood—as the sharp stubble above Nonni's upper lip pierced my upper lip, causing intense pain and sometimes bloodletting, or the intense pressure of the kiss itself made my front teeth penetrate the skin inside my mouth. My front teeth and the inside skin of my upper lip compressed together at a force no child should have to endure. Sometimes both types of injuries occurred so that I had outside and inside bleeding. So, twice a trip (beginning and end – hello and goodbye) I had to endure the bayonet kisses of my super strong and powerful Nonni.

Time crawled at a glacial pace during the drive and the visit to my Nonni's house.

School field trips went faster, and were certainly much more fun. When you were on a bus with your buddies, and you are going to Stornetta's Dairy or the Old Bale Mill, time flew by. Sometimes I was so excited that I would jump the gun, demonstrating how slow even the fun trips were. I just couldn't get there fast enough. When the school bus, on the way to Stornetta's Dairy, passed the old abandoned Stewart's Dairy, I started to scream with excitement. I saw an "S" on the sign and "Dairy" following the word that began with an S and that was enough for me to believe we had arrived at our destination. Most of the rest of the kids on the bus followed my fallacious lead, and also began screaming in joy. Only those brainy brats who could read knew we weren't there yet. The only thing I proved was that I couldn't read. I was only a first-grader, after all.

Longer trips—even to nice places—seemed to take centuries. My family took two vacations when I was growing up. One was to the Oregon Caves, and the other was in 1955 to the brand new Disneyland (the happiest place on Earth, if you can ever get there). Knowing we were going to Disneyland made the trip longer than ever. I must have asked my parents, "Are we there yet?" a million times. Time really varies in its speed with regard to trips, depending on the destination as well as the route.

Time also went slowly for doctor and dentist visits—especially *my* dentist. His name was Dr. Theodore Werner.

I am convinced he was a Nazi war criminal. He did NOT use novocaine. I kid you not. Five minutes in the chair with Dr. Werner was like five years. I would have done anything to avoid seeing Dr. Werner. He had a deep, calming, and soothing voice, but to me, that was just an indication of how good his con was. He could fool you into thinking he was a nice, gentle man. No way. Also, he must have dyed his hair. It was completely black, but his age belied the color of his hair. He probably was trying to look like he was too young to have been in WWII. You may as well call it a disguise. Come to think of it, he probably had some plastic surgery as well. It didn't work, though, because jet-black hair on a ninety-year-old man just made him look like a wooden puppet. He didn't look real. He looked ridiculous.

He tried everything to hide his true background, I am certain. He even had an attractive blond, blue-eyed dental assistant named Greta. I fell head-over-heels in love with her, but I believed this was just part of his game. He acted so nice and gentle, and he made sure his assistant was a beautiful, tall, strong, woman who seemed kind and nice. I am sure she was really an Eastern European scrubwoman who was part of the super race, determined to extract American secrets along with my teeth. The whole setup was an enemy front.

I know for sure this was true because Dr. Werner did NOT use novocaine! Poor Mom didn't know it, but I would have turned her over to the Nazis just to get out of that chair. And, he could have used Fraulein Greta as his means of persuasion. He didn't have to resort to torture.

He gave some explanation of why novocaine was not needed, but it was not very cogent. It had something to do with the cavity not being very deep, so he could drill without novocaine and it won't hit the root and therefore not cause any pain or something like that. How did he know for sure it wouldn't cause me any pain? It was my mouth, and if there was even a chance it could cause a split-second of pain, then I wanted novocaine. I mean, any discomfort at all was too much for me. Was Dr. Werner being cheap, so that his services were attractive to his clients? I know Mom was happy to save on the cost of novocaine. Let's just say that mom wasn't cheap, but she was sure frugal. So, I would just have to man-up—but, he did NOT use novocaine. As to the issue of time, I think it is self-evident that time moved like a snail during dentist visits.

Time moved extremely slowly for special occasions as well. Those occasions could not get here fast enough and, as a result, time was slowed almost to a halt. For me as a kid, it took forever for Christmas to get here. And the closer the holiday got, the slower time passed. Time varied, depending on the holiday, with Christmas taking the most time to get here. Then came Halloween and then Easter. Thanksgiving didn't take long (probably because no gifts were exchanged in this holiday). Halloween had candy treats, and Easter came with an egg hunt. These provided great fun, so time moved slowly.

It also took forever for my birthday to get here. My favorite way to celebrate my birthday involved going to the movies with my friends. Mom would provide lunch for my friends and me; following cake and ice cream and opening of presents, we would walk the four blocks to the theater and watch *Wings of Eagles* with John Wayne or *Abbott and Costello Meet Frankenstein*. I loved my birthday. It just never got here soon enough.

All time went slowly, even enjoyable times. Weekends lasted forever. Saturday mornings lasted about thirty-six hours. I had time to sleep in. I had time to have a feast of a breakfast made by Mom, who was a superb Italian cook. Unfortunately, I also had plenty of time to go to catechism class at St. John's Church on Main Street. I even had time to walk there (I always took the shortcut through the train trestle with its hobo-laden weeds and riverbanks). I would get back from catechism in time to see part of the Notre Dame football game on television. Then, after lunch, Mom would send me outdoors to play.

I never minded going outside, because that meant unrestricted freedom. Besides, there was nothing on television that interested me that early in the day. There would be some grown-up stuff like farm reports, but otherwise there were test patterns.

Because time moved so slowly during my childhood, we had abundant time to engage in various activities.

In the '50s, we did have the time, and out of necessity we did create our own games and our own fun. There were no computer games or programs for kids to occupy our time, and not many organized sports or music lessons. With so much time on our hands, we made up games or took off on adventures with our bikes.

Staying home by myself led me to different activities. Outside, sometimes I would just play with dirt. I know that sounds weird, but sometimes I would just play with dirt and sticks and let my imagination take over. Mine wasn't the best imagination in the world, so I usually ended up just building a fort and holding off the enemy of the day (Indians or Nazis). Many times, I would play baseball by myself, inventing my own rules so I could have actual games.

Across the street from my house, at the main entrance of the fairgrounds on Fourth and Burnell Streets, was a concrete block wall that ran on both sides of the archway of the grand entrance. On the Burnell side, I would throw my ball (either a fly league ball or a hardball) against the wall. If I caught the rebounding ground ball cleanly, then it was an out. If not, then it was an error, and the pretend runner was on first.

After fielding all the balls I wanted, I would go back across the street to our driveway and hit rocks with my wooden bat at the corporation yard that was across the street from my house. If the rock cleared the chain-link fence into the county corporation yard, it was a homerun. If it hit the fence, it was a single. I loved this game more than throwing the ball against the concrete wall, because I got to hit the rocks with my bat and because I would announce these games.

When my pal Billy Forsythe came to my house to play, he and I made up a variation of playing catch. When my team (which was just me) was up, I could surprise him by throwing him a ground ball or fly ball, at my option. He could do the same when his team (which was just him) was up. We created a full roster of players with fictitious names. We played this game so much that I never forgot them. They almost became real to me. My starting lineup consisted of Ron Newdnick batting leadoff and playing second base, followed by Eddy Hatrack playing shortstop and batting second. Ignacio Spermentata (an all star) played left field and batted third, because he carried the best batting average on the team (Ignacio Spermentata was my made up name for a real ball player named Minnie Minoso, who played for the Chicago White Sox in the American League). Batting fourth and playing center field was our cleanup hitter, Duke Storage-Cell (also an all star). He was named for my favorite center fielder, Duke Snider, of the Brooklyn Dodgers. Batting fifth and playing first base was Bernard Fartquard (the third all star on the team). Batting sixth and playing right field was Oily Slenson. We always said he was our "slick" fielding outfielder. Batting seventh was the third baseman, Hobie Mantrash. Behind the plate and batting eighth was Gossey McCullen. Our pitching staff consisted of right handers, Tommy Weatherwax, Dickie Capochalaou, and Harry Hosenose. The only lefty on the staff was Bee Bee Eyes Badashes, who possessed a high-velocity fastball. Johnny Mudbutt was our relief pitcher, known for his curve ball that seemed to break four feet and leave batters helpless. On the bench were utility players Ed Fictaseous and Freddy Fringo.

Announcing these games while playing them with Forsythe in my yard was great fun, and we played a full nine innings—unless we were rained out.

Inside my house, in the basement, I could use the bed as a trampoline, and string up rope around the four big wooden posts that held up the house, in order to create a boxing ring. I was a champion boxer, as long as no one was throwing punches back at me. Sometimes I would just explore all the nooks and crannies of the basement. There was a room in the very back of the basement, where the cement floor ended and the dirt floor began. That room was filled with empty gallon wine jugs. It was amazing how many empty jugs there were. Enough to destroy more than a few thousand livers, would have been my estimate.

Sometimes I would just roam around in the dark basement if I were depressed because I had a dentist appointment. I would try to kill time before Mom transported me to visit Dr. Nazi. I don't know why I had to keep going back to see him. I told him every secret I knew. I was an empty vessel of knowledge, valuable or otherwise. I was willing to name names, but apparently he wanted Mom and Dad to live, since they paid his bills.

When not in the basement, I would be upstairs, engaging in a game with my army men. They were all made out of plastic and all painted an olive drab green. Army men came in a set (I had combined my set with my brother's set, so I truly had a battalion of army men). The army men were made with different poses. There was the grenade thrower, the machine gunner, the rifleman, the army man on his belly crawling (he was doing the alligator crawl), the bazooka man, and so on.

There was, unfortunately, a marching army man that I considered a waste of a soldier. He wasn't doing anything to help win a battle. His rifle was not in a position to shoot, as it was permanently affixed to his shoulder. All he could do was march. I didn't want my men for a parade; I needed them to fight! I ended up using the marching guy to be the designated casualty anytime I sent my guys into battle. Frankly, I didn't mind if he got shot. I could afford to lose him. Besides, the poor marching army guy never, ever had a chance to survive. When you just stand there on the front lines with your rifle resting on your shoulder, you won't last long. He was always the first to go.

My plastic cowboys and Indians also provided hours of fun for me. Some of them were made out of hard rubber, with their legs spread so that they could be put on plastic horses. I loved those guys. The Indians were painted with bright colors and always wore their war paint. They were tough fighters, but suffered from a distinct disadvantage in that they only had knives and bows and arrows against the cowboys' rifles and six-shooters. They fought some valiant battles, but the cowboys always prevailed. Bringing a knife to a gunfight is not a recipe for victory.

My brother built model cars that were so perfect and beautiful that he could be proud of them. He displayed his models on his bookcase. I loved to look at them and play with them when he wasn't around. I couldn't wait to build my own model cars or even airplanes. I decided on model airplanes, because my brother didn't build model airplanes. I thought I would have the market on airplanes. That would be my thing.

Unfortunately, unlike my brother, I was never, ever neat. I got glue everywhere. Glue on the model planes and glue on the table where I worked and glue on my clothes and in my hair. These models were so pathetic looking that I wouldn't even display them. I couldn't clean off the glue from the planes; they were ruined. I rationalized that maybe there was something different about planes than cars, so I then tried building model cars. Same result, however. Glue all over everything. I just wasn't neat. In fact, I was downright sloppy. That was the end of my model-building career. It was a frustrating experience.

The only thing I enjoyed about model building was the heavenly smell of the glue. No one told me that it was bad for you, so I inhaled it every time I got frustrated with my building project—which was constantly. It is fortunate for my long-term health that I gave up my model-building career as soon as I did.

I also copied my brother in painting. He used to get paint-by-numbers kits to create a pretty landscape or a horse, or whatever the kit painting was that he purchased. Again, my brother's finished product was really nice. Mom loved them so much that she would hang some of them in the house.

Well, maybe model building was not something that I had an aptitude for, but I figured I might very well be a regular Vincent van Gogh at number painting. I started with the smallest kit, a 4x6 number paint kit. I decided to go slow and not rush it, but my nature is one of impatience. Also, I become frustrated quickly, so number painting proved not to be for me. I had painted both inside and outside the lines. I had paint in one section mixing with paints in other sections, thus producing new and different colors that weren't meant to be in the painting. I also had colors on the table and my clothes and in my hair. I wouldn't mind the mess, if only the painting had been beautiful. But it wasn't. It was awful. Even I knew it. I didn't even ask Mom if she would like to put my picture on a wall in our house. The worst thing was the paint did not smell delightful, like the model kit glue. I couldn't even get a high from this stupid exercise. I hated art.

I wasn't the only guy who played with disappointing games or activities. My best friend Paul had an electric football game with players uncontrollably going all over the place. It had an annoying sound that droned loudly as the game board vibrated the little players across the board. The sound got old fast, sticking in my head, almost driving me mad. Combining electricity and football didn't work. It seemed so frustrating that I didn't envy Paul for having the game. I didn't bother to tell my mom about it or put it on my Christmas list. Paul used his football cards to select eight teams by draft, and had a starting lineup, but it was still a mess. I didn't want to spend my rainy day hours over miniaturized electric versions of one of my favorite outdoor games. Football was not meant to be played this way.

Paul also had a card game for baseball with balls, strikes, hits, outs, etc. Players would turn the cards over and follow what they said. The game included red cards for stealing, hits, runs, and sacrifices. These games were perhaps an early form of fantasy games.

Paul had another game that he usually played alone, but could also play with his best friend (me). It was the Mother's Cookies racing car card game. You used a ruler and two dice. Each roll equaled inches for each of maybe ten car cards. A race would take place from one end of the room to the other.

Paul also engaged in model building—hot rods, tanks, battleships, and so on—and also wasn't very neat, getting glue everywhere. However, Paul kept his unpleasant-looking, glue-covered models until his teen years, when he shot them up with his BB gun or blew them up with firecrackers. I applaud Paul for finding an excellent use for these models, which were otherwise a useless waste of effort and money.

A solitary activity that Paul engaged in was to run around his house and touch the top of the door opening, trying to touch every one without missing. Later he would try to touch the beams, and as he got stronger he went for the ceiling. I don't know if these activities helped him develop his vertical leap but Paul had the greatest vertical leaping ability of all of Napa's athletes of our time.

Making up games was not limited to Paul and me. At about the same time we were playing games independently of each other, kids in every neighborhood, all over Napa, were doing similar things.

CHAPTER 6

Free To Play All Day, All Over Town

Mom was a protective Italian mother, but in those days, going out to play meant that I didn't have to be back at any certain time, other than before dark. I could ride my bike anywhere I wanted to. I would be gone for an eternity. In fact, Mom encouraged me to go outside and stay outside.

"Raymond, get out of the house, it's a nice day!"

I heard this thousands of times, even when the weather wasn't so nice. Still, I never minded going outside, because that meant unrestricted freedom to explore the neighborhoods of Napa.

Because time moved so slowly during my childhood, we had abundant time to engage in various activities. And, out of necessity, we did create our own games and our own fun. With so much time on our hands, we made up games or took off on adventures with our bikes. And, if you put playing cards on your spokes, you felt like your bike was motorized.

There were no guys to play with in my immediate neighborhood, so I usually had to bike up the hill to Alta Heights and take a chance that I might see guys I knew and get into a pickup game.

The community standard for Napa kids playing outside in the '50s was to be gone for the entire day, except for any specific time our mom needed us. So, as a result, we would be out of the house by 9:00 AM on a Saturday and not expected back until 5:00 or, if it was summer, until dusk. We were absolutely encouraged not to be back until the end of the day.

There were exceptions, if you had a doctor or dentist appointment or some other dreaded thing where your mom told you to be home by a certain time. Or, God forbid, you got in trouble with the police. They had more time on their hands, too.

It seemed like everything was treated as a big deal. Break a window, call the cops. Throw a ball over a grouchy old man's fence, call the cops. Sometimes the cops brought you home early, or called your mom and she had to come and get you, or worst of all, your father had to come to the station.

Someone in an airplane looking down on Napa in the '50s would have seen kids playing outside in various areas of town. The activities would have been similar in many parts of town, but some would be different, due to geography. For example:

EAST NAPA

Alta Heights Area

One day, brothers Steve and Dave Ceriani rode their bikes from their house up in Alta Heights down the hill to their cousin Larry's house on Marin Street, across from the gym at Napa High School. The three of them walked over to the back of the gym and started throwing a golf ball up against the wall of the gym. They soon discovered some small tile-like panes of glass in one area of the gym wall. These panes were high up on the wall, and many were broken.

Well, the boys took this as an invitation to become members of the "break a pane of glass" club, and started aiming their golf ball at the non-broken panes. Soon, one of the kids broke a pane, and before anyone could say, "We'd better get out of here," a police car rolled up near the gym. Apparently someone from the fire station, which was so close to the gym you could almost touch it, must have seen the criminal activity and called the police.

I personally believe that the firefighters may have broken the other panes of glass and saw their chance to put all the broken glass on the shoulders of the young kids who wouldn't be believed. Of course, my theory was very biased in favor of my friends. In any event, Dave and Larry had to get in the back of the police car, while Steve, oddly enough, was made to ride his bike to the police station with the patrol car acting as an escort.

Steve never forgot the stupid grin on Dave's face as he looked out of the rear passenger window of the patrol car. The stupid look worked on Steve, because he started laughing; this was interpreted by the police officers as disrespect and not taking the situation seriously. When they got to the police station, the officers called Steve and Dave's parents. Their father, home on his lunch hour from work, came down to the station.

Roland Ceriani was not fond of lawbreakers, and he would not tolerate this conduct in his sons. They both had to endure a long and angry lecture, especially Steve, because he was the older brother "who should know better"—even though Steve was only eleven months older than Dave, the two of them being only nine and ten at the time.

In a subsequent case, Roland Ceriani was extremely angry with his boys when he found out that they were possible suspects the case of "Arson at Alta Heights." The double doors to the lower classrooms at one end of the breezeway had been deeply scorched by someone who set it on fire either intentionally or negligently. Either way, the fire department was seriously investigating the matter as a possible arson. Steve and Dave's uncle, Elmer Stallings, a Napa Fire Department marshal, had informed them of this ongoing investigation.

Then, one day, a mutual friend of ours, Clark Lunty, who later became a California Highway Patrol Officer, dropped by the breezeway to see what was going on. Maybe a pickup game? Who knows? But Clark brought with him his brand new bike that, of course, had brand new handlebar grips. Maybe the boys were not in the mood for a ball game, or didn't have enough players for a modified game, or maybe they were just bored. But whatever the reason, the boys decided to engage in the prudent act of sticking a firecracker in the handlebars and lighting it off. According to all eyewitnesses within earshot of the blast, it made a hell of a noise.

The school custodian heard the sound, came out and spotted the Ceriani brothers, and turned them in to the authorities. This meant, of course, another trip to the police station. At the station, while being interrogated, Steve did not remain silent. In fact, Steve asked some questions like, "Are you investigating a possible arson case here?" The police officer looked at Steve and asked him how he knew about that. This made Steve a suspect in the officer's eyes, until Steve told the police that his Uncle Elmer of the Napa Fire Department had told him. The police subsequently released the boys to their father, who gave the boys an even bigger lecture than the time before over the broken windowpane. The lecture included the usual stuff like Steve should know better being the older brother, and should have protected Dave from this exercise of poor judgment.

With time on our hands in the summer, it was always better to hook up with other guys for a conventional game with rules that everyone knew. This reduced the chance for disputes and fights. Also, the organized conventional games themselves were not usually dangerous. Baseball, basketball, and even tackle football would not be high on a risk-assessment list compared to the games guys came up with when left to their own creativity. When left to their own imaginations, their minds drifted to the thrilling, and sometimes dangerous.

The red wagon game comes to mind. In this game, the guys went across the street from Steve and Dave's house to Alta Heights School. In the front of the school was a circular driveway bordered with juniper bushes. The object of this game was simple. It was to destroy or damage as many of the juniper bushes as possible. Each guy took their turn riding in the red wagon, purposely crashing the wagon into the juniper bushes. The handle had broken long ago; what was left was just the steering wheel shaft, which in effect, was like a sharp metal stick pointing at the driver. I am sure the parents of these boys would have loved to know that a stake was pointed directly at their child's heart, throat, or face, depending on the size of the kid. It should be noted that our parents really had nothing to worry about, because we all (or most of us anyway) had enough wherewithal to know that a sharp sick pointing at us was dangerous. Accordingly, just before we crashed, we would throw the handle overboard so as not to be impaled during the crash.

Some kids came home early if beaten by some hood or bloodied in a sports or bike accident. None of us carried Band-Aids, so we had to go to the closest friend's parents' home to be tended to medically. That parent then usually called the injured kid's mom and snitched him off. Then, his mom usually required his immediate exit from whatever fun activity he was engaged in. As a result, one did not ask for medical attention unless one couldn't walk.

However, except for these fairly narrow exceptions, we were free men. We had a "hall pass." Of course, we needed our bikes to get to places where we could meet up with our friends. Amazingly, usually nothing was planned ahead of time. We just sort of met up with each other at certain places and soon we were engaged in an activity.

For example, Paul used to go down to Alta Heights School from his home on Sproul Avenue in the hope that someone would come along to get a game going. He usually didn't have to wait at all. There were almost always kids at the school playing in a pick-up game. Paul was playing tackle football at a very young age. He played with older guys playing at the schoolyard who let him into the game. Most kids Paul's age probably would have shied away from engaging in such a game with seriously older guys such as

Max Newberry and Les Womble. But the older guys (about four years older) liked helping such a young kid, who was a natural athlete, develop under their tutelage.

Paul wore his helmet, plastic facemask, and shoulder pads. He learned how to tackle big guys there. That was the beginning of a career that led to a 5' 9" kid becoming an All-American. Before entering Silverado Junior High School in the seventh grade, Paul caught an elbow in the face playing the day before opening day of school, which resulted in a black eye. His mom, Betty, was horrified that he had a shiner on his first day of school. However, the Silverado football coaches were not so horrified. In fact, Coaches Burl Autry and George Cammerota thought Paul was tough, so he got their attention right away. The coaches were correct. Paul was tough as nails, but you would never, ever know it from his demeanor outside of the game of football, where he was easygoing, friendly, and genuinely nice.

Sometimes guys ventured out beyond their home territory. Paul, for example, went across town to Memorial Stadium where the Napa High Indians played football. He biked his way to the stadium and ended up in a pickup game with other players from his side of town in a game against a team of players from the other side of town. It was full tackle with kickoffs and extra point attempts. It had all of the aspects of a legitimate football game.

Steve and Dave Ceriani also went across the street to Alta Heights Elementary, where hanging around almost certainly produced a pickup game of baseball or football. During summers at the Alta Heights fields, they played at least one pickup baseball game every day starting around 10:00 AM. If they didn't have enough players for a full game then they would shut down an outfield area. For instance, if they only had seven players instead of nine, then right field would be out of bounds or foul territory.

Many other kids I grew up with played in these pickup games, like Mike Kerns and Ron Weien (another friend from Alta Heights). Kerns, who was a fine all-around athlete, credited these pickup games for helping him develop his athletic abilities. Mike lived with his family on Spring Street in Alta Heights, a few blocks from the school campus (until his parents divorced, later on). In the morning he walked over to the school, and more times than not, saw Steve and Dave Ceriani at the school playing catch or doing something in the field of sports. Before you knew it, a modified game of baseball, basketball, or football would begin. This kind of regular practice really helped all those boys develop their skills—plus it was fun.

On rainy days they would take their game to the breezeway, which was a spacious, wall-less, roofed area of the school connecting one building to the next. Here they used a regular bat to hit a tennis ball. If they hit the ball over the rail, it was a home run. They would play these games for hours.

Another game we made up was a rip-off of carnival bumper cars. We called it Crash. It was played on the school grounds, usually on the blacktop areas. It involved riding your bike around the school and crashing into each other, just like bumper cars. The real difference between bumper cars and Crash was that you never knew when the crash was coming. In bumper cars, you are in a round ring where you can see all of your opponents in their vehicles. Not in Crash. In this game, you could hide around a corner or a tree and come out riding straight into the side of your opponent's bike knocking him over. It was thrilling and fun, in part, because there was an element of danger.

It is weird, looking back, that there weren't more wrecked bikes or injured kids. We didn't think of Crash as dangerous, although it was self-evident, given the very name we gave to the game. It should have been, at least, a hint.

Some games seemed safe, but in truth and fact were dangerous, at least if anything went wrong. There was the driveway game, also played at the Cerianis' home at 16 Montecito Blvd. The Cerianis had a steep driveway. The game was played by a guy on his bike at the top of the Cerianis' driveway pedaling down that driveway and into the street, where he was required to stop pedaling. He would coast from there on out, crossing Montecito Boulevard and riding into the school's circular driveway and proceeding completely around the curved driveway to the exit leading back to Montecito. If the competitor pedaled after reaching the Cerianis' side of Montecito, he lost. If he didn't make it all the way around the school's circular driveway, he lost.

We guys were not reckless participants. We ensured that this game was played safely. The game included one of the non-participating younger boys to be posted at the top of the street, on Montecito, as a lookout. If everything was safe then he would yell, "The coast is clear!" and the person whose turn it was would take off on his bike to see if he could make it around without pedaling. If it wasn't safe to proceed, the boy would yell, "Wait!"

What could be safer? What could go wrong? If the boy didn't watch closely, or even if the coast was clear, it would be possible that a speeding car could come around the curve above the school. Or, a bike racing down the mountainside could be approaching unobserved. Things like this could possibly cause a problem, but other than this the game was perfectly safe. Right?

Happily, other than some very close calls, nothing tragic happened. I am pretty sure, though, that our parents would not have been pleased knowing about these games we made up.

As for injuries, at least in my part of town, the only one I know of was to me, and that was because of carelessness and gluttony. Mom was making some cupcakes, and had just finished making the frosting with her Sunbeam Mixmaster while my friend, Dave Mello, and I were watching. Our intention was to lick the residue frosting out of the bowl once mom was done, and also clean and devour the frosting off the two mixer attachments. However, when Mom left the kitchen for a moment, I immediately started to scrape the frosting off one of the mixers before she had detached it from the machine.

Dave, Napa City's future Fire Marshal, did what any curious young kid might do in this situation, and turned on the Mixmaster precisely at the time my right index finger was intricately inserted in between the attached blades of the mixer. The blades commenced to twirl, but instantly locked on my finger that was wedged in between them. I was stoic for less than one second, and then began to scream, quickly followed by crying. Mom came running back into the kitchen and turned off the machine but couldn't dislodge my finger. After tugging gently on my finger and having no success she turned the machine back on and yanked on my finger, freeing it from the machine. My finger was sore and red, but intact. Unfortunately, I had to use my left hand to eat the rest of the frosting. This was one of my worst injuries, and it had nothing to do with made up games or sports—only my craven desire for sweets.

Those of us from Alta Heights also enjoyed hiking the mountains behind the school and the residences. There was a favorite rock formation known as the cup and saucer. As a kid, visiting the cup and saucer seemed like an all-day hike, climbing the mountain to reach this great destination. I thought of it as climbing the Matterhorn in Switzerland, sans the snow and potential avalanches.

On the trek up there, we were always on the lookout for toads, lizards (including alligator lizards with their sharp teeth), and snakes. The only difference between my buddies and me was that they wanted to catch these creatures, whereas I was looking for the reptiles so I could stay clear of them. I was scared to death of snakes and alligator lizards. Hiking with my buddies was a great adventure, and in my case, an act of great bravery due to my phobia of creatures that slithered or crawled with sharp teeth, tails, and little legs.

While these games and adventures were taking place in the Alta Heights part of town (the East Side), kids in other parts of Napa also played games (made up or otherwise) based, in part, on their geographical location.

EAST NAPA

Monticello Road, Vichy Springs Area

On the East side, but further out in the country in the Monticello area, a good friend of mine, Doug Murray, could be found in the '50s doing some similar, and some different, types of activities amid the slowness of summer time.

In Doug's words:

> Summer fun in the '50s amounted to going over the back fence and down to the creek to catch frogs, snakes, and turtles. During the hot summer nights I would hang out on the street with the neighbor kids, because it was too hot to go inside and to bed.

> In particular, the usual neighbor kids were the Reid brothers, Tom, Jim, and Rick. They were all fine athletes. We would spend endless hours shooting hoops in the driveway. I can still hear my mom yelling at me because the ball usually bounced off the cement pad and into her rose bushes.

> The only distractions were our own inventions and imaginations. Boredom was a frequent theme, but danger—whether self-induced like drugs or alcohol, or the threat of violence, perverts or whatever—was basically not a part of our childhood, at least one I was ever aware of.

> I loved going up to Vichy Springs swimming pool and spending endless hours around the pool with the gang of guys that grew up in that area. We

loved swimming, the arcade, and the cute girls. It
was a great place to spend summer days.

Steve Ceriani and Doug were very good friends. One summer
day, the two Silverado Junior High friends were sitting around one
of the public swimming pools on a hot, sunny day. Bored,
competitive, and looking for amusement, they agreed to see who
could spit the furthest out into the pool. Doug managed a
respectable shot, but Steve hawked up a juicy one and then let it
fly. Before, it got out to almost mid-pool, a guy named Krause, from
Steve's younger brother Dave's age group, was swimming across
the pool underwater. When he reached his air limit he came to the
surface, mouth wide open as he drew in a big breath of air. Yep,
you guessed it. Steve's big loogie went right down his throat. Steve
and Doug looked at each other for a split second and then fell out
of their lounge chairs laughing so hard they were crying. Krause
looked at the two of them, wiping the water from his eyes,
choking, and as he began to figure out what happened you could
see him turning green.

Steve and Doug still get a good laugh out of it when reminded.

CENTRAL NAPA

Glenwood Drive and the Alphabet Streets

Wayne Davidson, a lifelong Napa resident and one of my all-time
best friends, moved with his family to Glenwood Drive in 1952
when he was eight. Glenwood Drive is located near Central Napa's
Alphabet streets. Wayne and his brothers and friends were totally
free to ride their bikes all over the Alphabet streets. They played
hide and seek at night, right up to midnight in the summers. Today
this seems unconventional and dangerous, yet it was normal. We
lived in a safe community then.

From his Glenwood Drive home, Wayne rode his bike to Fuller Park late at night and never felt anything but safe. Their bikes had lights and little bells on the handlebars, but they were bikes, nonetheless.

Wayne's cousins, George and Frank Davidson, lived on E Street. Wayne and his cousins would travel to the end of E Street. There was no California Boulevard back then. Usually, Pinky and Penney Forester (neighborhood girls) would hang around the guys. At this site, where California Boulevard would someday be, and where there existed railroad tracks, the kids would dig large rectangle-shaped holes in the ground and cover them with cardboard. Voila, they had themselves an underground fort.

The Davidson boys, joined by the Gunn brothers, Ron and Bob, would walk the train trestle until they heard a train coming; then wait until it was absolutely necessary to get off the trestle (think of the movie, *Stand by Me*).

Going from York Street to E Street west until you ran into the tracks, there was a creek underneath the train trestle. From there they would walk along the creek or play in the creek. They left their bikes by the trestle, as no one had any concern or worry about his bike being stolen. Sometimes they walked along the creek from E Street and what now would be California Boulevard all the way to downtown Napa.

Ron Gimple, the neighborhood bully, would chase them around the creek and shoot them with his BB gun.

As little kids, on rainy days they would play neighborhood games inside one of the kid's homes. Wayne and cousin Frank remember playing Monopoly with their buddies, or a game called Wham. They seldom watched television (unlike me). Another board game played by the kids in central Napa was called Star Reporter, a game by Parker Brothers, copyright 1954.

All the guys had baseball or football card collections that came with packs of gum. We could trade cards with our friends, or just enjoy looking at our collections over and over again.

Wayne was not alone very often, because there were always lots of kids in and around his neighborhood. While neither of Wayne's parents were around during the day, since they both worked, the neighbors provided a very informal neighborhood watch. For example, Wayne and his friends used to play on his roof. Some neighbor would call Wayne's father, Glen Davidson, who was working at Busby's Furniture Store at the time (Busby's was located at the old Gold's Gym area across from Napa High School). Mr. Davidson would come home promptly upon receiving the phone call, and bust the kids while they were playing on the roof.

Wayne's dad: "What are you doing on the roof?"

Wayne: "Playing."

Wayne's father would dish out the appropriate discipline and go back to work. This kind of incident would happen in the middle of the day and it seemed as if Wayne's father had some super power that allowed him to know when his son or sons were doing things that they should not be doing. Wayne never figured out during his youth that some unknown neighbor was snitching them off.

Who knows who the snitch really was? Wayne never found out. However, one neighbor, Mr. Flint, a retired elderly gentleman, lived directly across the street from Wayne and was at home most of the time. Also, Mr. Flint's home had a front porch with two old Morris chairs on the porch. At any given time during the day one might see Mr. Flint on one of his Morris chairs. At some point during his youth, Wayne's parents thought it would be good for Wayne to mow Mr. Flint's lawn for free as a service to the elderly gentleman. Wayne started mowing the old man's lawn for free, and when he finished mowing the lawn he would join Mr. Flint on his porch, sitting in one of the Morris chairs and enjoying a glass of lemonade while talking to Mr. Flint. This became a regular routine for the two of them.

After every mowing, the old man and the young boy would sit in those chairs drinking lemonade and talking. Mainly, it was young

Wayne listening to Mr. Flint talk about his jobs, his life, and his family. Both Wayne and Mr. Flint enjoyed these conversations. Soon they became friends, despite their age differences. As years went by, Wayne continued to check on the old man on his own. He didn't need to be told to do so by his parents.

When Mr. Flint passed away, Wayne received one of the old Morris chairs from Mr. Flint's estate, based on specific instructions from Mr. Flint. Wayne still has the chair.

The kids in the Glenwood Drive and Alphabet neighborhoods played baseball in the streets. They were able to do this because Glenwood drive was a circular court, large enough for a game to be played. Playing with a regular baseball quickly led to disaster, with broken windows and damaged landscaping. With primitive ingenuity, the boys modified their baseball games to use wet newspaper balls, but they fell apart almost instantly. The creative juices started flowing and soon balls were made with scraps of leather from the leather factory where Mrs. Gunn worked. The balls were secured with string. They worked far better than the newspaper balls, which didn't make it through one smash with the bat. The new and revised leather balls worked well for up to ten to fifteen whacks with the bat before falling apart. At that point of disintegration, you would have to reconstruct the piñata-like scraps back into a leather ball before the game could resume. The kids were ready for this, as they had four or five leather balls at any one time ready for use.

Wayne believes that he and his buddies were the first group of kids to make a leather baseball that didn't go far and was soft enough not to break windows. To Wayne's thinking, his group of friends created the first safe alternative to a hard ball that could be played in the streets lined with residences and cars without danger to property or any risk of injury to people. The need for some kind of safe alternative to a hardball for informal play in residential areas was later recognized by professional entrepreneurs. These professionals made a fortune by creating the very popular Whiffle ball. Our Napa boys' invention predated the Whiffle ball. Our guys got there first but, unfortunately, they were just kids.

SOUTHEAST NAPA

South Coombs, Shearer School, and Imola Avenue

In the southeast part of town there was another group of kids engaging in their own games. The first guy that comes to mind is Terry Simpkins, who lived in the famous log cabin at the corner of Coombs and Pine Streets. It seemed to me that everyone knew of the log cabin house, and Terry got lots of attention because of where he lived. There were stories about the log cabin, including the one that Abraham Lincoln built it and lived there.

That theory was believable only to the most gullible and uneducated kids. That theory, however, was dispelled easily, unless it was asserted by a bully, in which case consensus was quickly reached that the log cabin had indeed belonged to our sixteenth president.

The guys in this part of town used to go to Shearer School to hang around until something developed—usually a pickup game of some sort. There was a big grass field in the back lot of the school that was bordered by a fence. The kids played baseball there, but not many kids could even get the ball to roll to the fence, let alone go over it. That is, hardly anyone could get the ball over the fence until the guys decided to slant the odds in their favor by using golf balls. This improved the power shots considerably, until enough citizen complaints were lodged sufficient to ban the use of golf balls at Shearer School.

In this part of town, football games were played by youngsters nine to eleven years of age at Kiwanis Park on Coombs and Elm Streets, one block away from Terry's log cabin. Kiwanis Park was a softball park by design, but kids played football there in pickup games. Terry's group played their football games in right field, which presented the kids with one unique problem. The players had to deal with the right field light pole. This group of guys varied, but Terry recalls that regulars included Dennis Landucci (I remember Dennis as a real big guy—though I have to admit that most guys seemed big to me), George White, and Dave Hood.

George White was a gifted athlete. He went on to star at Ridgeview Jr. High School and later at Napa High School. George was an all-around athlete who starred in football as the quarterback, baseball as shortstop, and basketball as point guard. Terry said the kids he hung out with referred to George with reverence; they also called him the true Napa Indian. This was, in part, because he was the best all-around athlete in school. However, this particular reference was also because his mother was part Native American.

Dave Hood was also a fine athlete, and may have been great if he could have stayed out of trouble. His last name fit him. Luckily, he never pounded me. I was probably too small to be bothered with. Truthfully, however, it seemed like whenever we would get together with other kids from other parts of the town to engage in unorganized, non-sanctioned games, there was usually no trouble; if and when there was, we were able to work it out.

The game in right field at Kiwanis Park was tackle football, usually consisting of three players on each side. The positions were quarterback, combination center/tight end, and running back. The center blocked, but was eligible to go out for passes. A typical game would see, on one side, Dennis Landucci at quarterback, Shelby King as a running back, and Terry Simpkins as the center/tight end. The other side would be, for example, George White at quarterback, Dave Hood as the running back, and Skip Quigley as the center/tight end.

Landucci invariably called the same play every down. Terry was in the huddle with Landucci and King when Landucci would rise to a standing position and look back at the other team as if he, at ten, was sizing up the defense of a poorly coached, unsophisticated three-man team of ten-year-olds; then he would re-huddle with Terry and King, and say "fullback delay," which Terry says was essentially a fullback draw play. Terry says there may have been other plays they used, but he recalls that Landucci called that play the vast majority of the time.

Terry's first real exposure to football, in seventh grade, was because of the Franco family. Terry was a friend of Daryl Penzotti. One Saturday morning, Terry and Daryl went to Memorial Stadium at Napa High School to throw a football around. Daryl saw a friend of his named Vic Franco, and introduced Terry to Vic. One thing led to another, and soon the guys were in a pickup game of tackle football. One thing that distinguished this game from other pickup games was that there was a semblance of organization to it. It seems one of Vic's older brothers, Jim Franco, was volunteering to supervise and coach football to these kids. Jim was much older and very experienced in the game. The group of kids ranged from twelve to about fourteen; most of them were Catholics from St. John's School. All the Franco brothers (Ross, Jim, Les, Vic, and Bob) were Catholic, and all had attended St. John's over the years.

The kids may have snuck into Memorial Stadium to access the field and ran into another group using the field. This other group consisted of all girls. They were an official group, and they were very organized. They were Barbara Mercer's Pepperettes—a group of girls ranging from very talented fire-lit baton twirlers all the way to beginning baton twirlers.

Barbara Mercer was no pushover, but neither was Jim Franco. They may have butted heads over who had the right to use the field. The football team remained on the field. The two groups reached some amicable agreement as to when each could use the field (even though the Franco group may not have had any right or permission to use the field).

Even though the boys' group was all Catholics initially, they started letting in non-Catholic kids. Jim Franco was the coach and he turned Terry, a non-Catholic, into a center/nose guard. Vic Franco played quarterback, and Penzotti was a running back.

Terry said he learned a lot about the game from the good coaching of Jim Franco. All the kids had to bring their own equipment, and it seemed as if some kids would bring something that would stand out from the rest of the kids—sort of their signature piece of equipment. For example, one kid got a bright white mouth guard that really stood out from the others. Everybody had different equipment, but they all had helmets, mouth guards, and kneepads.

Not only did Terry learn a lot about the fundamentals of the game, but he also learned some tricks or tendencies that players are inclined to follow, that helped him anticipate what his opponent would likely do. Terry was taught to look at his opponent's eyes for signs of how the play may go. He also learned to try to deceive his opponent on offense by looking with his eyes in the opposite direction of where the play was going. He said he used this trick successfully years later in high school ball.

Another of my buddies who lived out in this area of town was Fred Teeters. Fred lived on Terrace Drive near Imola Ave and the Napa State Hospital. Fred had been a Yellowjacket with me in Fly League baseball. Fred divided his time between earning money (which he had to do from age eleven, if he wanted to wear clothes of his choosing), and having fun with his friends. The kinds of jobs he worked at were picking prunes (Fred was paid thirty-five cents a box, which he claims was the highest wage paid for that work) to cutting grapes.

The kinds of activities he did by himself or with others included going hunting. Hunting to me always meant going out in the country to shoot a BB gun. But not to Fred Teeters. Fred lived in the country in that area of town back in the '50s. He would go bird hunting with his BB gun at first and later at twelve with his shotgun. He got his first hunting license at twelve, and his bird license at ten. He would tote a .12-gauge shotgun with him down Shetler Avenue to near Soscol Avenue and shoot birds with it.

He would also fish in the nearby creek that was near Soscol Avenue. This creek fed into the Napa River. You could pick it up at the end of Coronado Street, which, at the time, dead-ended at the creek. There was nothing west of Coronado—no houses at all, until you got to just east of where the old Ford dealership used to be, and then there was a little house off of Soscol Avenue. *One* house. This was a different time. Across Soscol Avenue, where the Gasser building is now located, was a vast amount of property owned by Mr. Gasser. Now this property contains a Home Depot, Target, and other stores, in addition to a hotel, movie theater, health club, restaurants, and more. But back then, that wide open space was where kids would hunt.

Fred hunted for rabbits and pheasants. Across from Napa State Hospital, where the college is now, was vacant land; kids would hunt for rabbits there. And where the Ford dealership had been located, Fred would hunt for pheasant, dove and quail. He would hunt by himself or with his friend David Brown, and sometimes David's father.

While it is true that most of this surrounding area consisted of fields and vacant land, there still was some danger to citizens in hunting here as a boy. For example, Fred was shooting for birds with his shotgun, and he had an opportunity for a "triple" when three birds flew overhead. Fred's shotgun was a bolt action so it was naturally slow in getting off each shot, but Fred managed to do so, allowing himself an excellent chance to get all three birds. However, by the time he focused in on the third bird, he was aiming directly at a motel located on the east side of Soscol Avenue, bordering the creek. The location was near Jack's Club (an old bar on the other side of the creek) across Soscol Avenue from where the Gasser Building exists today.

The shot aimed at the third bird showered the motel with pellets from the shotgun blast. Fred was twelve at this time, and he sensed that he might have gone too far. When he heard sirens, he was sure of it. He started to run and made it home, where he sat in his living room, peeking out now and then to see if anyone was coming to get him. No one ever did.

When Fred was eleven, before shotguns came into his life, he participated in a hunting competition with his pals, David Brown and Mike O'Brien. Each of them agreed to go around the block, with their BB guns, from Fred's house on South Terrace Drive, and whoever could kill the most birds would be the winner. The kids would proceed to Shetler Avenue, to Coronado Avenue, to Imola Avenue and back to South Terrace. Fred won the competition by bagging twenty-three birds—mainly little wrens. Imagine today walking around your neighborhood, shooting birds off of the telephone poles. No one cared that kids shot birds or squirrels or rodents, but it would never happen today.

At ten and eleven, Fred and Mike O'Brien would catch king snakes and gopher snakes and bring them home, put them in the back yard, and throw their knives at them. This is what they did for fun.

For Fred Teeters, the rules were simple. His father worked at Napa State Hospital as an electrician, and the Teeters family lived close by the hospital grounds within earshot of the whistle that regulated Fred's life. The whistle blew three times each day on the hospital grounds. Once at 8:00 AM, once at noon and finally at 4:30 PM. As long as Fred was home when the 4:30 PM whistle sounded, all was fine with his parents.

Even activities that involved a parent in the '50s would probably not be allowed today by a normal, reasonable, loving parent. For example, it was not unusual for Fred's father to drop Fred and his buddies off at the east end of Lake Hennessey at a certain hour to allow them to hike and fish, and then come back the next day to pick them up at a set time. What parent would do this today?

Yet Fred's dad was a normal, reasonable, loving parent. For kids who hunted and fished their whole life, it was nothing to be on their own and camp out. And, parents didn't think anything about it, either, because they knew their kids were prepared for this. It was not viewed as dangerous. It was part of growing up.

In the country there were many feral cats, which were a nuisance to residents in the area. Fred told me that he knew a kid that caught a feral cat, swung it around by the tail, and let it fly into the middle of Lake Marie, located where Skyline Park is today. Even a fish might drown under these circumstances. The poor cat must have become very disoriented by the spinning, and then to land in the middle of the lake must have been terrifying, if not fatal. According to what I was told, this was not a one-time act on the part of one misguided boy only. It was not uncommon for some boys to mistreat feral cats in this manner. Nowadays, this conduct would be prosecuted criminally.

Another activity that used to occur was with firecrackers and cherry bombs. Some of the boys would put a cherry bomb in a wad of bread, light the bomb, and throw it at a goose. Some would take the bread and have their heads blown off. I am not saying this was great fun, or that those who did it were well-adjusted young boys, but when routine games and activities got boring, some would step it up a notch.

BB gun wars were popular as well, in this part of town. Clark and Jack Luntey, Stan Fahnholz, Ron Wincomb, and Fred would all have wars with their BB guns. There were rules, of course, for everyone's safety. No shooting above the waist. I don't remember ever telling my parents about this particular activity and I don't know anyone who ever did. But the wars existed, and were particularly exciting because they were real. It was an activity that was widely engaged in during this era and, surprisingly, no one got hurt or had an eye put out.

As for sports—the pickup kind—the kids from this part of town would go onto the State Hospital grounds to use their ball field. It was a beautiful ball field at the time. They would play football and baseball with whoever showed up. One of the older kids was Carol Nelson, who later married our gym teacher, George Cammerota. Carol lived on one of the streets in the neighborhood. She became an all-world star pitcher in softball. Fred's older brother would play there, and other older guys like Ron Collins, Bob Boals, and Don Lemmon would all play football and baseball in pickup games.-

Again, a different time meant a different norm and different rules.

SHIPYARD ACRES

The Shipyard Acres subdivision was a World War II temporary housing development designed for Basalt Rock and Kaiser Steel employees who helped in the war effort by being ship builders. The houses were put up quickly and were rented faster than they could be built. Some good friends of mine came from this small, inexpensive housing development that seemed so unique.

Shipyard Acres was located south of town—south of Napa State Hospital where the Memorial Gardens is located today. The original units were built as four-plexes. They were made with a slab concrete foundations, stucco walls, and tar and gravel flattop roofs. They sort of looked like an old-style motel with the four-plexes strung together. These original units were one or two bedroom units, with some studio units as well.

Later, a newer division of Shipyard Acres was built. These units were larger, built out of wood, and some had three or four bedrooms. The Acres, as it came to be known, had a school that went from kindergarten through the sixth grade, as well as a general store and its own post office.

Jerry Boswell was a friend of mine from Shipyard Acres. He was a superb athlete, especially in football. He was a big, tall, well-built, strong farm boy, who could run like a deer. He later became a starting halfback on our North Bay League Championship Football team.

Jerry had one traumatic childhood incident while living at Shipyard Acres. He lost the tip of his index finger by putting that finger inside the spokes of a bicycle when it was upside down and being spun by a friend. The next day, after stitches and a splint, another friend didn't believe him, and pulled on the finger and pulled the stitches out. Jerry was really a tough kid, but that had to be excruciatingly painful. By the way, Jerry's mom was not happy about this entire incident. Most of the time, however, our unsupervised play was without injury or incident.

Ellwin Jobe, another childhood friend, came from Shipyard Acres, as did Tom and Jerry Davis, Mike Howard, Dale Smith, Jerry Boswell, and others.

WEST NAPA

Pueblo Vista Area

When it came time to move from the Acres, coincidentally Jerry Davis' family and Ellwin's family both ended up in the same Pueblo Vista residential area at about the same time. This was the west and northwest side of town.

The Pueblo Vista Subdivision, formed in the early 1950s, was constructed differently from the streets in the downtown area. While most of the streets in the subdivision were normal linear streets like Carol Drive, Janette Drive or Kathleen Drive, the subdivision also contained seven streets configured as courts. Three sets of two courts faced each other, and a seventh court opened to a street that led to Carol Drive, which led directly to Redwood Junior High School. Those courts were just big enough for young guys to play whatever sport was in season, until they got too big and had to go to the nearby school.

As a five-year-old, Ellwin could freely go on his own to visit friends after school, even though some lived as many as five blocks away, and play before returning home in time for dinner. It was not because there was a lack of parental supervision (just the opposite, in fact, since he grew up in a strict parochial environment). If he came home after dark, though, there was the usual concern and some sort of punishment. Can you imagine a parent in today's culture freely, without significant concern, allowing their very young ones to wander their neighborhoods?

Ellwin's family lived in Shipyard Acres for almost three years, but his parents enrolled him in St. John's Lutheran parochial school in the first grade, before moving to the Pueblo Vista area, where his parents bought their first home, located in a court which had eight homes. Many children lived within that court: Jamie Sutton lived three houses away from Ellwin; Dennis Pallet lived next door to Jamie. Jerry Marco lived across the street. Jerry Davis lived in a court two blocks away. Those kids were very capable, and later, actually became some of the more elite athletes in high school sports.

During their younger days, most of their sports, be it football, baseball, or kickball, occurred right in the court, and other kids from neighboring areas would congregate where the activity was. There was plenty of room, and everyone learned to play within the physical boundaries, so that no houses or cars would get damaged by footballs, Fly League balls, or kickballs.

Ellwin drove by his old court recently, and found that each of the eight homes in the court had at least two or three vehicles parked in the driveway or in the court.

"There is no way that kids now could play these pickup games that we did then," said Ellwin. "Maybe the kids don't want to because they have organized sports but these pickup games forced us to organize the games themselves and make all the decisions regarding the fair make up of each team, being on your honor as to whether someone was safe or out, or if it was a ball or strike. Every argument necessitated a solution that we had to reach. Also, we played because we wanted to. There was no parental pushing to get us to play."

As the kids of Pueblo Vista grew older and the residential courts no longer met their needs, they moved their activities to two local schools and even to Memorial Stadium (across the highway) to play football and baseball. It was okay to have all the sports activities in the court when the kids were younger, but not all the adult residents were happy when an occasional ball would break a window. The kids had to learn to hit up the middle or pay for a broken window.

It seems as if no matter what area of town you came from, nearly every day was spent outside. There was always something to do, although most of it entailed walking someplace—sometimes for great distances.

When not playing games, the kids of the Pueblo Vista neighborhood would go to the Napa High School swimming pool. They might do this as often as three to four times per week in the summer. For ten cents (until age twelve when the price went up to a staggering twenty-five cents), it was a great deal and it got the kids away from home, so the parents were beneficiaries as well.

Swimming was definitely a fun activity in summer, but it was totally taboo on a game day.

Personally, I preferred the atmosphere of Vichy Springs, Oak Park, and Mt. George Resort swimming pools to the big pool at Napa High School. I compared the seriousness of the Red Cross swimming lessons I took at the Napa High pool, to the fun I had at the other pools. The arcade at Vichy and the snack bars and picnic grounds at all of those pools, were much preferable to the business-like feeling at the Napa High School pool.

I have one negative memory with respect to one of those three wonderful swimming holes. That chilling memory was of the water at Mt. George Resort. It was so much colder than the water in the other parks. I am relatively certain that it had icebergs floating in it. Other than that one drawback, those three swimming pools were far superior to the Napa High School pool.

The main reason I disliked the Napa High School swimming pool was the 5,000-foot elevation of the high dive. My first time in the deep end I was scared to death at the thought of having to climb up the high dive ladder without a safety net. It might have been the first time that I actually thought I might die. Just looking at the high dive up close caused a tremble that could have been mistaken for a seizure by others.

When I was forced to climb up the ladder to the diving board, it was like a vertical Bataan death march—only much slower. I got very tanned during the summer, but the sight of me climbing up to the high dive must have looked like some kind of brown animal with very white paws, especially around the knuckles, which had turned that way because they were so firmly clutched to the rungs of the ladder. Once the ascent to the top of the ladder was achieved (in about an hour), I had to stand up on the diving board. As I looked down, I immediately felt a weird tingle in my genital area. I had only felt that strange tingling once before, standing on the top of my garage looking down, when I was pretending to be Peter Pan. I didn't like it.

Exiting back down the ladder was what I wanted to do, because I could once again hang on to the ladder with the same intense constriction of a boa. I was in a dilemma, however. If I climbed back down the ladder to safety, I would not pass my swimming lessons, and I would have to repeat them, if I wanted to get my certificate of completion. That seemed like a no-brainer to me. Safety first. Maybe in a year I could try again without the tingling genitals. Maybe I just needed a year of maturity. Yes, that was the ticket. I would gladly waive my rights to a certificate for only one more year.

The truth is, I knew deep down that I couldn't do that, because I would never hear the end of it from Big Al. Comparisons to the Cowardly Lion were already going through my head. It was safe to assume that I either did the high dive now and pass the course, or do it in a year and endure a year of psychological abuse from an expert who could really dish it out. If I ever wanted to be certified by the Red Cross (and Big Al insisted on this), I would have to leap off the high dive.

I defied death that day, but not because I was the brave young boy who laughed at danger, snickered at catastrophe, or chuckled at peril. No, I was petrified. Once I actually got to the top of the ladder and climbed upon the platform letting go of the last banisters of the ladder, everything went completely in ultra-slow motion. I did not hop onto the actual diving board and run full steam ahead, commencing a bounce that was designed to achieve maximum height before the dive itself. To the contrary, I inched my way to the end of the board, which took another interminable period of time.

From there I carefully tried to not bounce, jump, or make any movement, for fear of falling. Passing the swimming test did not require that you run or bounce on the diving board before diving into the water below. In fact (thank you, Jesus) you didn't even have to dive in. I was certain that a belly flop from that height would have meant instant death. Your guts would surely catapult upon impact with the water from your stomach through your back, breaking every bone in your body. It was bound to be fatal. Besides, death would be the best outcome one could hope for. The end of life would certainly be preferable to sucking your meals out of a straw for the rest of your life, with a completely immobilized body.

The fact is, I was allowed to just fall in. I wasn't trying to be hyper-technical with the rules, but rules are rules, and if I could pass my class by jumping off feet first, that is what I was going to do. So, with my chubby body for all to see, I stepped off the high dive feet first, holding my nose so my sinuses didn't explode upon impact (I was told this had happened by kids who claimed they had witnessed or heard of such tragedies).

With this one act, I bravely jumped into the pool from the stratospheric height of the high diving board at the Napa High School pool. I got my certificate of completion.

The northwest Napa kids would walk everywhere from their home area around Pueblo Vista all the way across the freeway to the pool. Other days might include a special adventure to purchase a new Fly League ball. That outing would take them to only one place, Yates and Cochran's Sporting Goods Store, commonly referred to as Cochran's, generally recognized as the only place kids would go to marvel at all types of sporting equipment: balls, bats, gloves, fishing equipment, sling-shots, knives, and BB guns. It was heaven to kids. Yates and Cochran's was in downtown Napa, and therefore quite a trek for kids as far out as the Pueblo Vista area, but the truth is, a lot of kids walked all over the place from age eight on.

NORTH NAPA

Beard Road, Bel Aire, and Parts North

Bob Benning was one of those north Napa kids. Bob was raised in what is now a chocolate-colored house behind the Trancas Steakhouse on Beard Road. Across the street was a prune orchard, where Bob played hide-and-seek and established tree forts. The structure of the forts was very crude, with no nails used. The kids mainly balanced boards to create the forts. Since the forts weighed nearly nothing, and there being little likelihood that they would destroy any trees, the landowner was very understanding.

All good things must end, however, and that was true for the hide-and-seek games and the fort building. It was a very sad day when the bulldozers arrived and knocked down the prune orchard and commenced building the Pleasant Valley Subdivision. Little did Bob know at the time, but before his very eyes, Bob was witnessing a change in Napa agriculture.

Prune picking had been a primary source of income for many kids in those times. It was backbreaking and dirty work, but it was something a kid could do to earn income. Bob rode his bike as far as Christian Brothers—Mt. LaSalle to pick prunes. The prune crop was of such importance to the town's economy, that the beginning of the school year could be delayed if the prune harvest came in late September. When the Sunkist dehydrator on Yajome Street cranked up, you could smell drying prunes all over the town and valley.

The Napa River played a big part in outdoor activities for Napa kids in the '50s. Bob has a unique perspective, because his time growing up in Napa was shared living on Beard Road and also on Jefferson Street in the newly created Bel Aire subdivision. Both locations gave him excellent access to the Napa River. The river, in turn, provided kids a venue for many different activities.

When Friday rolled around, it was not uncommon to see Bob and other kids from the neighborhood carrying fishing poles and sleeping bags to stay down at the riverbank overnight, and fish and build campfires just north of the Trancas Bridge. They even watched the new bridge being built from the area underneath. They caught catfish and some largemouth bass.

The river was dirty, but they didn't care as long as they did not get any of the river water in their mouths. As they got a little older, they would bring 20-gauge and 410 shotguns down to the river, and walk the riverside north up to Oak Knoll Avenue, looking for carp. The 410 guns did not make as much noise as the 12-gauge, but maneuvered well for quick shots at fast-moving carp. Some of the kids even tried their hand at bow-hunting carp, with open-face fishing reels attached just above the handle of an old fiberglass bow.-

Since the Bel Aire boys were new guys on the block, it was not uncommon for them to run into the Crescent Park boys who lived north of Bel Aire around Sierra Avenue. One thing always seemed to lead to another, and before you knew it a full-blown rock fight would break out. For Bob it was very fortunate that the only hits were on the appendages and not the head areas. Some ideas were just not thought out properly.

After dinner, if there was still sunlight, kids went outside to play football. In the mid-50s, Jefferson Street stopped at Trancas, where the county fire station was located. To resume onto the new section of Jefferson, a driver would have to continue west on Trancas and turn right onto Baxter Street, which was the opening of Bel Aire. From Baxter you would turn right onto Rubicon and drive east to Jefferson Street. Rubicon ended there, except for a couple more houses.

Gasser's cow pasture bordered the back of all the east side houses (think of the Lyon Estates subdivision in 1955 in the movie *Back to the Future*). The traffic volume on that new section of Bel Aire was nonexistent, except for neighborhood traffic. The recently installed median had grass; and it made for an extremely narrow football field with very few traffic interruptions. Kids would play there in the evenings until they received a sign that it was time to stop, in the form of a parent yelling, "Time to come in!" Many times, however, the most convincing indication that it was time to stop came when an incoming pass hit one of the kids in the head due to darkness.

Baseball was also popular on Jefferson Street, but kids had to play in and around parked cars. Parked cars seemed to be a universal concern, no matter what part of town you lived in. Bases would include fire hydrants and any other object in the general proximity of the baseball diamond.

After Christmas, the kids from the Bel Aire neighborhood would go around the subdivision and ask for the old Christmas trees. The neighbors were thrilled not to have to dispose of them. The kids would then drag them down to the vacant lot between Trancas Street and the new section of Jefferson Street. There they would stack them up and build hideouts where they could—and would—spend hours. Bob Benning said the best part of these forts was the smell of pine.

There is no better or more accurate way to sum up a kid's life back in the 1950s, than to say that our lives were primarily spent outside. Our mothers sent us outdoors, with the firm instruction to come home in time for dinner.

Our only goal, once outside, was to have fun—and we made our own fun. We invented games and rules, and had to work out all of the details among ourselves. We had to work out all disputes between ourselves. I believe it was a good foundation for adulthood by learning to make compromises, the benefits of teamwork, and, on a very fundamental basis, the art of mediation. These activities were all done without the benefit of organized events that exist today and occupy most of our youths' time. This is not to say that one was bad or one is good. It was just different. There were and are benefits to both.

CHAPTER 7

The Dreaded Virus

"Get in bed now, boys!" Mom would say.

"But Mom, I don't want to yet. Can't we go out and play?" I pleaded.

"Absolutely not. You must rest, or you might get sick. Now quit fighting me on this and go to bed right now!"

My brother also fought Mom on this.

"But, Mom, it is two in the afternoon! We aren't tired!" Eugene whined.

I was bothered by how unfair this was. All of my friends seemed to be able to go play in the afternoons. Most of the time I did what Mom said, but sometimes I just had to vent about why we seemed to be the only kids who had to rest every day after lunch. Mom always insisted, however, on this rest period, and if either of us was too argumentative, she would threaten to tell Dad about how unpleasantly quarrelsome we had been. That threat would immediately put a halt to our complaints on our most feisty days.

I hated her spot checks, also, because I couldn't rely on her leaving us alone once we got into bed. Sometimes she wouldn't come into the bedroom, but would shout from the kitchen.

"Raymond, are you playing with your Army men?" It was usually true that I had been playing.

"No, I am just resting. My Army men are already taking their naps," I replied as I quickly put them back in their box and shoved them under my bed as quietly as possible. I wasn't always so lucky, especially when she would just walk into our room. One time I was caught red-handed in the middle of a ferocious battle between the Americans and the Nazis, with American troops and Nazi casualties scattered all over the floor.

"Raymond, I told you not to get out of bed," Mom said sternly. "Get back in right now. I'll get your toys; you just do what I said— GET IN BED NOW!"

It was clear to me that she would rather that I rest than pick up my toys. Usually, I was made to pick up my toys and put them away. I knew she must be very worried, but I really thought she was freaking out. She also remade my bed and piled all of the blankets back on top of me.

It was the summer of 1955. The dreaded polio virus was upon us.

I was confined to my bed every day at 2:00 PM. It wasn't because I was sick. I was as healthy as a horse. School was out and that meant it was time for kids to play. This particular summer, I got to play outside, but only in the morning. Noontime always meant I came inside to have lunch. Then, after lunch and some time to digest it, I would have to rest. I didn't have to nap or actually go to sleep, but I had to rest for about two hours. I could quietly read a book in bed, but I could not get up from bed, except to go to the bathroom. Thereafter, I could rise from the bed, but even then I had to be subdued in my activities. These were Mom's rules, and she meant them and solidly enforced them. My brother and I had to follow her rules to the letter because she was concerned and frightened for us.

Many summer days were hot, and because we had no air conditioning, it was quite uncomfortable to lie in bed under the covers. Mom believed that in order to be safe, her sons had to be under mounds of blankets. Mom acted as if this was so logical. Like, duh, if you don't stay under the blankets, the dreaded virus will get in bed with you. Imagine my state of mind while I lay under enough blankets to result in physical bruising to my body, while it was 110 degrees outside. I remember feeling perspiration dribble down both sides of my body from each of my armpits. The sweat was not coming from any exertion on my part. I had to lie still like a corpse. The sweat just boiled over from the sheer heat generated from the tonnage of blankets.

The early- to mid-50s was an era of fear in our country, and Napa was not spared. Polio hit every town, small or large. Polio was very contagious and spread by contact with contaminated feces or oral secretions. The truth is, back then, no one really knew where it came from or how it spread. They just knew they had a potential epidemic on their hands.

For whatever reason, it seemed that children were the most vulnerable. The virus inflamed the nerves in the brain and spinal cord, causing paralysis of the muscles in the chest, legs, or arms in severe cases. In minor to moderate cases, there may be weakness to one area alone with no paralysis. Sometimes braces were used to stabilize the affected limb. In the worst cases, where the victim suffered with chest paralysis, a special device was used to exert a push-pull motion on the chest. This device was the Drinker respirator, more commonly known as the iron lung. Anyone who spent time in the iron lung would never forget the experience. It was the size of a subcompact car. Today, of course, there are respiratory devices that are very portable and the iron lung is no longer needed. Not so in the '50s, however.

Polio has haunted our country at different periods of history. It is believed that the first case of polio in the United States was reported in 1894. It was thought that improved hygiene was the culprit, since, previously with contaminated water supplies, infants developed an early resistance to the virus. That wasn't the case with cleaner water supplies. It also reappeared in the 1920s. The organization known as the March of Dimes, which many people know today as an organization that raises money for many childhood illnesses, began in 1926 to assist in the fight against polio.

In 1938 President Franklin Roosevelt founded the National Foundation for Infantile Paralysis. The rehabilitation for the victims of this virus was very expensive, and was simply not affordable for most people, especially during the Depression.

In the '50s, polio made a comeback of frightening proportions. In the United States, from the late 1940s to the early 1950s, an average of 35,000 cases of paralytic polio per year were reported, according to the Centers for Disease Control and Prevention. Outbreaks of polio were widely reported in the newspapers. In department stores pictures were posted of polio victims with leg braces, crutches, or, worst of all, the iron lung. These pictures or posters were designed to encourage donations in the effort of researching and fighting this dreaded disease.

The March of Dimes posters featured the organization's beautiful, young children with braces and crutches who posed for fundraising pictures. A simple picture portrayed an adult woman with three children, an older boy, a young girl, and a little girl in the middle—all of them with braces and crutches. The poster simply stated, "Join the March of Dimes—They need YOU!"

I felt badly for these kids, and scared for myself. I was a frugal child, but even I donated a few coins from time to time. Many years later, as a public defender, I was appointed by the court to represent a criminal defendant charged with stealing the March of Dimes jar of coins at a 7-11 store. I had a difficult time hiding my disappointment in the young man, especially when he said he wanted a jury trial. However, after showing him the store's video of him clearly lifting the jar of money and putting it in his coat, he agreed to take the best deal I could get him. Little did he know I wanted the death penalty for him; however, probation, restitution, and a fine were his only consequence.

There was deep fear throughout the nation, which I was not aware of until it hit Napa, and even then I was oblivious until I was made aware of it in no uncertain terms after some of my friends became afflicted with the disease. However, before my awakening to life around me, parents and other adults were frightened by mosquitoes and flies that were believed to carry the virus. Also, although parents didn't know what caused it, they knew that flu-like symptoms were a bad sign. So, any symptoms remotely indicating the flu caused much angst among parents.

In disquieting conversations, Mom's friends spoke about someone else's kids having a stiff neck or coming down with a sore throat, or worse yet, getting a fever. These were not old wives' tales, because it was known that children who got the virus usually had a fever first, and then real polio symptoms like pain in their legs or back or neck. This was so scary because no one knew what really caused polio nor why it seemed to hit children the hardest.

Panic would set in, however, when someone in the community got the disease. So, if your parent didn't know what caused polio, but received some information here and there, coupled with your mom's gut instincts to err on the side of caution, you would be treated like you were very, very fragile—especially if your mother went to the movies and saw newsreels with terrible images of children in different states of paralysis or in an iron lung.

This is what haunted Mom.

It seemed to me that polio outbreaks were concentrated in the summer. So people just naturally associated the virus with summer activities such as swimming and picnics. The word around town was that kids weren't supposed to sit around in wet clothes or swallow pool water or even drink out of public drinking fountains. And kids were required to get rest and not get too tired. The fear was if your child got rundown or sick, he or she might get the virus. It must have been so frightening for parents to see a child with a fever or the flu or even a sore throat. Doctors didn't really know initially if the child was getting the virus. It must have panicked the adults and scared most kids—if they were listening.

I wasn't really listening, but I heard most of these rules from Mom, whom I am certain had heard them from her friend, Gussie Martini—who had five daughters. But Mom was not going to limit her sons to abiding by just these precautionary rules. She was going to protect her boys above and beyond the normal advice going around at the time.

Mom's fear of her sons getting polio had been exacerbated, because my brother, Eugene, had already been bedridden with tuberculosis a couple of years earlier. This deeply frightened Mom.

When the polio scare hit, she was worried that one of us would get it. She already knew that her sons were not above getting very sick, and Eugene's illness had shaken her to her core. She believed Eugene's lungs had been damaged from the TB, and worried that if he got polio, it might attack his lungs and that he might end up in the iron lung. That was a nightmare for her.

She had other rules as well. She kept us away from swimming pools. There were some great places for Napa kids to swim in the summer. Vichy Springs Resort was my favorite, but there was also Oak Park swimming pool and Mt. George swimming pool. In addition to these private pools, there was always the huge Napa High School swimming pool, where I had taken my American Red Cross swimming lessons (beginner, intermediate, and advanced). It didn't matter to me where I went, as long as I got to go swimming. Vichy was the best, because there were lots of pretty girls, and they had an arcade, and most importantly to me, they had great snacks.

Mom was not limited to restricting my access to pools only. I also couldn't go to the movies. I couldn't go anyplace where I might be exposed to a crowd of people. Under no circumstances were my brother and I ever to drink out of any public drinking fountains. And this is when the daily naps started.

Polio played no favorites. It attacked the rich and the poor and was seemingly impossible to stop without an effective vaccination. It was truly terrifying.

I can see why my mom was so worried. It seemed to her that people all around us had family members or friends who had the virus. And, if you got polio, it was terrifying, since it could have devastating results. The residual effects of the virus ranged from mild cases, in which one could recover with no lingering or permanent effects after several days, to severe cases, in which one could be partially or completely paralyzed.

One of my all-time best friends, Mike Kerns, contracted the virus. Unfortunately, it was before the vaccine had been fully developed. In 1954, seven-year-old Mike was invited to go camping by his friend, Billy Avery, and Billy's mother. Mike's parents allowed him to go. It was summertime, and it seemed like it would be an enjoyable experience for Mike. Mike was initially excited, not realizing how difficult it would be for him since he had never been away from home before. Ironically, a severe case of homesickness may have saved Mike from a more serious case of the dreaded virus.

Mike traveled with Billy and Billy's mother to Putah Creek for camping, hiking, and swimming. Mike and Billy both lived in Alta Heights and their homes were near each other, plus they were in Cub Scouts together. Mrs. Avery was a single parent who graciously invited Mike to go with them so her son would have someone to play with during a week of camping. Mike, having never been away from home before, became very homesick. He really missed his mom, dad, and sister. Because of this homesickness, Mike really didn't want to do much in terms of activities. He recalls mainly staying in their tent and reading comic books.

There were lots of kids in the campground, and because Mike didn't want to swim, Billy spent more time swimming in the creek than Mike did. It is unknown if this mattered, but Mike ended up with a mild case of polio, while Billy had a much more severe case. Billy played with the other kids and swam in the creek for most of the week. A day or two before the end of the week, Mike's spirits improved because he knew that the vacation was ending and he would be returning home to his family. Because his disposition improved dramatically, Mike started to play with Billy and other kids and joyfully went swimming in the creek.

Not long after returning to Napa, Billy and Mike became symptomatic. They were taken separately to Children's Hospital in San Francisco. Billy was hospitalized for a period of time. Mike was not.

However, while attending the Napa fair with his parents Mike did not feel right. He was talking through his nose and his parents questioned him about this. In fact, his mom told him to quit talking through his nose, but Mike couldn't help it. Whether this was a symptom or not, nobody knew. Nevertheless, his parents observed other flu-like symptoms. He didn't feel any pain, but he was run down.

Mike's parents thought something was wrong with Mike, so his mom took him to the doctor's office to be checked out. They must have suspected polio, because when they returned home from the doctor's office, his mom walked into the kitchen, tossed the car keys on the table and said to Mike's dad, "Well, he's got it." Mike didn't know what they were talking about.

Billy's situation was far more serious. He had to wear a brace for some time and he ended up with residual effects, including a permanent limp in his walk.

Mike was quarantined at home, and kept out of school for half of a school year. He couldn't go anywhere, and friends could not come over. Some of his friends' parents brought Mike lots of books to read, including tons of comic books—which Mike loved. Schoolwork was provided to him at home. Mike never had to wear a brace, but he had to lie on his back on the dining room table for physical therapy. The therapist made house visits to see Mike every other day. Mike was fortunate to have these physical therapy sessions paid for by his grandfather.

Mike did his physical therapy exercises regularly, and about the time that the second half of the school year was about to begin, Mike had fully recovered, with no residual effects.

Two friends in my neighborhood were afflicted with the disease. Mary Anne Behrens had a relatively mild case of polio, but the other case was a severe example of the deadly virus hitting very close to us. The disease found my friend and neighbor, Toni Williams.

The Williams family lived two doors down on Fourth Street. It was not the proximity to us that made this so scary. It was because Toni suffered a severe case of polio. She became paralyzed from the waist down and was wheelchair-bound for life. This was an example that no one in our neighborhood could forget. It probably helps explain why Mom became borderline psycho in trying to protect her children. Toni was a child with whom I often played. Toni waded with my brother and me in a small above-ground canvas swimming pool at our house. And, like so many ironic things in life, Toni was probably the nicest, kindest person you could ever want to know.

I don't know for sure how she got polio, but she had experiences similar to Mike Kerns and Billy Avery. Toni used to vacation at Pine Grove Resort in Lake County. Pine Grove had a pool that contained creek water with no chlorination. Once a week on Thursdays they would drain it and whitewash the whole pool, then refill it. It was super cold. Toni used to swim there before she got polio. Toni, Mike, and Billy all had the common experience of swimming in bacteria-infested creek water and fighting mosquitoes. Who knows?

Valerie Martini's mom gave Toni's mom Pauline a heavy wool blanket with which to wrap Toni. That is what neighbors did in those days. Toni was in an iron lung at Children's Hospital for a couple of years. Valerie would go to San Francisco with Pauline to visit Toni. Toni would continually ask her mother if she could go home; poor Pauline would do her best to comfort Toni, telling her that she would talk with the doctor. After Pauline and Valerie left the hospital, they would sit in the parked car for a time while poor Pauline cried.

When Toni finally came home, we neighborhood kids would sit with her in her room, and Ernest Mann, the physical therapist, would come over to help exercise her legs and arms. The neighborhood girls helped Toni do her exercises, but many times Toni said that she did didn't want to do them. Pauline had to get after her, urging her to keep trying. Pauline always gave us oatmeal cookies and pink lemonade. Once, while visiting Toni along with my brother, I said, "Come on, let's go out and play." As soon as those words came out of my mouth, I regretted saying them. I didn't want to cause Toni any pain, but those hurtful words hung there, reminding her just what she could not do.

In the summers, Jackie Martini and I often took Toni to the softball games held in the evenings at the fairground diamonds. Napa was a big softball town that had some very good teams in the '50s. Because the fairgrounds were across the street from where we all lived, we had easy access to the games. It was really fun for me because I could watch games with exciting teams from around the state. Napa played against Stockton, Lodi, Fresno, and many other teams. There was a concession stand that sold hot chocolate for ten cents, plus you could go under the bleachers and collect pop bottles, which we could then return to the Napa Liquor Store a block away on Third Street and recover the deposit. That was a great way to make money. Chasing foul balls was fun, too, if you were lucky enough to recover the ball (which usually required fighting off fans of all ages). We redeemed the balls for five cents.

One evening, Jackie was late getting to Toni's house, and by the time they picked me up, we were almost certainly going to miss the beginning of the game.

"Jeez, Jackie, now we are late and we are going to miss the start of the game," I rudely said. Not only did we need to get to the entrance, but there were other late-arriving fans, which meant we would have to wait in line.

"I don't want another second-inning start like last time when we missed Jimmy's home run," I continued. Jimmy Dykes was Jackie's uncle, having married Joyce Martini. Jimmy was an all-star legend in our neighborhood.

"Raymee, my mom wouldn't let me leave until just now. Give me a break," Jackie pleaded.

Toni watched as the two smallest kids in the neighborhood squabbled.

"Come on, you guys, this isn't the end of the world, we will see lots of the game," said Toni.

That sobered me up.

"Ok," I said, "but let's make up for lost time."

I don't know if Jackie felt guilty since she was the one responsible for making us late, but instead of just walking hurriedly like the other late arrivals, Jackie started to run as she pushed Toni's wheelchair. I was running beside the girls on the street.

Toni hadn't said a word, and I couldn't see if she was happy about being pushed so fast or not. I was too far behind them to see her face. Unfortunately, the road was in serious disrepair and had chuckholes. Suddenly, Jackie hit a deep one straight on. All I remember was Toni falling forward out of the wheelchair and going down in a heap. The wheelchair also tipped over and landed partially on Toni.

"Toni!" I screamed. I was about to yell for help, but there was no need. All of the late-arriving adults instantly turned their attention to Toni.

"Bob, give me a hand will you?" someone asked. Immediately, several bystanders were helping to lift Toni and the dead weight of her lower limbs back on to the chair, which was placed upright by others nearby. Incredibly, Toni was not badly hurt. She didn't feel pain in her legs and lower body, so except for some scrapes on her arms, she seemed fine. She didn't want to go back home.

"I am fine, I want to go to the game now," Toni declared to what seemed like a dozen people around her. The women in the crowd were very kind to her and checked her out.

"Aren't you Pauline Squicciarini's daughter?" asked one of the women.

"Yes, I am," replied Toni.

"I will take you back to your house, if you like," said the woman.

"No thank you," Toni said. "Please, I am fine," she continued, "I really want to see the game."

With that, some of the remaining adults pushed Toni in her wheelchair onward to the game. Almost completely unnoticed was Jackie. When the wheelchair pitched forward, dumping Toni, Jackie went head over heels over the chair and over Toni, straight onto the blacktop. While several of the late arriving male adult fans rushed to Toni's side, no one was checking out Jackie. Poor Jackie (called "Bones" because she weighed about thirty pounds soaking wet) was sprawled out on the road like a pancake. I went to her side.

"Are you okay, Jackie?" I asked.

Jackie was fighting tears and was obviously hurt. I felt badly that I had given her such a bad time about being late. I felt that this whole accident was my fault.

"I am okay, I guess," Jackie said, her voice trembling from the pain and fright.

"The adults are taking Toni on to the ball game. Do you want me to walk you home?"

"No, I want to go to the ballgame, too."

"But, you have cuts and are bleeding."

It was apparent that she had suffered the most severe damage of the two girls. Jackie had scrapes and contusions all over her arms and legs. The poor thing was a bloody mess.

"Don't you think you need your mom to clean you up?" I continued.

"No, Raymee. I am all right. Let's just go to the game."

"But I think you need to clean up and get some medicine."

"Raymee, I can cleaned up at the water fountain with napkins. I will be fine. If I need medicine my mom can put mercurochrome on me later, okay?"

This sounded like a reasonable plan, plus I really wanted to see the game, myself. If Jackie wasn't too uncomfortable to attend the game, then neither was I.

Before we could continue on, Jackie spoke up.

"Wait, is Toni really okay? I mean really, is she okay, or is she bleeding and hurt like me?"

"Really, she seemed fine. She didn't travel in the air as far as you, and I don't think she felt much pain. She didn't have many scrapes on her arms, either, that I could see. She wasn't crying. She seemed more embarrassed by the attention everyone was giving her. She is all right, Jackie," I explained.

With that, Jackie was ready to continue on to the ball game, which had just started. I went to the concession stand and grabbed a boatload of paper napkins. I wet several of them in the drinking fountain for Jackie to use and helped her clean up. The rest we used for drying. Then we all watched the game together.

Toni's last name belies her Italian heritage. The maiden name of Toni's mom, Pauline, was Squicciarini. Many years later, sometime in the early '90s, I went to Pauline's house to make a house call in my capacity as a lawyer to draft some documents for her. As soon as I entered her home, I was right back in the '50s, as a little boy who would go over to Toni's house to visit. It was the sensory perception that took me back.

Pauline was making pesto, the Italian dish of her heritage, and the fresh smell of basil transported me immediately from the front door to the kitchen, my favorite room in any house. Toni's father, Al Williams, was a record-setting track star from Vallejo High School. At one time, he held the track record for the 100-yard dash (I think it was a 9.7 time).

Toni also had a younger brother, Tommy, who we called T.J. This was a wonderful family. The polio tragedy that hit them affected the entire neighborhood.

However, due to the strong character of Toni Williams, her response to this affliction wasn't to give up; it wasn't to lean on others; and, certainly, it was not to feel sorry for herself. Toni's response to this challenge was to maintain herself and move on with life as best as she could. She even reassured those of us who felt so badly about what had happened to her.

While visiting at her bedside we found her to be cheery and fun to be with. Her response to this situation was an example of strength and courage and was simply inspiring. She did not look back.

As anyone who knew her would expect, Toni grew up and married a wonderful man. They had three children that they raised in our community. Toni also obtained employment with the county of Napa as an eligibility worker and was promoted to a supervisorial position. She made a full life for herself because of her love, faith, and strength. She was a spiritual person and an inspiration to all of us who had the privilege of knowing her.

Sadly, her polio came back in her later years and eventually took her life. I am still inspired by her courage and strength. She is one of the best examples of the human spirit that I have ever seen.

Although polio never devastated large numbers of the population like the plague or influenza, the medical threat of polio was significant because it was a frightening, highly contagious disease with no known cure.

Dr. Jonas Salk developed a vaccine in 1952, but the serum was not introduced to the world until 1955. Finally, the country had an antidote to the dreaded virus. Initially, it came in the form of shots. The Salk serum contained the dead virus.

Later, Albert Sabin created a vaccine that contained the live virus, which proved to be even more effective. The vaccine came in the form of shots and later orally with sugar cubes. The oral vaccine was more effective because it got into the body faster, and was cheaper to produce. In my opinion, eating sugar cubes was a great way to get vaccinated as opposed to needles and shots.

However, I tried to use the polio shot to my advantage once to avoid a beating from Dad. He beat my brother for fighting with me, and then it was my turn. I exclaimed, "Dad, don't! My polio shot, my polio shot!!!"

I hoped that this plea would prevent him from hitting me at all. I attempted to show him my reddish colored left arm as he raised his fist. It didn't even slow him down, so, after being hit once, I jumped into an open closet and faked crying. He couldn't get much leverage in the closet so I avoided a prolonged whipping. From then on, I was a sugar cube proponent all the way.

You would think that once the vaccine was invented everyone would have been relieved to know that this contagious disease would be stopped in its tracks. However, this medicine brought its own fears and stress to various communities around the country.

In 1955, vaccinations were suspended because of the California Cutter Laboratory incident, when eleven people died and hundreds of others were paralyzed because of faulty vaccines.

Napa was certainly one of the towns where residents worried about the vaccine, whether or not it was safe. There had been reports in other communities that there were bad batches of the vaccine and that some of these bad batches were infecting people with polio instead of insulating them against the virus.

The April 27, 1955, issue of the Napa Register had the following headline:

INOCULATED NAPA TOT GETS POLIO; SCHOOL SHOTS CONTINUE: PINCKNEY

The article explained that some of the serum was under suspicion and that the Public Health Service in Washington, D.C., had ordered the temporary withdrawal of the Salk vaccine manufactured by Cutter Laboratories in Berkeley because of seven cases of paralytic polio among children vaccinated with it. One of the cases was in Napa.

The article went on to say that Napa County's mass vaccination of first- and second-grade school children was not affected by the order since the vaccine being used was from the Eli Lilly and Company laboratories. Private physicians in Napa, however, had received 300 cc's of the Cutter product, which was enough to give 150 children their first and second shots, on April 14. Most of the doctors reserved the remaining vaccine for the children's second shots, due to be given four weeks after the first shots. Because of this disclosure regarding the tainted serum from Cutter, the physicians returned the serum to the Cutter laboratory in compliance with the national order.

The last part of the headline referred specifically to Dr. Edward R. Pinckney, the county health director. He was quoted as saying that only the Cutter product is being questioned and that the National Institute of Health has found nothing wrong with the Lilly vaccine being used in the school vaccination program. More than 1,000 first- and second-graders in the county already had been vaccinated by the time of the Cutter disclosure but it was with the Lilly vaccine. Dr. Pinckney urged Napans to continue with the inoculation program that was scheduled for the very next Friday.

The lead story in the next day's Register, on Thursday, April 28, 1955, was headlined, **"FAITH IN VACCINE UNSHAKEN HERE."**

The article explained that, while eight families had cancelled their children's shots, thirteen more had signed up, and that overall, Napa County parents continued to demonstrate their confidence in the new Salk polio vaccine despite the eight cancellations. Of 200 first- and second-graders already signed up for the shots at the Napa County Health Department, only eight mothers cancelled, while thirteen new children came in with consent slips not previously signed. Dr. Pinckney had expected a wave of hysterical cancellations and expressed his gratitude for the attitude of Napa parents.

"The parents agree that they want their children protected if there is polio in the area," Dr. Pinckney told the Register.

The Napa girl who was the victim of bad vaccine was twenty-one-month-old Gail Kunkel. She became ill one week after receiving the vaccine, when she started showing signs of the illness. She developed a temperature of about 102 degrees, which later ran up to 104 degrees. At this point the girl's mother, Mrs. Kunkel, called her husband, Arthur F. Kunkel, to come home from his workplace at Berglund Tractor. The little girl showed no signs of improvement over the weekend and on Monday she showed the first real signs of polio—pain in her back and legs. Mr. Kunkel said his wife couldn't pick up his little daughter because it hurt her to be touched. The Kunkels took their girl to Dr. Olive Jack, who performed a spinal tap and sent it to the laboratory, which reported that it was polio. She didn't have the use of her left arm and her shoulder was partially paralyzed.

An argument ensued between the doctors in the various counties about vaccination programs. Dr. J.C. Geiger, public health director of Oakland, gave the impression that vaccinations with all the commercial vaccines should be stopped and said counties that began the program went into it too hastily. Dr. Pinckney felt much differently and was very critical of Dr. Geiger. Dr. Pinckney stated that with the backing of the United States Public Health Service, the State Department of Public Health and Napa's own local medical authorities, Napa County was justified in continuing the program.

The 150 children in Napa who did get their initial shots from the suspected vaccine from Cutter Laboratories were advised by Dr. Malcolm H. Merrill, state health director, to "let the children continue their normal activities but observe the usual precautions taken during polio season—such steps as seeing to it the children avoid excessive fatigue and chilling, and that they get proper rest."

Imagine the stress on parents in Napa and other counties where bad batches of serum had been discovered. Now parents had to decide whether to give their children the polio vaccine, or withhold it because it might cause polio. This was the stressful choice of parents at the time—a real dilemma, to choose between two equally unsatisfactory alternatives.

Dr. Dwight H. Murray of Napa, chairman of the board of the American Medical Association, pointed out that only the Cutter product was in question and it was the Lilly vaccine that was being used extensively in Napa.

"If there is polio in the area," Dr. Murray said, "certainly the vaccination program should be continued without losing any time."

The father of the young victim, Gail Kunkel, expressed faith in the Salk vaccine. "I have all the faith in the world in this serum," Mr. Kunkel said. He said he and his wife were going to give it to their older girl, Patricia, who was six-and-a-half, although he wouldn't allow the use of the Cutter Laboratories product.

In the end, after the Cutter Laboratory scare, the school polio shots ended with ninety-four percent of Napa's first- and second-grade children being inoculated with the vaccine. Most parents decided to protect their children from polio with the vaccine and bank on the serum from Lilly Laboratories not being contaminated.

The Register reported on Monday, May 2, 1955, that a second child had died after receiving the Salk vaccine. Nevertheless, it was apparent that our community had made its overall decision to risk possible contaminated vaccine as opposed to not taking it at all.

Parents today face similar decisions regarding vaccinations for all types of diseases. The decisions are the same, but for one thing. In the '50s there was a real terrifying, highly contagious virus that was, in some cases deadly, and in other cases severely paralyzing, staring right at them, with no known cure and, at first, a suspect solution.

This was truly an era of fear.

CHAPTER 8

The Best Invention Of All Time

The '50s brought changes, many of which were fun, exciting, and, for the most part, surprisingly affordable. Every man, woman, and child had a chance to get their own new and different toy.

For the traditional man of the '50s, there was hardly anything more exciting than the modern cars and trucks that flooded the new decade. The traditional stay-at-home mom, recently stranded in a new locale called the suburbs, discovered that access to town was difficult without a second car. The all-American domestic engineer had an array of modern appliances, purportedly to make her life easier, as well as lots of time-saving, convenient and healthy ways to prepare full meals without slaving over the stove for hours on end (for example, Swanson's TV Dinners).

For kids, there was an abundance of toys. There were cap guns, BB guns, slingshots, Davy Crockett apparel (particularly the popular coon-skin cap), Erector sets, Electric Football, Hula Hoops, Magic 8 Ball, Monopoly, Mr. Potato Head, Play-Doh, Pogo Stick, Silly Putty, the Slinky, Radio Flyer Wagon, and a host of other things. It was the age of consumerism.

But nothing was more exciting for the whole family than the introduction of television to American society. The TV had been around for some time, but it wasn't until the '50s that television came into its own as a cultural phenomenon.

Immediately after World War II, production of TV sets started in the United States. In 1946, when I arrived, only 44,000 homes in the U.S. had TV sets; by the end of 1949, 4.2 million homes had television. By 1953, fifty percent of all American homes had TV.

People became enthralled. This was so much better than radio. The first time I saw a television program, I was in downtown Napa with Mom, standing outside a store window, trying to catch a glimpse of the show. The main character was a smiling puppet. I begged Mom to go inside to get a better view of the screen and hear the sound.

"Please, Mom, let's go in and get closer. Please?"

"Oh, Raymond, if it is that important to you then fine, we will go in, but only for a few minutes."

She gave in to my nagging, partly because she wanted to see it for herself. This was a marvel to her. Mom sensed that this was a snapshot into the future and all we had to do was step inside.

We left the rest of the crowd milling around in front of the store window and went in. The merry little puppet was Howdy Dowdy, the star of my first television experience. When my family eventually acquired our own television set, it became my favorite show. What was not to like?

Buffalo Bob Smith hosted the show, from 1947-60, with the Peanut Gallery, which consisted of children lucky enough to be selected as part of the show. Other characters included Flub-a-Dub, who was a combination animal with a duck's bill, seal flippers, and dog's ears. The show had a villain—another puppet, Mayor Phineas T. Bluster, who had a South American cousin, Don Jose Bluster, who was just as evil. A beautiful puppet named Princess Summer Fall Winter Spring was an Indian princess with whom I was infatuated. There was also Dilly Dally, a little kid puppet with a baseball cap, who may have been the first creature (human or puppet) to wear his cap sideways. They also had special short films like *Tons of Fun*, which featured three fat guys doing a brief skit. The name was not politically correct, but this was the '50s, and political correctness did not exist.

Before my family acquired a television, I went to Ernie and Gussie Martini's house around the corner on Third Street to watch television in their basement, which functioned as their family room. There, in a basement full of people, including Ernie and Gussie's five daughters, I saw the Brooklyn Dodgers and New York Yankees play in the World Series. Gussie was so nice to me, providing delicious sandwiches and strawberry soda. I just sat and enjoyed the ball game. What could be better?

Despite being treated so kindly at the Martini house, I very much hoped my family would get a television of our own. It wasn't long after seeing that television in the store that my father purchased a TV. He was hooked as soon as he saw it.

My family became very popular, very quickly, once we had a television. More people visited our house in 1954 when we got our first television (a Zenith twelve-inch screen in black and white) than at any other time in my childhood. It was like Grand Central Station, with some kids I didn't even know sitting next to me on my couch sharing my TV with me. I didn't mind, however, because it was fun and I felt special.

Television was not on twenty-four hours a day, seven days a week, as it is now. In the early days of TV you had to wait patiently between programs. TV was on most afternoons and evenings. Between those times all you would see was what we called snow on the screen, except on CBS, which continued to show a large Native American in full head dress. I became such a TV addict that I watched the most acceptable program on at any given time. If the choice was between snow and the Native American, I chose the Native American. There were only black-and-white TVs in the '50s for the most part. At the very end of the decade and the early part of the '60s color TV started to become more common.

The only way to get reception for your television was to have an antenna mounted on the roof. They were large and ugly, and Dad bought the biggest and ugliest so he could get maximum reception. It was perched high above the roofline of the house and looked like a metal tree with bare branches and no leaves. The only way to obtain good reception was if the antenna was pointed correctly in the direction of the signal to properly receive the local TV station. The problem was that sometimes the signal came from San Francisco and sometimes from Sacramento. As a result, one constantly had to adjust the antenna.

In my family that was my father, not an even-tempered fellow when he got frustrated, and this could be a frustrating job. My assignment was to remain inside, looking at the TV and yelling out the open window to Dad, informing him if the picture was better or worse. Somehow, Dad made me feel that it was my fault if I had to deliver the message that the picture was worse instead of better. Dad was the kind of guy who didn't mind shooting the messenger, if the messenger was the only one around to blame.

Dad would be on the roof, adjusting the antenna, as I yelled out an open window, "No, Dad, too far, come back a little." Out of frustration, he would sometimes yell, "Come on Raymond, you mean it isn't better yet, for Christ's sake?" The timbre of my voice gave away my lack of confidence in my response. I would say, in a voice that had all the bravery of the sound of a timid French horn, "Yeah, Dad, you can come in and see for yourself, but it is fuzzier than ever, sorry."

As soon as my father learned that some antennas were manufactured with remote control, enabling you to change the direction of the antenna from the comfort of your couch by just turning a dial, he was all over it. After he bought and installed it, the acid dripping in my stomach dissipated to controllable levels.

However, when Dad purchased our next television, a bigger-screen Zenith, it came with a remote-control channel changer. This turned out to be terrible for poor Mom. Once Dad obtained a new and larger TV set with channel-changing remote control, watching TV in the Guadagni household was never the same. The frustration filtered down to my brother and me. Dad was so impatient that as soon as a commercial came on he would change the channel and, of course, wouldn't change it back in time to pick up the show that the rest of us were watching. This was maddening, but Dad was the unquestioned captain of the remote.

Of all the new toys and games and inventions that flooded the market for people in this new decade, none was more important, fun, and entertaining to me than television. Not the Hula Hoop, Slinky, Silly Putty, my Army men, cap gun, or bow and arrow with stupid rubber suction cups replacing the sharp point of the arrow. Nothing compared to the joy that TV brought to me.

Maybe that was because I lived pretty much alone, except for all the Italian girls in my neighborhood, most of whom were older. My brother was almost four years older, and siblings do not always see eye to eye. My brother and I hardly saw each other because we lived in different worlds.

Maybe it was because I just loved the dreams, fantasies, and the entertainment of seeing so many different adventures from different parts of the world (most shows were shot on Hollywood sets and locations, but I was blissfully ignorant of that). I was mesmerized. I couldn't get enough TV. And, when the program ended and the snow or Native American returned, I could go out and play the part from whatever character I had just watched on TV.

There was an early television series called *Jungle Patrol*, where the men wore Australian hats with one side folded up. They drove tank-like jeeps in the jungle and fought the bad guys. I have never known anyone who remembers the program; I thought that I must have dreamed it, until many years later when my buddy Paul informed me that he loved it, too.

The '50s television shows included many Westerns. The oldest running Western was *Gunsmoke*, which was a radio show before becoming a Western television drama. It took place in Dodge City, Kansas, during the settlement of the Old West, and it starred James Arness, a six-foot-five-inch tall actor who played the lead role of Marshall Matt Dillon. Dennis Weaver played Dillon's sidekick

Chester, who had a lame leg. The show enjoyed great success. In fact, for a while, it held the record as the longest running show on television, and still holds the distinction of being the longest-running Western television series ever.

My all-time favorite cowboy was *Hopalong Cassidy*. My brother and I had watched Hoppy movies before we had a television. We used to go to Ernie and Gussie Martini's house on Saturday evenings to watch Hoppy movies on Ernie's home movie projector in their big basement. It was so exciting, even if we had to watch it with Gussie and Ernie's five daughters.

Hoppy was portrayed by William Boyd, a former silent screen actor. He may have been a little old for the part, as he had a completely white head of hair, but he played the role to the hilt and was very energetic. I did wonder how he could beat up tough cowboys at least twenty years his junior. I figured it was experience. He must have had thousands and thousands of fights in his day, given his age, and must therefore have become a very accomplished fighter. One thing was for sure about Hopalong Cassidy, and it is absolutely why I loved him: he was always on the right side of justice. He never lost his moral compass. He was the best role model a kid could hope for.

He had an all-white horse named Topper. He hung around with a young stud named Lucky and an old timer named California. Hoppy shot his movies on location in Lone Pine, California, and consequently, the scenery was real and beautiful—not just a Hollywood set with paintings for the background. I also liked Hoppy because he had a great, contagious laugh. But the main reason I liked him over all the other cowboys was that he didn't sing.

Roy Rogers sang. Roy had a girlfriend, Dale Evans, who also sang. Also, Roy Rogers was not really from the Old West because he had a sidekick named Patrick Aloysius Brady. Patrick drove a Jeep, which had a name too—Nelly Bell. That was not Old West enough for me. I did like the fact that Roy had a wonderful horse

(Trigger) and Dale had a cool horse (Buttercup) and they had a great dog in Bullet. So to me, there were all the trimmings of a great cowboy family, but the modern-times flavor of automobiles diminished Roy as a genuine cowboy (they called him the King of the Cowboys, which I strenuously disagreed with) and the singing finished him off as a serious threat to Hoppy. Roy Rogers was no Hopalong Cassidy.

The same has to be said of Gene Autry. In fact, Gene Autry was known as the singing cowboy. I hated that aspect of his show. I liked him as a fighter and his sidekick, the stumbling bumbling Frog (Smiley Burnette) was entertaining and funny. Gene had a great horse named Champion, but I just couldn't abide all the possible action we missed because so much of the show was taken up by terrible singing. I can't count the number of times when just as something dramatic was about to happen, old Gene would break out into "I'm Back in the Saddle Again" or "Mexicali Rose." He even yodeled from time to time and that was awful.

Like Roy Rogers, Gene was a little too modern for me as well. There would be cars, trucks, and even airplanes. Gene would go into nightclubs (a perfect foil for him to be asked to sing) and he would dance or have dinner with a beautiful girl and talk with some questionable bad guys who were not dressed like cowboys at all. They wore modern business suits and had mustaches and slicked back hair. They were always from back East and they were evil, but they were not bad-guy cowboys, which is what I expected, and wanted, to see. They were bad guy Easterners who didn't fight well enough to really be a match for Gene. They had to resort to trickery and deceit. It just wasn't the same as good cowboys fighting tough bad cowboys.

Every Autry show opened with a song within minutes, if not immediately. There were always one or two songs in the middle and always a song at the end as the heroes (Gene and Frog) rode off into the sunset. The other usual ending was when Frog got trapped by an old cowboy woman (who looked like a hag and not very much like a woman) who was trying to get him to marry her or kiss her. The last scene was Frog running off the set screaming and the rest of the citizens including Gene and the beautiful young woman, holding Gene's arm, laughing their butts off at Frog. No matter how the show ended, however, the singing started again as the episode came to its conclusion.

I also loved the mysterious Westerns. *The Lone Ranger* is a classic example. Here was a great Western featuring a masked hero and his Native American sidekick, Tonto. It was a little confusing to me because the Lone Ranger was played by two actors over the years (Clayton Moore and John Hart) but the Native American was genuine—Jay Silverheels. Also, I wasn't as confused as my friends about the Lone Ranger and exactly why he was the Lone Ranger, because mom bought me the 78 record of the original story of the Lone Ranger and how he came to be alone.

He was originally a Texas Ranger; he and his fellow Rangers were all ambushed by the Hole in the Wall gang and all the rangers except for Clayton Moore were killed. Thus, Clayton became the Lone Ranger. However, he may have not had a chance to be the Lone Ranger were it not for Tonto, who happened to ride upon the slaughtered rangers and was able to determine that one of them was still alive. Tonto nursed the Lone Ranger back to health and they became partners and buddies in fighting crime and bad guys after that. For some strange yet wonderful reason the Lone Ranger felt compelled to wear a mask to hide his identity. It was for a good reason, and although I heard the reason many times because it was on my 78 record, it never made sense to me. I am sure, however, that it was a hot, uncomfortable, and silly-looking mask.

Silver was the Lone Ranger's horse and Scout was Tonto's horse. At the end of the show when the Lone Ranger rode off someone would say, "Who was that masked man, anyway?" Tonto called the Lone Ranger "Kemosabe," which allegedly meant "trusted friend."

I loved the fact that the Lone Ranger was the only cowboy to use silver bullets. I don't know why, though. It could only have brought headaches to him. I am guessing the Lone Ranger used them to establish a trademark. But, from my way of thinking, silver bullets were much more expensive. I thought it was a waste of money. I guess that other cowboys were a bit wiser economically. Another big disadvantage for the Lone Ranger is that it would be easy to frame him because of the silver bullet. Any autopsy performed on a dead cowboy in whom a silver bullet was extracted by the coroner would be strong circumstantial evidence supporting an inference that the Lone Ranger must have been involved in the killing. I know that the Lone Ranger was on the side of right and would never have committed murder, but when the bullet matching your gun is recovered from the body, a criminal investigation must ensue with the masked man as a suspect.

The show opened with a narrator announcing in a manly voice, "A fiery horse with the speed of light, a cloud of dust and a hearty 'Hi-Yo-Silver.' With his faithful Indian companion, Tonto, the daring and resourceful masked rider of the plains led the fight for law and order in the early West. Return with us now to those thrilling days of yesteryear. The Lone Ranger rides again!"

The theme song was the *William Tell Overture* from Rossini's opera, which was a fast and exciting piece of music that played as you watched the Lone Ranger galloping on Silver, presumably chasing bad guys. Most of my friends and maybe adults, too, identified that music with the Lone Ranger instead of Rossini's overture.

Though I never understood why he wore a mask or why he had to say "Hi-Yo-Silver, Away!" instead of just digging his spurs into Silver and riding off, it was one of my favorite programs. Originally a popular radio program, this American Western television series was by far the highest-rated program on the ABC network in the early 1950s and its first true hit. The television show was not as good a show as *Hopalong Cassidy*, but it was still enjoyable to watch. The introduction to *The Lone Ranger* was the best of any Western television series ever. I still have one burning question: Did Tonto ever *not* get beat up in any episode?

Zorro was another Western I loved. Zorro also wore a mask; behind the mask, he was Don Diego de la Vega. Zorro was skilled with a whip, an expert with a sword, and wherever he went to oppose the corrupt tyrants of Spanish California, the masked swordsman left his mark, which was the letter "Z" carved into some conspicuous place at the scene of his latest triumph.

I understood the need for his mask, because Don Diego de la Vega was an insider and thought to be on the side of the tyrannical Spanish government. He had to have a disguise. I didn't think, however, that his disguise was adequate. However, the Don Diego de la Vega character was a very passive, almost cowardly Don, and the mask and the machismo of Zorro was such a different character, that people bought it. I think I must have been a particularly bright ten-year-old, because I was pretty sure I could tell that he was the same guy. He was always picking on a bumbling, grossly overweight, Spanish Army officer named Sergeant Garcia.

Many of the Westerns of this era had either stupid opponents or comedic, bumbling sidekicks. *Wild Bill Hickok*, played by Guy Madison, had a sidekick in the rotund, obese Jingles, played by Andy Devine. The show was sponsored by Sugar Pops ("Sugar Pops are Tops"). Gene Autry also had a fat comedic sidekick named Frog, played by Smiley Burnette. Roy Rogers had Pat Brady, who, while not fat, was a complete screw up. Chester, Marshall Dillon's sidekick on *Gunsmoke*, was slim, but had a left leg that did not bend at the knee. Chester didn't even carry a gun.

It was difficult for me to fantasize that I could fill the role of the hero in any of these Westerns. I looked more like Sergeant Garcia. In fact, I actually played a similar part in our Cub Scouts' production about the Alamo. I was a Mexican soldier storming the Alamo. As one of the Mexican soldiers who killed my hero Davy

Crockett, I went through a period of self-disgust after the show that lasted an entire weekend. In reality, I looked more like Gingles than Wild Bill Hickok; I looked more like Frog, than Gene Autry. The hero cowboys were all handsome and well built. Unfortunately, I was like the fat, useless sidekicks. Still, denial is very powerful, and I somehow managed to believe that I was really a handsome, brave cowboy under my less-than-attractive human exterior.

Although I did not like my cowboys to have modern inventions like cars, or have dealings with the Nazis or anything remotely to do with modern times (making the show less authentic), there was one exception that I allowed. That was the *Sky King* show. Sky King was a cowboy who owned the Flying Crown Ranch. He had a truck and even an airplane that he called the Songbird. He lived on the ranch with his nephew, Clipper, who was the wimpiest kid I ever saw. He wore new cowboy clothes, which made him look ridiculous. That is like being a football player with a clean uniform. It proves you are a bench warmer (I know this from my football career—I used to leave the bench to fall in the mud so it looked like I played in the game). Sky King also lived with his niece, Penny, who was good looking. Although she couldn't have been more than twelve, I always felt that she and Sky would become an item (unless, God forbid, they already were). I didn't mind the modern conveniences or modes of transportation because Sky King had everything a person could want. He would get in his plane and fly after bad guys. He had a truck. He still had a horse and he lived on a beautiful ranch in the country. The show was sponsored by Lorna Doone, which were delicious cookies, especially when dunked in a cold glass of milk.

I loved all of the Westerns, to some degree. Whether it was *Maverick*, starring James Garner; *Bat Masterson*, starring Gene Barry (who also starred in the 1953 movie *War Of The Worlds*—my favorite science fiction movie); *Lawman*, starring John Russell; *The Rifleman*, starring Chuck Conners; *Wyatt Earp*, starring Hugh

O'Brien; *Have Gun Will Travel*, starring Richard Boone; or *Rawhide*, with Clint Eastwood, I loved them and watched them all.

Westerns, while one of my favorite genres on TV, were not the only programs I loved. That was my problem, according to mom. I loved everything on TV, even the Native American logo.

The Adventures of Ozzie and Harriet completely fascinated me. This was an early American sitcom, first airing on ABC in 1952. It featured the real-life Nelson family. The series starred Ozzie Nelson and his wife, singer Harriet Nelson, and their young sons, David and Ricky Nelson. This program portrayed the ideal American family life.

It was the polar opposite of my family. For one thing, Ozzie never raised his voice or made any life-threatening remarks to his kids. Also, Ozzie was always around the house. I never did know what he did for a living, but the family seemed quite well off. I thought maybe Ozzie was a drug dealer. Maybe he paraded around in a cardigan sweater and lived in suburbia as a clever disguise for his subterranean work as a drug lord, but I never did find out. He was portrayed on the show as a bandleader, but you never ever saw him leading or rehearsing a band or being in a recording studio.

My father, on the other hand, was never around, even on weekends. That was good in a way, because whatever threats he made on Monday morning, he had forgotten by the time we saw him next.

Even hygiene was different. Ozzie was impeccably well-dressed, even when being informal around the house. He even wore a tie.

Dad was personally a very clean person, but anyone who worked at a wrecking yard had smelly automobile grease, gas, and transmission fluid fumes emanating from his person. Couple that with all the garlic he ate and he was never mistaken for Ozzie Nelson.

Mom could be like Harriet Nelson in that she was so kind and nice. Comparing mothers, however, Harriet Nelson wore beautiful dresses, even when at home. She accessorized with beautiful jewelry and high heels (even while doing housework—although I never saw her do housework). Mom, however didn't own a dress as nice as the most casual clothing in Harriet's wardrobe.

Also, Harriet was beautiful, and though I loved my mom dearly, she was not comfortable with her looks. She was under five feet and very stout. She had a true Italian nose and was prematurely gray (I am sure because of my father, brother, and me). There was nothing that reminded me of my parents when comparing them to the Nelson parents.

The same can be said for my brother and David Nelson. David always was the wise older brother who was so handsome and always had girlfriends. He was neatly dressed, well-groomed, and wise beyond his years. My brother, Eugene, did not live up to this description. He was a kind-hearted person and generous, but he was neither a cool, well-dressed teenager, nor a ladies' man.

However, the only real comparison I cared about was the one with the younger son—the baby of the family like me. That was the ridiculously cool Ricky Nelson. He played guitar, sang, had the coolest pompadour hairdo, and was strikingly handsome. He was popular with the guys and the girls. When he would sing at a high school production, the audience of coeds would all sway back and forth in their theatre seats and clap to the rhythm of his song. He was amazing.

More than anyone else—more than Wally Cleaver, Beaver's athletic and handsome older brother; more than Spin of *The Spin and Marty Show*; more than James Dean—I wanted to be Ricky Nelson. In fact, while I dreamed of being any of those neat guys and having their life, I actually fantasized about going to Hollywood and changing places with Ricky.

I pictured myself getting to Hollywood and going onto the set where the actual Nelson family would be rehearsing, and approaching Ozzie and Harriet themselves. I knew I would have to get Ricky's parents' permission. I would explain to them how Ricky had his time with the family and his life was all set and now it was my turn. And, how I could play a musical instrument like their son even though it was the accordion and not a guitar. Still, I could entertain even though rock and roll songs do sound a bit different on the squeezebox than on an electric guitar.

I waited and dreamed for this chance and desired it with my entire being. I would promise Ozzie and Harriet that I would not let them down. I would be a devoted son. I knew my chances were bleak, but it was the life I wanted and deserved from my self-involved point of view.

Being a realist, I was prepared with a contingency plan if they turned me down, which was to pose as a long-lost cousin who suddenly appeared on the show in a new episode. In that way, Ozzie and Harriet could keep their precious star baby boy Ricky, but I could at least be on the show. Maybe a cousin from Italy (we could always say that Ozzie had some Italian in him), and then I could become a regular on the show.

My third alternate plan was to have them let me appear in sporadic episodes—say, every fifth episode. I actually would have been satisfied with that.

My fourth alternative was to have them at least give me a picture of Ricky Nelson, autographed, "To my best pal, Ray Guadagni."

Finally, if they rejected all of my requests, I would make my last stand and beg them not to call my parents (especially Big Al). Please, just kick me off the premises.

That was my fantasy, which I planned to the last detail. Sadly, I never got the courage to trek off to Hollywood to actually attempt to implement my fantasy and it is probably all for the good. I may have gotten in big trouble, maybe even a juvenile record or, worse yet, never been allowed to watch any television again.

I Love Lucy took the '50s by storm. The show starred Lucille Ball as Lucy; Desi Arnaz, Lucille Ball's real life husband, as her television husband, Ricky Ricardo; Vivian Vance, as neighbor Ethel Mertz; and William Frawley, as Fred Mertz. The show was about Lucy, who was always conniving to become a star with her bandleader husband, Ricky, and, as a result, she was constantly finding herself in hilarious situations. Lucy was the star, but she had one of the most talented supporting casts imaginable. The show even took advantage of Desi Arnaz's Cuban accent by playing on his broken English with Lucy making fun of him. The program showcased the traditional roles of men and women of the times, with Lucy not so effectively going against those traditions. *I Love Lucy* was a great American television sitcom.

It was clearly one show that my brother and I and our parents all agreed upon. This was rare indeed, because while my brother and father and I might all enjoy a Western, we still didn't have Mom aboard. My brother, father, and I also loved detective stories, but again, Mom was not a fan. She loved music, which might get my dad's vote on occasion, but unless it was Elvis, then that usually left my brother and me out of any consensus.

Leave it to Beaver comes to mind, as well as *The Little Rascals*, *The Honeymooners* with Jackie Gleason, *The Life of Riley*, starring William Bendix, *The Red Skelton Hour*, *The Ernie Kovacs Show*, *Father Knows Best*, *Dobie Gillis*, *The Untouchables* with Robert Stack as Eliot Ness, and many more. These were all great shows.‐

There were particular genres, like science fiction, that were so exciting and yet so scary. Shows like *Twilight Zone, hosted by Rod Serling; Alfred Hitchcock Presents;* and *Alcoa Presents: One Step Beyond*, which frightened the crap out of me.

Another genre were animal shows such as *The Adventures of Rin Tin Tin*, about a kid orphaned due to an Indian raid and his German Shepherd dog, who were adopted by the troops at Fort Apache in Arizona; and, of course, *Lassie*.

I loved the cartoon genre: *Heckle and Jeckle; Mighty Mouse; Woody Woodpecker; The Deputy Dawg Show; Rocky and His Friends; Quick Draw McGraw*; and *The Huckleberry Hound Show.*

Certain programs that targeted adult audiences, such as *Perry Mason* and the hip *Peter Gunn*, constituted another type of program that I loved to watch.

Finally, one more show that meant so much to me was *The Adventures of Superman*, starring George Reeves. In this program, a man of steel fought crime, when he wasn't cleverly disguised as a reporter at the Daily Planet. His disguise didn't fool anyone in the television audience, but the opening narration was memorable:

FASTER THAN A SPEEDING BULLET,
MORE POWERFUL THAN A LOCOMOTIVE,
ABLE TO LEAP TALL BUILDINGS IN A SINGLE BOUND;
LOOK!
UP IN THE SKY!
IT'S A BIRD,
IT'S A PLANE;
NO, IT'S SUPERMAN.
YES, SUPERMAN,
STRANGE VISITOR FROM ANOTHER PLANET
WHO CAME TO EARTH WITH POWERS AND ABILITIES
FAR BEYOND THOSE OF MORTAL MAN.
SUPERMAN,
WHO CAN CHANGE THE COURSE OF MIGHTY RIVERS,
BEND STEEL IN HIS BEAR HANDS, AND WHO,
DISGUISED AS CLARK KENT,
MILD MANNERED REPORTER
FROM A GREAT METROPOLITAN NEWSPAPER,
FIGHTS A NEVER-ENDING BATTLE
FOR TRUTH, JUSTICE AND THE AMERICAN WAY!

I got the chills watching this program. Each episode was filled with amazing feats of strength performed by Superman. The ability to fly was a super power I wanted, as well as great strength, of course. But X-Ray vision would have been my choice. Wow, as a young kid I couldn't imagine a better, more exciting, or more desirable super power, which I could have put to great use. If not great use, then, at least, extensive use.

I loved sport shows. On *The Wide World of Sports*, each program started by showing a skier flipping out of control, breaking every bone in his body. Just as the skier lost complete control and went airborne, flopping around, the announcer said dramatically that athletes enjoy the thrill of victory and the agony of defeat. I would watch the show just for that beginning.

I also loved *Gillette Cavalcade of Sports*. On Friday nights they had the Gillette's Friday Night Fights, and Dad and I did one of the very few things we ever did together—we watched the fights. I loved the fights. This was one ritual with dad that I really enjoyed. We both would sit on the edge of the couch rooting on our boxer. Even if we didn't know the boxer by reputation, we would look at the fighters as they entered the ring, and pick the one we liked by his looks or record or whatever information we could get. We usually picked the same boxer. The show featured some great fighters: Chico Vejar, Willie Pastrano, Harold Johnson, Benny Kid Paret, Emile Griffith, Joey Giardello, Jose Torres, Sugar Ray Robinson, Carmen Basilio, Chuck Davey, Kid Gavilan, Tony Demarco, Gene Fullmer, and Dick Tiger.

Dad would sit on the couch in a boxing position with his guard up. He would duck and weave and throw punches as if he were in the ring. It looked as if he knew how to fight. Had he boxed, he would have been in the heavyweight division, given that his weight was more than 200 pounds. This may have been a real problem for Dad, considering that he was only 5' 6" tall. Still, in our house he was unbeatable. He was the undisputed and undefeated heavyweight champion. He was able to box well sitting down with a beer in his hand. I figured anyone who can box competently while swilling beer and yelling must be very skillful and probably a decent fighter without those disadvantages. Basically, with a beer in his hand, he was a one-handed fighter but he never lost.

Imagine Dad with the use of both hands. Of course, no one was throwing any punches back. That may have made a difference.

Dad and I worshiped Rocky Marciano. First, he was Italian, and second, he hit like a mule and had a great chin. You could hit the Rock with a brick and it wouldn't hurt him. And to our enormous delight, Rocky Marciano trained in Calistoga, Napa County, for his fight in San Francisco with the British heavyweight champion, Don Cockell. The Rock became the only heavyweight world champion in history to retire with a perfect record. His impressive record was 49–0 with forty-three knockouts. Dad and I were faithful fans of Friday night television fights. My memory of this time was positive. The fights on television were a special time for Dad and me.

Finally, early television should not be discussed without mentioning some of the worst programs.

The Lawrence Welk Show was loved by Mom and enjoyed by Dad, if it didn't conflict with a Western. I hated it. There were sissy dancers (real cowboys didn't dance), awful singers, and even accordion players. Lawrence Welk was a not-very-good accordion player born to German immigrants in the German-speaking town of Strasburg, N.D. One of his performers was Myron Floren, an excellent accordionist, but this was only enjoyable if you liked the accordion. If I had to sum it up I would just say you have never heard such square music in your life.

The Hit Parade was another show that I didn't care for, even though I would watch this over *The Lawrence Welk Show* anytime. Mom loved *The Hit Parade*, which had singers who would do their rendition of the top songs of the week as rated by the Hit Parade. This meant that if the number one song in the nation per the Hit Parade were "April Love" by Pat Boone, then Snooky Lansen (one of the featured singers on the show) would do his arrangement of "April Love."

These songs were choreographed as well. If the hit were "Love and Marriage," the song would be sung while a couple was walking down the street with a baby carriage. Mom loved these arrangements. These singers were all trained professionals, so the songs were usually sung well.

However, many of the renditions were terrible, not because the singer didn't have a quality voice, but because the singer's style was ill suited to that type of song. It was like a podiatrist working in the emergency room. Some of the songs were passable but, if, God forbid, the hit song that week had been made famous by a singer whose style was unlike the regulars on the show, then not only was the song rendition bad, it was very often unrecognizable.

For example, Little Richard, a popular African-American singer among teenagers, had a hit song, "Tutti-Frutti." It was an early rock and roll song and very, very popular with the young crowd. When Snooky Lansen belted it out on the Hit Parade, it was unrecognizable and completely embarrassing. This was not about race, with white singers doing African-American singers' songs; the Hit Parade singers also butchered many of Elvis Presley's hits. "Hound Dog" with Snooky Lansen in a cardigan sweater singing to a basset hound was musically unendurable, and in no way resembled the rock and roll song.

These were some of the few show times when I was glad we had a remote control channel changer. If I could steal it away from Big Al (who many times had dozed off to a peaceful slumber), I would turn the station to anything other than *Lawrence Welk or Hit Parade*.

Mom loved another terrible show, *The Liberace Show*, featuring a piano player who was very flamboyant. He wore extraordinary glittery costumes and capes. He was a real showman and an exceptionally talented pianist. He also seemed to be very effeminate. Mom, however, would defend Liberace and say that he hadn't met the right girl yet. She never saw it coming that maybe Liberace was gay. She just thought he was dramatic. She acknowledged that people made fun of him, but she would always say that Liberace's retort to this was to say that people may laugh at him, but he laughs all the way to the bank. I thought he was really good at the piano, but to me his show was so boring that I thought about poking my eyes out.

There were other shows that Mom liked, which is another way of saying there were other terrible shows.

Queen for a Day, hosted by Jack Bailey, rewarded the winning housewife—usually the one who cried the most—with lots of prizes and a ride in the show's solid gold Cadillac.

This Is Your Life featured a surprised guest who would come on the show and learn for the first time that the entire evening would be dedicated to a review of his life. Relatives and friends would be summoned from all over the country to pay tribute to the honoree. This was not a show of my choice but, as I said, I would watch the most tolerable show on at the moment or the show that I was allowed to see by my parents. I have to admit that I liked the show on occasion and even got emotional sometimes when a long-lost relative was brought on stage to see the honoree.

What's My Line? and *I've Got a Secret* were also favored by Mom. And, there was widespread popularity for the quiz shows like *The $64,000 Question*, until those shows were exposed as fraudulent. Apparently, the winning participants were supplied the correct answers.

Mother loved the Perry Como show because of her unrequited love for Perry Como, and she enjoyed the Ed Sullivan variety show. I don't list the Perry Como show as a terrible show out of respect for mom and because Perry used to be a barber, a profession I loved. I also enjoyed the Ed Sullivan Show because he would produce Elvis or the Beatles from time to time. That was exciting and it was a show that our whole family would watch together (this was a very rare event).

I was on a television show when I was at Silverado Junior High. The show was called the *Dick Stewart Dance Show*. Not to be confused with the nationally famous *Dick Clark Dance Party*, the *Dick Stewart Dance Show* was a Bay Area television program broadcast out of San Francisco. I was one of several students selected to go on the dance show and represent our school. I was also given a school pennant to present to Dick Stewart. We had one problem. The show was on from 4:00 until 5:00. School didn't get out until 3:30 in Napa so we arrived at the show with only about fifteen minutes left in the program.

When we arrived, right after a commercial break, I was interviewed by Dick Stewart on the air. He asked me in front of the studio audience and the television audience why we were so late. Without an ounce of diplomacy, I resorted to the truth and told him and everyone listening that the school officials would not let us out of school early.

When I started to get on the bus in San Francisco to travel back to Napa, Austin Kelly, the Dean of Student Activities, was shaking his head at me and repeated what I had said on the air. He told me that blaming the school administration was not the wisest thing to say. I was too frightened to ask him what I should have said, seeing how what I said was the complete truth. But poor Mr. Kelly seemed so frustrated with me that I thought it best if I leave that alone.

The Dick Stewart Show allowed me to dance with Bonnie Kreitzer, who was a pom-pom girl at our school, and absolutely beautiful and nice. She was, of course, taller than me and I had no chance with her in a million years, but if it weren't for the Dick Stewart Show I would have never danced with her. So, on balance, my television experience was worth attending. After my fifteen minutes of fame on this show, I started watching it regularly. It was not a very good show to watch but even bad shows were better than no show at all.

187

Whether it was an awful program or one of my favorites, I loved television (and still do). Television is the best invention of all time.

CHAPTER 9

Bombs Away

When the United States bombed the Japanese city of Hiroshima in August 1945, the atomic age had visibly arrived. This single atomic bomb killed 80,000 people instantly. Three days later, a second bomb was dropped on Nagasaki, killing another 40,000 people. In the aftermath, approximately 100,000 people died slow, agonizing deaths as a result of radiation poisoning. These bombings are the only nuclear attacks in the history of the world.

In the late 1940s the Soviet Union successfully detonated its own atomic device, spurring both the United States and the Soviets to create even more powerful fusion weapons called hydrogen bombs. The nuclear arms race had begun, while the horrible effects of the atomic bombs touched off a debate in the scientific community.

Robert Oppenheimer, the leader of the Manhattan Project that developed the atom bomb, opposed the development of the hydrogen bomb. Joining Oppenheimer in opposition were scientists Enrico Fermi and I. I. Rabi, who wrote, "Since no limits exist to the destructiveness of this weapon, its existence and knowledge of its construction is a danger to humanity."

Scientist Edward Teller, however, pushed for its development, as did the military, which felt that this was a necessary weapon to stay ahead of the Russians. None of the opposition prevented the creation of the hydrogen bomb, as President Harry Truman ordered its development.

On November 1, 1952, the United States tested its first hydrogen bomb on Elugelab Island in the Eniwetok Atoll of the Marshall Islands. This explosion was more than 450 times the power of the bomb dropped on Nagasaki, and it vaporized Elugelab Island, leaving only an underground crater. It also destroyed life on the surrounding islands. Those who had witnessed previous atomic tests were stunned by this blast. The cloud, when it reached its furthest extent, was about 100 miles wide and twenty-five miles high.

The crushing blast was described in the Napa Register seventeen months later, in 1954, after the official motion picture of the explosion was released by officials of the Federal Civil Defense Administration, who stated they believed it was necessary for the American public to know the facts about the destructiveness of nuclear weapons.

The headline from the April 1, 1954, Napa Register stated, "H-Blast Wiped Out Island!" It went on to say in the first paragraph, "The government disclosed today details of the world's first hydrogen explosion—a searing and crushing fury that wiped out an island in the twinkling of an eye and spawned a gigantic fireball big enough to engulf the heart of New York City."

However, in 1952, the big problem for the U.S. in development of the hydrogen bomb was that the bomb tested at Elugelab Island was in no way transportable. In that sense, it wasn't even a bomb. It could not be dropped from an airplane, or even moved easily when on the ground. This device was massive and complicated. In fact, it took thousands of military personnel plus civilians to detonate this bomb. The only way this bomb could kill your enemies would be if they were willing to accept an invitation to come to the bombsite and stand next to it while it was exploded. However, this test did provide the U.S. with a short-lived advantage in the nuclear arms race with the Soviet Union.

Only nine months later the Soviet Union, determined to not be outdone, exploded its first thermonuclear device, greatly surprising and concerning the United States military and government. The concern stemmed from the issue of portability. Unlike the U.S. hydrogen bomb, which could not be transported, the Soviet bomb was no misnomer—it was a true bomb because it was a deliverable weapon. This meant advantage Soviet Union, because it had something the U.S. did not have—a transportable hydrogen bomb.

There was already an arms race going after the development of the atomic bomb, but when the Soviet Union exploded their hydrogen bomb, it touched off a nerve-wracking, anxiety-producing arms race that was escalating to dangerous and unimaginable heights. The race was clearly on to develop as many weapons and arms of mass destruction as possible. In short, the race was on to find the biggest, baddest, maximum casualty-producing weapons known to humankind, with the intent to annihilate as much human life as possible.

I am as competitive as the next guy, but this is one game that should not be played. I like winning, but I don't want to obliterate, exterminate, or abolish my opponent. Besides having to deal with a long period of self-disgust, I would not be able to gloat about my victory if my opponent was dead. Likewise, if I lose I am dead, which is no fun, either. This game should not have been—nor should it ever be—played. The consequences are unspeakable.

There was no turning back. The United States evened the Soviet advantage when it developed, in 1954, its first deliverable thermonuclear weapon, which was tested at the Bikini Atoll, in the Marshall Islands. The bomb yielded much more than its expected power and, unfortunately, became the worst radiological disaster in our country's history. The combined results of both a huge blast as well as poor weather conditions contributed to widespread radioactive nuclear fallout that contaminated more than 7,000square miles, including Marshall Island natives and the unfortunate crew of the Fukuryu Maru, the infamous Japanese fishing boat with a name that ironically translates to "Lucky Dragon." This tuna boat and its crew (as well as the Marshall

Island natives) were covered in a snow-like mist of radiation. Even though the natives were quickly evacuated, they received so much of the radioactive fallout that they suffered cancer and birth defects in subsequent years. These contaminated islands are still uninhabitable today.

The supremely unlucky Lucky Dragon was about ninety miles east of Bikini Atoll at the time of the blast. About two hours after the bomb exploded, the "snow" of the radioactive ash, composed of vaporized coral, was falling on the crew. Within a few hours members of the crew became nauseous and their skin darkened. In a couple of days their hair started to fall out. Many crewmembers were hospitalized; one went into a coma and died.

The Marshall Islands was not the only nuclear testing area used by the United States. Starting in 1951, the Nevada Test Site in the desert had become the primary location for hundreds of U.S. nuclear tests. It was important for the purpose of killing humankind that these weapons worked, and to observe how the blasts behaved under various conditions. To do this properly these tests had to happen.

To be clear, the goal of killing people was not shared by all Americans. Quite the contrary, the moral aspects of these dangerous weapons had been debated since the first atom bombs were dropped on Japan to end World War II. However, the explosion of the thermonuclear bomb at Bikini Atoll raised many questions about how humankind could survive a nuclear war. Debate raged about what fallout and dust from a full-scale nuclear war would do to the whole world, not just the cities and countries directly bombed. Speculation ran amok.

Supporters said that the opponents were overly concerned and being too emotional and dramatic about it.

Opponents believed that their speculation was based on reasonable assumptions, and made the point that the terrible long-term effect on human lives of the Japanese population could never be justified.

Supporters said the alternative to not using the atomic bomb on Japan would have resulted in an Allied invasion of Japan (it was clear Japan was not about to surrender until the U.S. used the atomic bombs), which was expected to cost hundreds of thousands of lives. From their point of view, the U.S. was justified to use the bomb—and perhaps immoral not to use it—to end the war as quickly as possible.

Though the back and forth debate continued over the use of nuclear weapons, it became clear that the fate of the world was tied to the actions of the bomb-hungry superpowers.

The fear of Communism also affected the arms race. I became knowledgeable about the Red Menace when my friend Donnie Accomando and I were in the seventh grade at Silverado Junior High. One day, as we were walking down the hall, he turned toward me and said, "My mom sees red everywhere." I had twelve years behind me at that point in my life, but I have to admit I had no idea what he was talking about. Rather than ask him for clarification, I figured he meant that Nadine Accomando had some type of eye disorder where she only saw the color red instead of the broad spectrum of colors that we all see. Poor lady.

Alternatively, I also knew that "seeing red" was an expression meaning a person was extremely angry. I learned this from Mom, who used to say, "Your father is seeing red right now so leave him alone." This was always said when Dad was angry (which in my memory was twenty-four/seven). Consequently, I figured Nadine might have had anger issues.

Either way, I felt bad for Donnie. His mom was either someone who couldn't appreciate the beauty of multiple colors, or she was pissed off all the time. Neither alternative was good for her—or Donnie.

As Donnie continued talking, it became clear that he was talking about the Red Menace. This was something that sort of rang a bell with me, but not really. I finally had to have Donnie explain it to me in as much detail as a fellow twelve-year-old could articulate. He explained to me that "Red" meant the Communists, who were bad people who wanted to take our property, do away with democracy, and take over our government.

Donnie said that Communism was indeed a bad way of life, but he was frustrated with his mom, whom he claimed was paranoid when it came to her fears of Communism. She suspected everyone who wasn't gung-ho about bombing the hell out of Russia as a Communist. Any statement that could be interpreted in a different way was seen by her to mean that the person sympathized with Russia. Her favorite U.S. Senator was Joseph McCarthy who, like Nadine, saw Communists everywhere. She thought several of her neighbors were possible undercover spies. Donnie was mature enough to believe that his mother was way off base and just scared. Still, paranoia and fears as reflected by Nadine Accomando were seemingly widespread and they did affect the arms race.

For example, those who opposed the efforts at bomb development were met with harsh criticism, and subjected to claims in which their patriotism was questioned. If opponents could be disgraced or shown to be Communist sympathizers, then the U.S. could continue to acquire as many nuclear weapons as possible, and the arms race would continue to escalate. This is exactly what happened.

Even a respected scientist and American hero such as Robert Oppenheimer, who headed up the Manhattan Project that lead to the development of the atomic bomb, was not spared from blistering criticism, with disastrous results to his career. The Atomic Energy Commission temporarily suspended Oppenheimer's security clearance, alleging that it was necessary in the "interests of national security." This suspension came in 1953 during the height of the anti-Communist feeling in the country known as McCarthyism—named after Wisconsin Sen. Joseph McCarthy.

The allegations against Oppenheimer were serious and pointed. He was accused of having associations with the Communist party over many years. The fact that he had an opinion against the development of the hydrogen bomb was also used against him, even though he opposed the bomb because of concern for the health and safety of our species. Apparently, Oppenheimer continued to be against the development of the hydrogen bomb even after President Truman signed an order to continue the arms program. This seemed to be unpatriotic to Oppenheimer's critics.

Finally, in 1954, after various security hearings, the temporary suspension of Oppenheimer's security clearance was made permanent. Even the board's decision, however, reflected the mixed emotions that the board must have entertained. While the security board members found Oppenheimer to be a loyal citizen and that the nation owed him a great debt of gratitude for magnificent service, they nevertheless refused to reinstate his security clearance because he did associate himself with questionable people, and that this reflected a serious disregard for the requirements of the security system.

This was a sad episode in American history, and it led to a big divide among the American scientific community. The various stressors of the '50s, including the nuclear arms race and McCarthyism, were, at times, intertwined.

What was the level of awareness of the Napa community to our country's fixation on nuclear weapons? Apparently, Napa adults were paying attention to what was going on in Nevada. On May 5, 1955, the Register's front-page headline was **"BIGGEST A-SHOT BLASTS TEST CITY."** The article set forth the testing that was taking place in Survival City, Nevada, and claimed that the nuclear fury in Nevada was greater than Hiroshima, and that the "dust pall filled all of Yucca Flat—twenty miles long and ten miles wide within seventy-five minutes after the 5:10 AM blast." It also pointed out how a 500-foot tower was completely vaporized. The burst jarred Henderson, near Las Vegas. Survival City was completely enveloped in dust, some of it radioactive, a few minutes after detonation.

The Register also reflected the concern and the hope of the times. Napa was attempting to be as prepared as possible in the event a nuclear bomb was dropped in the Bay Area. A front-page story in the May 7, 1955 Register was headlined, **"LAWSON BACK FROM ATOMIC GROUNDS."** This article was both promising and optimistic. It expressed how prepared the Napa community would be if we became bomb victims. The article indicated that Napa would be as prepared as any county in the state to cope with fallout, should an atomic bomb hit the Bay Area, because Harold Lawson, assistant rabies control officer and radiological chief for Napa County civil defense, spent a week and a half in Nevada working with the civil defense officials and bomb experts in evaluating equipment, instruments, operational plants, and training results. The article concluded with optimism.

"Should a bomb hit in any area near Napa, the radiological group headed by Lawson would go into action in an effort to detect fallout and move Napans out of the area where it might occur," the article reads. "Over 100 Napans already have been trained as volunteers in the field, and Lawson described the group as a fine nucleus for efficient operation in case of bombing."

On the same front page another article boasted that a pair of concrete-block houses built by Napa's Basalt Rock Company "withstood the powerful atomic blast at Survival City, Nevada, Thursday, the Civil Defense Administration announced today."

The article went on to proudly explain that the two houses "were erected 7/8 of a mile from the detonation site, and came through unscathed except where the windows and doors were buckled by the nuclear fury." Hector Maclean, a spokesman for Basalt Rock, explained that precast lightweight wall panels were made of a light aggregate with a very high compressive strength, and then were not only reinforced vertically and horizontally with steel, but were pre-stressed at 15,000 pounds per square inch.

"The walls then were welded at three spots at the corners, and also welded to piers sunk in the ground," the paper quoted Maclean as saying. There was a concrete slab roof that was also reinforced and stressed and welded to the house. There was a continuous concrete and steel beam "right around the top of the wall," Maclean said.

These articles depict a Napa community making genuine efforts to be as prepared as possible in the event of a nuclear attack, no matter how futile these efforts may have been, should the area be bombed.

Civil Defense officials around the nation talked confidently about building group bomb shelters for millions of people, but in some communities, people were becoming too nervous to wait and took their survival into their own hands. Bomb shelters costing from $100 to as much as $5,000 for an underground suite with phone and toilet were popular, selling as fast as they were being built.

I don't remember any bomb shelters in Napa, except for the one Terry Simpkins' family had at their house. Terry lived in that log cabin house on Coombs Street near the Kiwanis ballpark in the south part of town. Everyone in town knew that house. We all just called it the log cabin house. We all knew it was near Kiwanis ballpark. What we didn't know was the history of the home.

Terry said his log cabin house was built in the 1930s and had a bomb shelter when his family acquired it. I think most people really did think the home was built in the 1800s. At least, we kids thought so. In any event, the house was neat. The logs were real and on the inside of the house in the living room there was no sheetrock so you were able to see the beautiful logs themselves. The home also had a fireplace made out of rock from the river.

Terry said the bomb shelter didn't mean much to him until the Cuban missile crisis in 1962. During the very stressful days of the crisis when our country was on the brink of nuclear war, Terry claims his personal popularity soared. He had friends that he did not know. Even girls liked him. I guess a missile crisis will do that for one's popularity when you have something that could save lives. There were plenty of homes with concrete basements but a concrete basement did not equal a properly built bomb shelter.

My family lived in a very old rented home which had a partially finished basement with a concrete floor. However, that concrete floor would only ensure that we would be crushed like bugs (if not vaporized) when the rest of the old wooden house collapsed on us.

The stressors incorporated into the arms race, and the fear of being the victims of an atomic bomb attack or its dreaded fallout, were very much on the minds of the Napa adult community as evidenced by the local newspaper articles. I don't believe that it was a very prevalent subject in the heads of the kids and adolescents of the town. At least, it was not in my mind, except when I was made to think about it.

In truth, I never thought of the dangers of being bombed until the Cuban missile crisis. Before that, it just wasn't on my mind except at school, when the teacher, Miss Marabelle, had us practice bomb drills. My classmates and I were taught to "duck and cover" in case of nuclear attack. These drills should have been a terrifying exercise for me. But they were not, for two reasons.

First and foremost, when we practiced the drill, I always knew that this exercise was just a practice drill, and not the real thing. There was no visible panic among kids or teachers. This took all fear away from me. Also, ducking and crawling under my desk was fun. I usually got to pinch a girl or roughhouse with another boy.

The second reason I wasn't scared is that I was devoid of any discernable intellectual curiosity. If I thought or knew anything about nuclear weapons, one would know that the bank of glass windows that ran the length of the side of my third grade class room would have shattered and blown into my classroom like lethal shrapnel carving me up like a Christmas turkey. In addition, even if I avoided being shredded by the glass spewing out of the windows, I still would have been vaporized by the nuclear fury. But, because I never bothered to think about any of this, I went about these drills blissfully happy. If my teacher said that this duck-and-cover exercise would protect me from harm in case of an atom bomb attack, I believed her. Teachers knew everything, especially someone as beautiful and smart as Miss Marabelle.

The Cuban missile crisis was a different story for me. First, I was no longer in the third grade at Alta Heights doing duck-and-cover drills. I was at Silverado Junior High School and was more aware of the current events, especially the Cuban missile crisis, because it was on television and everyone was talking about it.

President Kennedy spoke to the nation on all three channels. I saw a worried expression on my president's face as he explained that an American U-2 spy plane photographed a series of launch sites for medium-range ballistic missiles that were now being constructed in Cuba. He told us that we believed that Russia was planning to put nuclear missiles on the island of Cuba, which was under the dictatorship of Fidel Castro, a Communist who was an ally of the Russians. The president said this situation was unacceptable to us and we had to take steps not to ever allow this to happen. He told us he planned a naval blockade around Cuba to turn back the Russian ships that were transporting the nuclear weapons.

Then the president said something that was not clear to me. He said that our country was prepared "for any eventualities." This phrase didn't make sense to me, unless it meant war. I was glad he was calm and not hollering, ranting, or throwing things like my dad when he became frustrated. Kennedy seemed collected in his thoughts and had a game plan, but he also seemed to be warning us of the possible directions this delicate situation could take. He seemed worried when he informed us that the wrong turn could lead to an escalation of tactics by both sides.

Mom said that meant war. She told me to be real glad we didn't live in Florida, because the poor people in that state were very close to Cuba, where the Russians had missiles ready to fire at us. Besides the president's troubling message, the television newsmen told us that these medium-range missiles could travel far enough to allow Russia to bomb many major American cities on the Eastern Seaboard if a nuclear war began. And this bombing would happen before we could prevent it, if they struck first.

This kind of information was troubling, even to a self-centered shallow person like me. My immediate knee-jerk reaction was to bomb them now so they couldn't bomb us first. It seemed like whoever was first would win. I thought the decision was easy. Had I been in charge of our country we would have wiped out the island of Cuba and taken out Russia's weapons along with Castro all in one attack. Perhaps it is good that I was not in charge.

President Kennedy went face-to-face with Nikita Khrushchev, and it is said that Khrushchev blinked first. But then a very strange thing occurred. The Russians sent two offers to settle the matter. First, a deal was worked out for Khrushchev to order the removal of all missiles from Cuba in exchange for a commitment by the U.S. not to invade Cuba (we had already tried this in the failed Bay of Pigs Invasion a year earlier). This was a great deal and one that the President was about to accept, when the Russians sent another message now demanding the U.S. remove all of its missiles from Turkey before any Russian missiles would be withdrawn from Cuba. Who knows who authorized these different offers (I bet the first guy was sent to Siberia). In any event, the president accepted the first offer publicly, and then privately accepted the second deal by sending an agent to the Soviet embassy.

This crisis was the closest the U.S. and U.S.S.R ever came to nuclear war. It was averted only because of a last-minute compromise by these countries. It was too close for comfort. The many   opportunities   for   mistakes   to   happen   or miscommunications to occur were truly frightening. One good thing that came of this was that both superpowers experienced the real danger of coming close to nuclear war; both countries worked hard to reduce their nuclear tensions following the crisis.

Looking back on this crisis, I always have the same two thoughts. The first, is that it is a good thing for our country I wasn't the president during the Cuban missile crisis. My second thought is that it is a good thing for our country that Dad wasn't the president during the Cuban missile crisis. Having to watch Dad, as president, on television ranting and raving and scared to death himself would have grossed me out and not have been very calming or comforting to the rest of our country's citizens. But worst of all, of course, is that with either me or Dad at the helm, our country would have been in a full-scale nuclear war.

The development of nuclear science came about for good reasons at first: To end a horrible war as soon as possible and save thousands of American lives in the process; to make scientific advances that could potentially save lives, make the quality of life better, and allow people to live longer. Then, as with all well-intentioned things, someone saw some real corrupt possibilities and it became perverted. The arms race and weapons of mass destruction became the rage. The more humans you could wipe out in a single weapon became the goal.

Not all nuclear developments have been bad for humankind. Medical advances from nuclear science have improved medical treatments and detection for people worldwide. M.R.I.s, CAT scans, ultrasound, radiation therapy, and many developments are offshoots of nuclear science. Now, if only we could forget about weapons of death.

As a kid, I appreciated nuclear science, not because I understood it, but because I loved that genre of movies. Without the Atomic Age,

I wouldn't have been able to see movie like *The Beast From 20,000 Fathoms*, a 1953 movie starring Kenneth Tobey, in which a ferocious dinosaur was awakened by an atomic blast in the Arctic. The dinosaur was really pissed off that his nap was disturbed, so he terrorized the North Atlantic and made his trek all the way to New York City for his revenge.

The Japanese, who were the tragic victims of two atomic bombs, came out with *Godzilla* in 1954, depicting American nuclear weapons testing as leading to the creation of a dinosaur-like beast that was pretty much invincible.

Also released in 1954 was one of my personal favorites, simply called *Them!* It starred James Whitmore, the wonderful Edmund Gwenn (who played the best Santa Claus ever in *Miracle on 34th Street*) and James Arness (who went on to star in the science fiction hit *The Thing* and the TV show *Gunsmoke*). The movie *Them!* was also about atomic testing in New Mexico, where the radiation caused ants to mutate into giant man-eating monsters that threatened civilization. Even Whitmore was eaten by one of the humongous ants as he saved a little boy.

Another movie that was not a big hit, but reflected the lingering feelings of World War II against Nazi Germany along with atomic power, was called *Creature with the Atom Brain*. Released in 1955, it was about an ex-Nazi who was a mad scientist. He used radio-controlled atomic-powered zombies in his quest to help an exiled American gangster return to power.

The mad scientist resembled Dad with the television remote control. If our television remote control was a lethal weapon or could convert normal people into slaves, my dad would have ruled the world. He could whip around stations like no other. He almost drove Mom completely mad with his use of his remote and his callous deprivation of her enjoyment of the *Perry Como Show*. Mom was allowed to see the opening sequence of the show with Perry singing a song like "Catch a Falling Star," but then as soon as there was a commercial break, Dad would change the channel, never to return. I am positive he caused my mom to break out in hives and reduce her to a blithering, drooling shell of her former self, ready to be molded by him into a zombie slave.

Another movie that enjoyed great success was *It Came From Beneath The Sea,* also starring Kenneth Tobey. Also released in 1955, it was about a giant octopus that had been affected by the radiation from the hydrogen bomb tests. This one scared me because it hit close to home. This particular giant octopus was in the San Francisco Bay and rose from there to cause chaos and havoc on our California coast. It wrapped itself around the Golden Gate Bridge, lifted itself out of the water and started chasing and crushing people on the streets of San Francisco. The giant octopus would have probably made it to Napa, too, until some Army men on shore chased it back into the sea with flame-throwers. Finally, Kenneth Tobey blew the monster up with a torpedo from his Navy submarine. That was too close for comfort.

In 1957, a movie scared me on a different level. I really didn't want what happened to the man in the movie, to happen to me. It was based on height. I was always the shortest guy in my class. That is a distinct disadvantage for a guy who wants to have a girlfriend. Being fat didn't help either, but I could theoretically lose weight (not that I ever did)—but there was nothing I could do about my lack of height. This movie was *The Incredible Shrinking Man.* The title character slowly started to shrink due to exposure to a complicated mixture of radiation and insecticide.

Holy crap, I never touched a container of insecticide again. The movie also scared me, because I realized that if I did shrink, I would have to combat spiders like the guy did in the movie. I *hate* spiders. And these spiders were like monster spiders to the guy in the movie who was no bigger than a thimble. It is one movie I wish I hadn't watched, because, as opposed to other movies where a combination of scientists and military personnel usually figure out a way to resolve the problem, in this movie the dreaded shrinking condition absolutely stumped all of medical science, and even the military was useless against such a condition.

I never saw the 1951 film *The Day The Earth Stood Still* in the theatres because of my age. However, I have seen it a few times on television. This film might have been Hollywood's attempt to insert itself into the political discussions of the day. It seemed to be directing a message to U.S. and Russia to make peace and knock off the fighting among the powers on Earth. The movie was about an alien, far superior to Earth people, who landed in Washington, D.C., and told the people of Earth that they must live peacefully with each other or be destroyed as a warning to other planets. Was this a message being sent to the superpowers? If it was, they weren't listening, or just didn't get it.

Finally, my all-time favorite science fiction movie was *The War of the Worlds,* starring Gene Barry (who later starred as Bat Masterson on television). Released in 1953, it was about Martians invading the Earth. Nothing worked against the Martians. I remember everyone in the theater clapping loudly when the movie depicted the U.S. Army being called in to drop the atomic bomb on the aliens. But nothing worked against the Martians— not even the atomic bomb. Those bastard Martians had some kind of invisible shield that was impenetrable even against the power and force of an atom bomb. This scared me. Besides, the Martians were real ugly and frightening. They could just vaporize Earthlings with their superior weapons—they had ray guns.

I went to the theater to see the film with my brother, Eugene, and my neighbor, the beautiful Jonette Pittore. We went to the afternoon matinee, and when it was over, Jonette and my brother decided to watch it again. I stayed too. After the second showing, it was about 5:00 PM when we walked home.

After two doses of the most exciting, scary movie of my life, I was less than stoic when I got home. I was okay when I was in the house with my brother and my mom, but not when I was alone. I decided I would not ever be alone again. However, I had to answer nature's call every once in a while. The first time I went to the bathroom I just kept my head down the whole time and never, ever looked out the window that was above the toilet. There had been a scene in which a scary Martian suddenly appeared in the window, and the woman screamed like a baby. So I had another rule, which was to never look at the window when I was alone.

Soon I was establishing too many rules, but I had to get through life somehow on my own, when my brother or mother weren't there to protect me. Unfortunately, I had to pee after dark; I just couldn't help myself, and looked up at the window above the toilet. Luckily, I didn't see anything, but I was sure I would see a Martian any second. I couldn't stand it anymore.

Dad didn't help me because he was always at work, and besides, if he were there, he would go into a rant against the ugly Martian, which would bring an entire squadron of Martians to descend upon us and quickly vaporize us. It was an advantage to have Big Al at work.

I confessed to Mom that I was scared to go into the bathroom by myself because of the big window. I asked her if she would go into the bathroom first and check it out, to ensure that there were no Martians in the bathroom (I was more scared than ever as the evening progressed), and also to make sure they weren't perched right outside the window of the bathroom. Mom sensed that I was truly scared, so she did it a few times but after a while, I think she got tired of all these various trips for brushing my teeth, taking a bath, or peeing.

I tried drinking less, but that didn't stop the number of trips to the bathroom that became necessary. After two days of this, Mom had enough. She said if I couldn't go to the bathroom by myself, then I couldn't go to any more scary movies. At first, I didn't know what I would do. I knew I wanted to go see more scary movies, but I also knew that it would be hard not to have my mom go on a reconnaissance mission first, before I went in alone.

Later in life, I wondered if Mom objected to going into the bathroom first because she must have realized how willing I was to sacrifice her to the Martians, to make sure it was safe for me to enter alone. It must have appeared that I didn't care about her well-being. The truth is I didn't care enough about her well-being because I was so terrified. Yes, I would have given Mom to the Martians to save my butt. Okay, I am a terrible son.

My solution to this dilemma was that I went back to putting my head down when I went into the bathroom after Mom's ultimatum, and finally, with time, I got over going to the bathroom alone. My mom honored her side of the bargain, and allowed me, against her better judgment, to go to the next scary movie that came out. All was well again in our household—until I actually went to the next scary movie.

CHAPTER 10

The Napa Junior Traffic Patrol

It was one of those rare programs that combined good social policy with good fiscal policy.

The streets around Napa's elementary schools were made safer because they were patrolled by student traffic guards. They were all volunteers, and the program was so popular that students waited in line to join the Napa Junior Traffic Patrol.

The Alta Heights Traffic Patrol.
I am in the first row, 5th from the right. Next to me to the right are
Wally Keller, Bob Blewitt, Steve Ceriani, and Larry Adams.

The student patrolmen were on duty every morning before school started, during the busiest traffic time, as children were being transported to school by car, truck, or school bus, and again every afternoon when school let out, when parents and the busses were picking up the children.

The Junior Traffic Patrol was created in 1955 as part of a larger, nationwide organization sponsored by the American Automobile Association. The uniforms and badges had the AAA logo on them. Each elementary school was assigned a police officer to organize and train students to act as crossing guards at their schools.

Officer Chuck Hansen and a squad of Junior Traffic Patrol Cadets.

Photo courtesy of Napa Police Historical Society

At the end of the school year, every patrol met for review at Napa Memorial Stadium. This was a really big deal to the kids. We all marched on the football field in front of our parents and various dignitaries of the justice system. The presiding juvenile court judge would attend, along with the Sheriff or Undersheriff, as well as the California Highway Patrol captain and the Napa Police chief. Also in attendance were the supervisor of the program, which was either Police Officer Earl Randol, who started the program in Napa in 1955; his successor, Officer Chuck Holden; or Holden's successor, Officer Bob Boals. These three men were the only supervisors of the program during its forty-five-year existence. The patrols were disbanded in Napa around 2000; however, a few schools still independently use the model.

Most kids thought it prestigious to be on the patrol. The Napa Police Department issued guidebooks to the guard members. The booklets had photographs of the correct way to hold the signs and instructions on marching and various commands. A police officer reviewed these instructions and taught us how to march properly. We learned all the drills you needed to march in step to the street corner to which you were assigned.

There was a hierarchy of positions, from student patrolman, to squad patrol leader, to sergeant, to captain of the entire school patrol. It was easy to pretend that we were in the Army. We got to wear good-looking uniforms that made us feel important. Students couldn't even be in the patrol until the fifth grade; the top ranks were typically not earned until the sixth grade (elementary schools at the time ran from kindergarten to sixth grade).

My friend, Don McConnell, attended Lincoln Elementary School, which was a large, imposing brick school. He recalls:

> One of the best parts of being on the traffic patrol was the quasi-marching to our posts. We were pretty spiffy at Lincoln. I recall the positive and elevating way Officer Earl Randol was with us. It was memorable having an actual policeman give

you some instructions on your duties as a traffic patrolman. I also recall Officer Chuck Holden being part of the traffic patrol. From my first meeting with the officers it was a positive experience. It was a good opportunity to learn responsibility. Growing up and then staying in Napa for most of my life, I found a lifelong friendship with the officers.

Alan Barraco was our Patrol Captain. David Slaight was also one of the Patrol officers. He later became a Napa policeman. Wayne Davidson was in Slaight's class and was also on the Traffic Patrol. I looked up to those guys. There were no accidents while the Traffic Patrol was on duty, helping kids cross streets. The drivers were all good. It was a great experience on many levels.

Another friend, Frank Davidson, whom I met in the ninth grade at Silverado Junior High School, had been a member of the St. John's Catholic School Traffic Patrol. He recalls:

I was a proud member of the Traffic Patrol. I remember thinking how cool it was having 'police' powers. All the cool guys were crossing guards so it wasn't nerdish to be part of the patrol. We all proudly served. Earl Randol was with the police at the time and he was our trainer. I remember feeling the power when cars would stop for you. The only incident was one time a car didn't stop and I thought for sure when I reported this to Officer Randol he would hunt him down. Much to my disappointment, nothing happened. I did make sergeant so I had my own Patrol. I thought about making a career in law enforcement but moved on.

Bob Benning was a classmate of Frank's at St. John's, and recalls the student officers and their rank. It was a big deal at St.

John's, and it confirms that even the cool guys were in the Patrol. The officers in Bob's patrol were: Bob Albertazzi—Captain; Mike Lawler—Lieutenant; Bob Benning—Master Sergeant; and five sergeants, including Frank Davidson and Mike Howard.

Paul Vallerga, a patrol member at Alta Heights, said his patrol uniform was "pretty classy," plus he enjoyed getting out of class early to get to his post. However, a funny thing happened one day as Paul and Mike Kerns were in uniform and on the way to their crosswalk post on East Avenue. Said Paul:

> A rumor was going around about taking several quick breaths and holding your breath while putting your thumb in your mouth and blowing, thus creating a strain while holding your breath. This was to produce a dizziness that was supposed to be a cool feeling. Mike took five or more quick breaths and then inserted his thumb and blew hard. He passed out and busted his upper lip.

Poor Mike was forced to leave the Patrol for the day. His mother was called to pick him up; he was taken to the doctor, who, after hearing what happened, told Mike not to do that again.

I was a member of the Alta Heights Junior Traffic Patrol along with Paul, Mike, Steve Ceriani, Wally Keller, Dave Bastian, Mike Crane and a host of other buddies. I also loved the uniform, and was proud to be a member. I felt important and it was the first time I felt I had power over grown-ups. I couldn't believe that adults actually obeyed the stop signs I put out in front of them, requiring them to stop their cars.

The only traffic patrol incident I had involved my gluttonous tendencies. At lunchtime, I found that Mom packed a couple pieces of cold pizza for her supple little boy. I gobbled them down, and in my haste, the cap on my front tooth, which I had broken in a BB-gun accident, came off. I devoured the pizza so quickly that I ate the cap along with it. It was sometime afterward that I felt the pain of the exposed tooth without the cap when the air hit it.

I was a trouper, and completed my assigned duty after school, despite having to withstand the verbal jabs thrown at me by my good friends who were on duty with me. I think it was Wally Keller who said I looked like a hillbilly. Others said I looked like a pirate, or an upside-down ring toss. My buddies took no mercy, but I deserved it.

The Napa Patrol may have been ahead of its time by admitting girls, who were allowed to participate at some of the schools. This was unusual for the times. My wife, Ann, grew up in Sacramento and wanted to participate in the traffic patrol at her school in the early 1960s, but the program was only for boys. My friend and longtime Napa resident, Randy Snowden, who grew up in Berkeley and participated in the traffic patrol, said that it was boys only there as well. Not every elementary school in Napa allowed girls. The Alta Heights program was for boys only, as my Patrol photo verifies.

However, my friend Wayne Davidson, who attended Lincoln Elementary School, said that when he was in the sixth grade in 1957, the teacher in charge of the patrol announced that girls would now be allowed into the patrol. He still remembers some of the boys objecting:

> As I recall, some of the guys told the teachers that we didn't want girls in our patrol. The teacher responded by telling us, then the patrol would be only girls. When the teacher presented this ultimatum, the boys folded like a cheap tent and the patrol was integrated.

According to photos, some schools allowed girls to participate as early as 1957, according to Napa Police Officer Todd Shulman, a noted Napa historian, particularly with respect to local law enforcement agencies. Schulman dated the photos to 1957 based on the vintage cars on the street and the poodle-type skirts the girls wore. A year or so later the girls started wearing the same red uniform shirts as the boys, but with skirts. Then, in the 1960s the girls and boys wore pants with the red shirt, although some girls still wore skirts.

Junior Traffic Patrol marching on Main Street.
There were girls in the patrol by 1957.

Photo courtesy of Napa Police Historical Society

Janet Lipsey, who became a highly regarded evidence technician for the Napa Police Department, was a member of the Napa Junior Traffic Patrol, starting in 1965.

The Napa Junior Traffic Patrol was a worthwhile program for kids, parents, and the community. The kids put a lot of time and energy into assisting their fellow students to safely cross streets to and from school. Our community came to depend on the kids at all of our elementary schools. There was no possible way, without a great deal of manpower and a large expenditure of money, that the community could feasibly or economically provide the services that all of these kids provided throughout the school year.

For the duration of the Napa Junior Traffic Patrol program, the kids assisted in keeping our children safe. In the forty-five-year history of this Patrol, there were no injuries or fatalities while the Patrol was on duty. That is an incredible reality that the kids made possible and for which our community was extremely proud and thankful.

Most people have good intentions, but it takes more than good intentions to patrol our busy streets for an entire school year. The ability to start a job and stick with it is a great asset. The kids had to arrive at school forty-five minutes to an hour before school started, and stay thirty minutes after school. That was a major commitment. But these kids rose to the challenge and stuck with the job, rain or shine, hot or cold, sleepy-eyed or not.

The kids were leaders at their elementary schools. When the kids moved on to middle school, some of them continued with their commitment of community service, as leaders, and as good examples for their peers.

The parents also benefited from the kids' sacrifice of time and energy. This was a way for parents to give their children an experience that had many benefits. All parents sacrifice for their children, but rarely does it have–such an immediate and profound effect on our entire community.

This program saved lives. The patrol kids protected all the children in our community and gave them safe passage under hazardous conditions. They saved drivers, also, from close calls, not being sure where students might walk. Most of all, the patrol kids saved all of us from the tragedy of having an injured child, or worse yet, a fatality.

Special thanks must be given to those officers who coached our patrol kids. The good look of the patrol and the precision of their movements were vital to drawing the attention and respect of both drivers and students crossing the street. The high quality of

Napa's patrol was a testament to not only the patrol students, but also to their coaches. Unfortunately, the three program champions (Earl Randol, Chuck Holden, and Bob Boals) have passed away, but our community was made safer because of these men and all the other police officers that worked with the Napa Junior Traffic Patrol.

CHAPTER 11

Accordion Melodies

I know why the accordion was so popular with youngsters growing up in the '50s. "I can do it all by myself!" was the proud announcement from many a youngster to his parents and friends.

Plus, kids could show off all their control and ability: there is the treble and the bass, the keyboard for the melody, and the bass buttons to complement, enhance, and complete the melody and astonish and impress the listeners. It was indeed a portable piano, but with so much more. The portability aspect was much appreciated by parents who wanted to show off their "talented" child.

Napa also had a large Italian population, and this instrument appealed to their nostalgia, because if you were Italian, and you had an accordion and a mandolin, you had a party!

There were three prominent accordion teachers in Napa: These were Teresa Greco, Art Kunkel, and my teacher, Willie Ferranato. Not surprisingly, two of the three, Teresa Greco and Willie Ferranto, were Italian. Perhaps other accordion teachers were hidden somewhere, but I doubt it because it's hard to conceal an accordion.

Over the years, I must have been invited to play at every service club in Napa: Kiwanis, Native Sons, Elks, Moose Lodge, Rotary, Lions Club, The Women's Club, The Blind Club, The Druids, Sons of Italy, and more. I also volunteered at the Napa State Hospital because Mom always urged me to play for the mentally ill patients.

Performing at the Vallejo Fair in 1957,
with my music teacher Willie Ferranato and a fellow student.

"Those people are locked up because of their illness and they don't have much entertainment to make them happy," she told me. "You are doing a wonderful thing if you can bring happiness to them."

I played for large groups at local events, including the Napa Town and Country Fair and the County Fair in Calistoga, and I won prizes, including money! As a teenager, I joined the musician's union and formed a musical group called Ray's Combo. We were paid union wages—five times more than the minimum wage. We played at dances and weddings and actually made good money, most of which I banked for college.

In the twelve years that I played my accordion, I had a variety of experiences, not all wonderful, but always interesting, as I met so many people from various walks of life. Playing at the Napa

Town and Country Fair, I made it to the finals and then went on to become the winner of the entire talent show. Some, upon hearing how I won, might not quite believe that I deserved it. If the applause meter had the highest reading, that person won. Dad claimed that what won the contest for me was the screaming, clapping and thumping from him and his buddies. Nevertheless, I remained very proud of this accomplishment, and the big trophy and roll of carnival tickets proved my worth, at least to me. My parents shared my pride. It felt good.

I also entered the County Fair held at Calistoga Fairgrounds. I placed second in the talent show and got what was, for me, substantial winnings. I kept the $25.00 American Savings Bond until it matured and brought it out of my drawer every once in a while just to look at it. Again, my parents were thrilled.

I received several certificates and commendations over the years from Napa State Hospital for volunteering at least forty hours per year amid the lingering smell of urine, and the scary, sad people there.

My sorrow and pity for the patients was poignant, because I knew that each had a tragic, depressing life. On one occasion, I was the sole entertainment during the Ward A-7 Easter party. The wards were fairly small, and the patients sat around me in a circle. Mom, who accompanied me, told me to stand in the center of the circle and turn as I played so that all the patients would get a chance to see me. I was about nine at the time so I could play without sitting. I did exactly what Mom said. I went to the center of the circle and began my song. I slowly turned as I played. The ward was decorated with Easter-themed decorations. Pictures of bunnies and colored eggs adorned the walls. Crepe paper of pastel colors was strung across the walls and ceilings. It was actually colorful and pretty. It felt like a happy atmosphere.

As I kept turning I saw a woman with her arms cradled and going through a rocking motion as if she had a little baby in her arms. She had nothing in her arms. It made me so sad that I have never forgotten her. I wondered if she lost her baby and was so devastated that she became mentally ill. Is that how it worked? Could that cause mental illness? I knew nothing about it, of course, but I felt wounded. I kept turning, relieved that I didn't have to see that poor lady cradling an infant that she mourned.

As I looked ahead, I saw some smiling faces of patients talking to each other. I didn't know if they were talking about me or if they were just having a conversation. At some point while I was turning, I felt what I thought was a rock hitting me in the middle of my back. I heard something drop to the floor behind me. I kept turning, but looked down and saw I had been pelted by a hardboiled Easter egg squarely in the back. I was more shocked than hurt. It also scared me, because I didn't know if everyone would start pelting me. I looked up from the egg and saw some whiskered, toothless old man sharing a laugh with a couple of other guys. Next to this old man was a small basket filled with Easter eggs. He had a ready supply of ammunition. I feared the pelting would not be an isolated incident, so I stayed in that position for a little longer to ensure that I would be able to see, in advance, any more attempts at hitting me with eggs. After several seconds in place I commenced rotating as Mom suggested.

I cut short the medley of songs I was playing so I could finish quickly and leave. I hastily bowed in one direction and went from the center of the floor to where Mom was located. I didn't feel safe. There was only one guard for each group of twenty patients. I immediately asked Mom if she saw what happened.

"Of course, Raymond. I was so proud of you that you kept playing and continued to rotate so that all of the poor patients could see you."

"But Mom, the egg hurt and that man seemed like he might continue pelting me."

"I know, Raymond, but I was watching out and would have summoned the guard if it continued. You were a little trouper."

220

I didn't know exactly what she meant, and I wasn't thrilled at being stoned by a hardboiled egg. I now understand why she was proud of me, but at the time I was just "eggshell" shocked.

There were many performances at the State Hospital and most of them were on the wards with small audiences. The Easter egg incident was the only scary one for me, but regardless, I didn't really enjoy playing at the hospital. My performances were usually on a Saturday afternoon when all my buddies were out playing and having fun. Playing at the State Hospital was an act of charity, not fun. I used to get nervous and couldn't enjoy Saturday mornings because I was continually thinking about having to go to the ward to play for the patients.

Mom made it worthwhile because she never failed to praise me for making these sad people a little happier. Still, my experience when she would schedule a gig was that I was being made to feel guilty if I didn't go there to play.

"No, Mom, not again. I just played there last month. I don't like it. I want to play with my friends."

She would be kind to me, but she knew the power of guilt.

"Raymond, you don't have to play for these poor people, but then they won't get any entertainment or enjoyment out of their weekend. You are all they have. But if you don't want to play, I will tell the State Hospital people that you would rather not go to this event and that we are sorry. Is that what you want me to say?"

I might answer yes at first, but sooner or later I would tell Mom that I would go and entertain the patients. I would do it, but I never enjoyed it.

Not all of my musical performances at Napa State Hospital were held in the small wards. If the occasion was grand, like the annual Christmas show, the administration would hold these events at the State Hospital auditorium. This was a large building and could house patients from multiple wards on the hospital grounds. Such was the case at Christmas every year. On one particular Christmas I was again invited to play, and had despondently tried to reject the invitation. Once again we did the reluctance/guilt dance.

"Mom, I don't want to go."

"But, Raymond, these people will have no other entertainment."

"Okay, fine, I'll go."

The dance with Mom was actually more prolonged, but this is an accurate summary.

This particular Christmas extravaganza was held on the stage of the auditorium with all the patients sitting in the folding chairs in the audience. This event was so big that I was not the main attraction. In fact, the Napa Pepperettes were the main attraction; I was to play between their performances to give them time to change costumes. The Napa Pepperettes were a baton school for girls. Actually, boys could join the Pepperettes, but except for one lesson given to Mike Kerns (who nagged his mother after seeing a drum major in a parade) I had never even heard of a boy in the Pepperettes. After intense teasing, Mike quit after one lesson.

Mom brought me backstage, but then left to go out to the audience to sit with the patients so she could see my performance. Normally, I didn't like being left without Mom, but it wasn't too scary because no patients were allowed back stage, and the pretty twirlers in their little dresses made it an interesting experience.

The show went off without a hitch. I played several musical numbers spaced between the baton routines. I garnered the usual light applause after each of my songs. The rest of my time I spent watching the baton acts and lusting after some of the pretty girls. I also spent time trying to get to know some of the girls my age. I realized my good fortune in not having Mom nearby. I actually enjoyed this trip to the State Hospital.

When the show was over, the girls went with their teacher and exited the back of the stage. I was saying my good-byes when a guard came up to me and asked me to come with him. He took me to the front of the stage where Mom was standing on the staircase leading to the stage. The guard had asked her to remain there with another guard as he retrieved me.

"Son, is this your mother?"

"No sir, I have never seen this woman in my life."

"Raymond! What are you doing?"

I turned from looking at her to looking back at the guard.

"Sorry, this is not my mom. May I go now?"

The guard told the other guard to take Mom back down to the audience and find out what ward she was in. I am pretty sure that the way my poor mom was dressed didn't help matters. She never had any money to spend on herself; the earnings of a husband who worked at a junkyard didn't allow for flashy or even nice clothes. She was wearing an old well-worn cotton dress that never looked good, even on the store hanger.

As for me, I think all the suppressed residual anger from having to spend so many Saturday afternoons playing the accordion for patients in the mental hospital rather than playing with my friends boiled over into a rebellion against Mom and her manipulative ways. Poor Mom was caught so off-guard that she didn't know what to do. Within minutes, I went back to the front of the stage where one guard was allowing her to produce some sort of identification.

"Sir, she really is my mom. I am very sorry. I was just joking."

I smiled at Mom, but there was no return smile. When she finally took custody of me and got me out to the car, she looked me in the eye.

"Raymond, why did you do that?"

Instead of being mature and having an open discussion about the fact that I did not like being forced to play the accordion against my will, I chickened out.

"I thought it would be fun to see what happened. Sorry, Mom."

Once, when I was about eight, my accordion playing included a paid-for family vacation. We had only been on two vacations my entire childhood, and when we were invited to a festival on the Russian River, all of us Guadagnis got to stay in a cabin and dine at restaurants as part of the event. I got this invitation because I had been a member of a group called the "Stars of Tomorrow." There were local celebrities and various winners of beauty pageants from nearby cities such as Sebastopol, Vallejo, Santa Rosa, and El Cerrito. I felt like a star. I had to play my accordion on Saturday and Sunday in the show, but the rest of my time was free. It was super.

At a Russian River resort, I was joined by the Beauty Queens of 1954.
They were very healthy ladies.

I admired the lovely pageant winners. They were all, except one, Peter Paul Rubens women—large, buxom ladies. There was one who I thought seemed, at least by comparison, to be skinny, but when I look at my photo of these women, I still see that all were plump, hefty heifers. The one I deemed slender would not be judged skinny by today's standards.

When I was in the fifth grade, I appeared on the *King Norman Show*, a kid's show produced by a local television station aired only in the Bay Area. The show was named after the host and featured film clips of talented local children dancing or singing.

The King also had kids as guests who played various games, with the contestants getting a prize. There was also a talent show, where three kids would exhibit their talent and the audience would mail in their choice for winner. All the weekly winners would compete with each other in the finals for the ultimate King Norman Talent Show winner. I don't even know how I got on this show but somehow I was entered into the talent contest. I suspect that my mother thought I was so good that being exposed to television might be just the break her son needed to become famous. I was much older than the kids the show was for, since I was a fifth-grader.

My friends scorned this show because it was a little kids show. However, they certainly watched it when word leaked out that I was to be there. I was an embarrassed, nervous, and anxious wreck by show time. It was strikingly weird to be introduced to this large man with a full-length robe and full beard with a crown of jewels on his expansive helium head. The studio was surprisingly small and the live audience was just a handful of people. I followed the stagehand's instructions exactly. I stood in front of a microphone that was on a stand. The large television camera was directly in front of me and the lights were blinding, brighter than anything I had ever seen in my life, brighter than train lamps and even spotlights used at movie premieres. I couldn't see anything. I played whatever song I chose about three times faster than the required tempo.

Back at Alta Heights on Monday, I found out that a couple of my friends had seen me, probably because my mom told their moms. My friends were brutally honest with their reviews. One of them said he thought I was going to cry. Both of them said that they could see tears in my eyes.

Nevertheless, I knew I had a good chance to win when Mom spent the week filling out stacks of penny postcards, all of which were votes for me. I still can see her sitting at our yellow Formica kitchen table filling them out until her hand cramped. Mom explained to me that we had to fill out all of the postcards by addressing them all to the King Norman Show and each one had to cast a vote for me. She seemed to think that this was fair play, because she was sure that all the other parents of the contestants were doing the same thing. Besides, she said that she was just voting for all of our friends. I really had no idea that we had so many friends, but that is what she said.

The week passed, and at 9:00 AM the next Saturday I was sitting in front of the television watching the King Norman Show waiting to hear the announcement of last week's winner. I had to wade through all of the kid stuff and that week's talent entries. Finally, at the end of the show King Norman said that last week's winner was (drum roll): "Paul Gadini" from Napa. I wasn't sure I won because my name wasn't Paul, but then again I was the only contestant from Napa and "Gadini" was close enough to be Guadagni. I figured I had won. This turned out to be true!

I appeared again at the end of the month on the finals; this time, a panel of judges determined the winner. Their rejection of me was swift, and I went home with nothing—actually, less than nothing. All of those post cards cost my mom a few dollars when you included the cost of the cards and the stamps. It was a losing proposition, and I was humiliated.-

Playing the accordion around town (or even out of town, for that matter) was never a source of great enjoyment, and I began to resist invitations. Once, I was requested to play at Fort Baker in San Francisco for the veterans. The invitation came from "Stars of Tomorrow," led by an old woman named Ma Braden. I don't recall how I got hooked up with her, but I am sure Mom had something to do with it. My resolve was strong, and my refusal this time was unequivocal. Mom assumed that this was my common reluctance, not a genuine decision to not go. When it came time to leave for San Francisco I reminded Mom that I had never accepted the invitation and did not intend to play that evening. Mom was astonished at my vehement refusal. She was beside herself.

"Raymond, I am sorry if I didn't listen correctly, but I accepted on your behalf because I thought you said yes. You can't let them down now. They are counting on you."

"Mom, I wish you had listened better, because I never accepted and you need to just call them and tell them that I can't go. You can tell them I am sick, which is partly true because I am a little sick about this situation."

Then Mom deployed her guilt trip.

"Okay, Raymond, but you will be letting these soldiers down, and this is the only entertainment they get."

I was weary of this manipulation.

"It is a shame that soldiers (or mental illness patients or the like) get their only entertainment from me, but I never accepted this invitation and I am not going. Sorry."

Mom gave up.

"Okay, Raymond, I will call the show and let them know that you will not be attending." I felt very guilty but also relieved that I didn't have to play that evening and proud that I had stood up for myself.

Apparently, Mom hadn't really given up. She made a different call. This one was to my dad who was at work Saturday morning, and told him that I was refusing to play. Dad said to not worry, that he would make me go. When he got home that afternoon he said that he wanted to clean up and then we should leave in the early afternoon, so we could get dinner before the show, which started at 8:00 PM.

"I guess you haven't heard, Dad, but I am not going. I never accepted the invitation and so I am not going."

"You are going and I don't want to hear another word about it."

"But, Dad, I didn't accept the invitation. Mom misunderstood..."

That was as far as I got.

"Raymond, I told you that you are going and not another word about it. I don't want to hear any more whining. This is final."

Dad was beginning to yell. I knew that there would not be a rational conversation about this issue. Why should I expect that, anyway, when there had never been a rational conversation with Dad about any disagreement?

I had lost, so I put on my dress clothes and packed my accordion to the car and off we went. All the while we were in the car heading to San Francisco I kept thinking to myself that I should take a stand. I shouldn't go on the stage. I would tell Dad that I really mean it when I say no and I am not going on the stage. We can tell Ma Braden (who, by the way, looked like a dried apple doll) that I got sick and had to leave. I could do it! I kept saying that I must be strong and take a stand. I practiced my remarks all the way to the city.

Finally, we arrived at the fort and went into the auditorium to get set up. Telling Dad was not going to be easy so I put it off. It was never the right time. Finally, backstage with some of the other acts sitting around waiting for their turn, I felt I was safe enough to talk to Dad without him yelling.

"Dad, I am sorry, but I really meant it when I said that I never accepted this invitation and so I am not going on tonight."

Dad looked angry in the way he always did before he started yelling.

"Raymond, what is going on? Am I talking to the wall? We've been over this and you are going on and you will play. Now that is final!"

I could hear my heart pounding. I had never challenged my dad to this extent before.

"Sorry, Dad, but my decision is final. Just tell Ma Braden that I took ill. She will understand."

I anticipated that my dad would start his usual loud, vicious rant. Instead, he bent over from where he was standing to where I was sitting and he whispered in my ear.

"You are playing or I will end your life tonight."

I felt his garlicky warm breath as he threatened me. It gave me the shivers. I had never ever heard such restraint from my dad. And I had never ever heard the ultimate threat of taking my life, either. I sat there with fear and rage in my heart. How dare a father threaten to kill his son? I thought as a father he would be programmed to love me. I guess not. My mind raced with fleeting and mixed thoughts: get up and run away; scream and ask for help; tell Mom; just play the accordion and run away later. These and many more thoughts were considered in a nanosecond. I rejected them all. I didn't know what to do, but I couldn't believe that my father had threatened my life. It wasn't one of those frustrated emotional threats like, "Clean up your room or I'll make you wish you had," or "Mow the lawn or I'll throttle you." No, it was not a rant, this was a soft spoken calm threat to end me. Could he mean what he said? Would he actually carry out this threat?

With these feelings of fear and rage, I decided to go on stage and play my songs rather than risk an argument that, at the least would be abusive, and possibly violent. I went on the stage with a phony-baloney smile pasted on my face, tears in my eyes, and a well of anger in my heart. Discretion is the better part of valor, and his threat hurt me to the core. I lived to fight another day. That's what I kept telling myself, but I also felt like a coward who couldn't stand up for himself.

But I did learn an extraordinarily important lesson: I would not be such a father to my children. I have never threatened my children with violence, bodily harm, or death, and behold! They are the greatest joy any parent could experience, and also, they did not need this lesson to be wonderful nurturers of their own children.

A gig that didn't involve violent threats came when I played at the old Christian Brothers Winery for a goodwill tour. It seems that sometime in the late '50s, the new French president Charles de Gaulle had given the country of Madagascar its independence, and shortly thereafter the country became known as the Republic of Malagasy. My reputation as an accomplished accordionist was somewhat known around town. As a result, my agent (aka Mom) was contacted sometime around the late summer of 1960 by whomever was putting on the entertainment at the winery in honor of the King of Malagasy. Mom told me that President Kennedy's administration was sponsoring this event and I would be playing for the king (I don't know if he was a king or president, but that is what Mom told me). In any event, I accepted the invitation and played my accordion for His Majesty. No one pelted me in my back with Easter eggs. Mom was so proud. I am sure the king enjoyed the sweet sounds of my accordion, having been plied with some of the best cabernet sauvignon in the valley.

My first music group was a trio formed in the fourth grade with Mike Crane on the trumpet, Gene Baker on the drums, and me on the accordion. We practiced a lot before we played in front of our class. Finally, we performed *Hot Diggity*, a song recorded by Perry Como that made the charts in 1956. Playing such a popular song, we were sure we would be a hit with our classmates. My biggest fear was if our audience wanted an encore we would have to play *Hot Diggity* again because it was the only song we knew. Many things that you worry about in life do not come true, and this was such a time. Surprisingly, to me, the class did not request an encore, nor did our teacher Mrs. Allen invite us to play more than the one song. It took longer to set up than it did to play the tune. Because of serious musical differences, the trio disbanded soon after our one and only gig.

I successfully integrated the accordion with my friends when I got to Silverado Junior High. This is where I met Bill Forsythe, an exceptionally talented musician. His first instrument was the trumpet, but he could play anything if he wanted to. He had perfect pitch, an extraordinary ear, and could improvise beautifully. Bill loved music and loved to clown around. He was a perfect match for me. After a while Bill and I brought our other friends into the group, even though all of them were without formal musical training and, in fact, most of them were without any musical talent, including the ability to keep time. Our only requirement was that we liked these guys. We had them play quietly. Paul Vallerga played the drums, Mike Kerns played the gut-bucket, and Mike Lawler played the cymbals. With me on the accordion (used like a keyboard) and Bill on the trumpet we called ourselves The Firehouse Five. Sometimes we had more than our original five, but our group name was made to accommodate that. If Donny Accomando and Don McConnell joined us, we announced ourselves as the Firehouse Five plus Two. We played anywhere we could get attention—Our goal was to play in front of girls. We hoped our audience included Gael Mosher, Ann Potgeter, Lana Bisson, Suzanne Fetters, Stevie Inman, Sandy Hicks, Bonnie Kreutzer, and all the girls of Silverado Junior High. We played after school and on weekends. Our favorite spot to set up was on the traffic island between Vallerga's Grocery store, the roller rink, and

Food Fair. It was located on First Street near Juarez Street and Silverado Trail. We thought we were so cool. We belted out "When The Saints Come Marching In" and any other song Bill and I knew. It didn't matter to the rest of the group because they couldn't read music and had their hands full with keeping time as they banged their instruments.

By the time I was fifteen, I finally started getting remuneration from gigs performed by the next musical group I formed, aptly called Ray's Combo. We played dances, weddings, engagements, anniversaries, and parties of all sorts. The amount of money we made was whatever I could negotiate.

The group consisted of me on the accordion, Bob Eggers on the stand-up bass, and Bill Forsythe on the trumpet. Like Forsythe, Eggers was an exceptionally talented musician. In addition to stand-up bass, Bob played rhythm guitar, and Bill also played piano. I played the drums, as well as the accordion. With such variety we could play many different kinds of music, from a Herb Alpert-type of rock with guitar, drums and trumpet, to the old American standards, with me playing an electric accordion chording behind Bill on his trumpet and Bob on the bass. This was a means of entertaining a variety of audiences, so demand for our performances grew.

I always kept our price low to attract business. It was not very long before I got a call from a representative of the musician's union for the Napa area. It was the president himself, Eddie Zaro, who was a drummer (I later learned in a sociology class at Cal that the vast majority of musician union presidents were drummers).

Mr. Zaro was very kind to me, but let me know that we must be in the union. Then, he explained that we would be getting union wages of $5.50 per hour (compared to the minimum wage of $1.25). I told him that was fine with me, but I was fifteen and the other two members of our trio were only fifteen and sixteen years old. I didn't know if there was a minimum age before we could join.

After some discussion, we were allowed to join the union upon receipt of fees and annual dues.

This is when our group really started to earn income. We played dances and other gigs for union wages. This was fabulous money, and because I was very frugal I just banked my share for college. It was my group, but the most talented was Forsythe and the next talented was Eggers. I was Ringo Starr to Lennon and McCartney. We split everything equally and I took care of all the arrangements and contracts, and ensured there was a piano and electrical outlets, microphones and everything we needed to set up properly.

Before long we got regular jobs. We played weekends at Catania's Pizza Parlor. It was a great gig, except that the PA system went through my amplifier. This meant when the proprietor announced through the microphone, "Pizza number 76, your pizza is ready, pizza number 76!" our band would not be able to hear ourselves for several seconds. It was odd and was a challenge to see if we were all on the same note and chord when the announcement finished.

Everything from then on was for union wages. I was making more money than I could believe. It made working at the Shell gas station for a minimum wage seem like a complete waste of time. Four hours playing at a dance (four hours was our usual minimum) was equal to 17.5 hours of work at the gas station. It hardly seemed worth it but I knew that the music gig might not last. If business went bad for the pizza parlor we would be the first unnecessary expense to cut back on. Catania could just use the jukebox, and dispense with us.

Nonetheless, I kept my job at Shell until I got an offer to work at the Napa Grocery Center as a box boy. This was not for music union wages but it was also not minimum wage. I had to join the Retail Clerks Union, so I was making $3.25 per hour. My choice of this job over the gas station was automatic. I could work for minimum wage at a greasy gas station where the only perk was to wash windows of a car in the summer months where the driver or passenger or both were pretty girls in bathing suits, or work at the Grocery Center where I made three times as much money (besides, pretty girls shopped for groceries, too). I was now making union wages as a musician and as a box boy. Now my bank account was really growing. I lived at home with no expenses for room or board. I save nearly every cent I earned.

In the summer between eighth and ninth grade, while I was saving my money from my various jobs, with accordion gigs being, by far, the most lucrative, my father left my mother. He found someone else with whom to utilize his skills of power, domination and unpleasantness.

Upon his departure, he was yelling at my mother and following her into their bedroom. Just before he entered their bedroom he stopped and looked over at me standing at the kitchen doorway. He noticed that I was crying, which prompted him to tell Mom, "I guess that one won't be much help to you." He didn't even say my name. This typical contempt for Mom and me evoked a silent vow to help my mom make it without him. We would all be happier.

Even though Mom was very sad for the family not remaining intact, she was also truly unhappy with him. I was relieved because things were more peaceful around the house, but I was also sad for Mom. Her identity was as a housewife and now she felt like a failure at that. Also, she had no employable skills. She took a typing class at the junior college, but the only jobs she landed were babysitting and cleaning houses.

Mom's childhood had been extremely difficult. She had lost two siblings when they were very young, and she had lost her mother when she was twelve. Her father died when she was seventeen, and she was left to take care of herself and one remaining sibling, her younger brother, Jim. She had already dropped out of school to help make ends meet when her mother died. When her father died, she took in wash and several other jobs to help support herself and Jim. She was accustomed to working hard, and was not afflicted with self-pity.

After he abandoned us, Dad did pay a meager amount for support but this was sporadic. Mom could not count on him for a regular monthly amount. Mom made things work, but she still had an emptiness in her life. She only wanted two things: a family and her own house. Her parents did not own their house, and throughout their marriage, my parents always rented. It looked as if her fairly modest wishes would never come true.

However, after a couple of years, the flame went out of Dad's new love life, and he came back, requesting/demanding another chance. I, personally, was hoping she would not take him back. The memories of Dad's new girlfriend calling up my mom and warning her to "watch her husband" and other taunts regarding Dad's indiscretions, were still fresh in my mind. I learned these things as I sat beside Mom, holding her hand, while she cried herself to sleep.

I hated Dad's girlfriend and I hated Dad. When I prayed I would propose to God that while I wouldn't murder this other woman, would it be possible for Him to kill her because of her commandment violations and unnecessarily cruel taunts to my mother? I felt she was truly evil. To an eighth grader this seemed like a reasonable request. Dad had destroyed Mom's dream of what she considered a family. Still, now that he was on his own, he was on his best behavior and at least claiming to be remorseful. Mom was a very forgiving person. After months of Dad's cajoling and begging, she agreed to give him another chance, but on one condition: buy a house for us.

Dad was intent on buying a house for her so he could come back. He only had a few problems in this regard. He had no money. He had a checking account but it was usually overdrawn. He spent money as fast as he earned it. He did not own his own home, and the land where his wrecking yard was situated was also leased. In other words, he did not have any collateral. His borrowing ability was nil. He did not have, as they say, "a pot to pee in."

I told Mom that if she really wanted to try to make her marriage work, I would support her by buying a house for her. She knew I was sincere because I had been bragging to her about all the money I had saved. By this time I had more than $4,000. You could buy a modest home in Napa for between $8,000 and $20,000. A down payment was usually only ten percent of the purchase price.

Mom didn't want to accept it, but she knew there was no way to get a house if she didn't take me up on the offer. She said she could not accept this money from her son. She knew I was saving it for college. She was in a real dilemma. She decided to accept my money as a loan that she would pay back, with interest. In that way, she could accept the money, not as charity, but as a business deal in which I would profit. I was glad that was the way the deal went down, because that way Mom never had to feel that I was financially supporting her. There were no papers signed, no collateral, and no handshake.

I never really expected her to pay me back, although for years she made small payments out of the paltry sums Dad gave her to run the household. She kept careful track of interest and principal payments. She did her very best to pay back the money. My father never made a payment nor did he ever mention the source. It was as if he had given her the money to fulfill the requirement to return, not me. Owning a house was only important to Mom, as Dad was indifferent. For her, a lifelong dream had come true. She was always so appreciative of me for staking her. Her house was her pride and joy. Her housekeeping was immaculate. This was no surprise to me because she was always a spotless housekeeper at the rental where I grew up. We didn't have a backyard at the rental, but there was a large one at her new house. She made a beautiful garden there, and fixed up a wonderful patio where she could sit on summer evenings and enjoy her backyard. She was overjoyed to finally live in her own house.

My music jobs kept money rolling in, and in later years I worked at Kaiser Steel Fabrication Plant in Napa, where the hourly pay was $3.75 an hour and double that if you worked the graveyard shift. The money from music, together with the money I earned from working at Kaiser, was enough to pay for college at the University of California at Berkeley and for my law degree at the Hastings School of Law in San Francisco.

When I reflect on playing the accordion, I have to conclude that it was not all that much fun for me. I didn't like playing at all of those organizations, nor did I enjoy traveling around and playing for audiences. I was always nervous being on stage, and there were always other things I would have preferred doing (like being with my buddies).

Still, I can't say I regret these experiences, because it led me to playing the piano by teaching myself the left hand. Nowadays, I play for my enjoyment, and I have enjoyed composing songs. Also, I have always been proud of being able to put myself through school. That could not have happened without my music.

Most importantly, however, my music allowed me to purchase a house for Mom. That fulfilled her life-long dream. She thrived in her house for the rest of her life. It was truly worth taking an egg pelting from a State Hospital patient, being on the King Norman Show, playing at the Fair, performing at service clubs and the Veterans Home, surviving dad's death threat, and giving up Saturday afternoons and weekend evenings, to see the happiness it gave my beloved mother.

CHAPTER 12

To Pompadour Or Not

In the '50s, the flat top was very popular with boys and men, particularly among guys who wanted their hair short and easy to manage. No combing, no grooming, no fuss, no muss. And all you had to say to your barber was, "I want a flat top, please." Oh, the barber might ask you if you wanted to leave the sides longer, in which case you had a flat top with fenders. That was it.

By the mid-1950s, it became the most popular men's hairstyle in the United States. Kids and adults alike were getting flat tops, which was a perfect hairstyle for hot summers. Even sports stars were wearing them, like Roger Maris, who tied Babe Ruth's record (although an asterisk was put by Maris' name because it took him more games in the 1961 season than it took Ruth in the 1927 season to reach and break the record).

His great teammate, Hall-Of-Famer Mickey Mantle, also sported a flat top from time to time. From the 1950s well into the 1960s, and to a lesser extent in subsequent decades, flat tops have remained in style. Many of the U.S. astronauts have worn flattops. Gus Grissom was a classic example. During Watergate, H. R. Haldeman was a total throwback to the '50s for flat top haircuts. And, one of my favorite basketball players on the Warriors, and another Hall Of Fame player, Chris Mullin, still wears a flat top.

Today, though, things are not nearly as clear and simple. For instance, recently at Sweeney's, a longtime sporting goods store in Napa, the thirty-something clerk had what looked like a traditional flat top haircut directly out of the '50s. I kept staring at it and finally told him I couldn't help thinking back to my favorite decade. I asked him if he called that a flat top or, more particularly, if his barber called it a flat top haircut. To my surprise, he said no.

He said he had to be very specific about what he wanted or it wouldn't come out the way he envisioned. Frankly, I couldn't believe this—it was just a frickin' flat top. I asked him to clarify, which he was more than willing to do. He said he had to tell his barber he wanted a "zero fade high and a number four on top." He explained that "zero fade high" referred to how high he wanted the short hair on the sides of his head to go, before fading into the top. He said "number four on top" informed the barber how long his hair should be on the very top of his head.

I asked him what he thought he would get if he just told the barber he wanted a flat top, with no other explanation. He said that a flat top is a military-style haircut with very short sides meeting a short, flat top.

I guess this is progress, as it does allow exact input from the customer so that he is pleased with what he gets, but it is more complicated than anything I remember. To me, it is more stressful trying to specify how high the sides are and whether a razor or clippers should be used and what the number should be on top. I preferred the simplicity of just saying flat top. Whatever I got was what I got.

As a kid, it was even easier than that. I had only to point to the picture on the poster behind the barber's station, to specify what I preferred. The poster listed the Forward Brush, Professional, Ivy League, Business Men's, Butch, Crew Cut, Flat Top with Fenders and the Flat Top. The poster also stated prominently off to the side, "We specialize in cutting hair correctly...the way you like it."

Yeah, right, where is Ralph Nader when you need him?

Those haircut pictures, compared to the results on my head, must have constituted consumer fraud, bait and switch, or some kind of negligent, if not intentional, misrepresentation. Something drastically illegal was going on, which leads me to the big problem I encountered at every barbershop I ever went to.

The same thing would happen, no matter what hair style I picked from the pictures on the wall (butch, flat top, or Ivy League, depending on the weather): the finished haircut did not resemble the guy in the poster. All the haircut models looked like a young Tony Curtis with black hair and blue eyes, as opposed to a short, chubby Italian kid. I thought if I picked that picture, a haircut would transform my face, age, complexion, weight, and eye color. I was wrong.

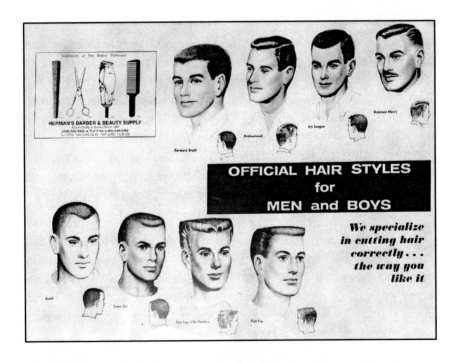

From this barbershop poster, I rotated between selecting the Butch, Crew Cut, Flat Top, or Ivy League hairstyle. I, however, never looked like these guys on the best day of my life.

I went to many barbers over the years due to my tireless quest to look like one of the handsome guys in the poster. The barbers were all nice guys engaged in what was a "clean" profession. I learned this from Mom, who liked the neat and clean barbering profession, as opposed to the dirty, greasy, smelly auto wrecker profession of my dad. Also, her favorite singer, Perry Como, used to be a barber.

I thought about becoming a barber because of propaganda I heard from Mom, and because of the fun chitchat I observed between the barbers and their older customers. It seemed like they were always discussing sports or other current events. It seemed like fun. Getting paid to shoot the breeze with friends and customers while you provided a service seemed almost too good to be true.

By the time I got to high school, my guidance counselor wasn't sure I would make a good anything, so I didn't even want to shoot for such a profession and fail. Further, I innately knew deep down in the recesses of my mind that I couldn't work with my hands very well. I just knew this fun picture of being a barber would end up with me somehow terribly butchering someone's hair or shaving a head inappropriately. Then the happy atmosphere would dissipate into a lonely Italian barber who had no repeat business, and would be unable to engage in interesting chitchat, unless he started talking to himself.

Nevertheless, I loved the barbershops of the '50s. As long as I stayed away from the butch style, which disclosed my misshapen head and was not a pretty sight, I was good. I figured there was no sense in making myself completely gruesome to the ladies. I was already being very unconventional by going back to short hair. I loved short hair. I was made for this era. I was a rebel.

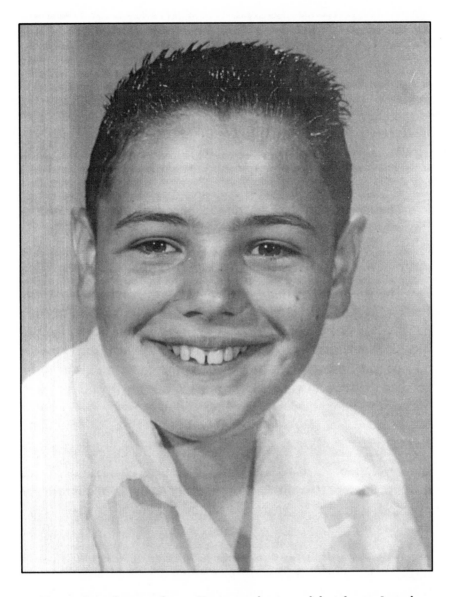

My version of pompadour—No matter how much butch wax I used,
I never resembled Elvis or Ricky Nelson. I am sure the chipped front
tooth from a BB gun accident didn't help my chances with the girls either.

All the barbers had neat names: Bun from Bun's Barber Shop; Gene and Shirley's, where Shirley was a guy who used to work for Bun before branching out with Gene; and Benny the Barber. The name sounded like an Italian gangster's name—a member of the Mafioso. However, Benny was 100 percent Filipino. His barbershop was located on Second Street (where Second Street intersected Main Street, dead ending at the river) with the Western Union Office on one side and the Napa River on the other. It was across the street from the Oberon bar (now Downtown Joe's).

The haircuts on their posters were described as "The Official Haircuts for Men and Boys." This would not, however, be an accurate description of all the hairstyles of the 1950s, unless mention was made of certain other popular looks of the time.

There were the pompadour hairdos of the rock stars, and the Duck's Ass Hair or Duck Tail—if one wished to be tamer in labeling it. This was one of the most popular styles for men of the entire decade. Tony Curtis wore this style. It looked like he parted his hair on one side, combed the top over to the other side, and then combed the sides straight back to meet in the middle of the back of his head forming the duck's tail. Hair cream or wax (usually butch wax or Dixie Peach) was applied liberally to hold the hair in place.

There were also other styles for older men who favored a very conservative look, with a short haircut and lots of cream to plaster it down. Most parted the hair on one side and combed it straight over to the other. The sides and the back were all combed down like Marlon Brando.

And then, there were unique hairstyles that were either throwbacks to prior decades or just defied derivation because they were so unique. Jimmy Stewart had his own type of hairstyle, for instance, as did Cary Grant.

Some men just combed the hair straight back like the vampires Bella Lugosi and Christopher Lee, or Robert De Niro in the movie *New York, New York*.

Regarding cool, greasy hairstyles, when my hair started to grow out, before I returned for my next haircut, I would experiment by trying to get the biggest wave in the front that I could get. The bigger the wave, the cooler you were. I plastered my hair with butch wax or Dixie Peach and combed a big front wave.

I would not have looked appealing with my version of the pompadour style. I have a rather large and broad forehead. Not a good start. I also had a widow's peak that looked pretty silly when the wave exposed it to the fullest. Besides, Mom didn't like me using hair wax. When I would sit up in bed to read a book or magazine, I would leave a rather large grease spot on the wallpaper behind my head. This left Mom vexed with disappointment. These fancy styles just didn't work for me.

I was only four feet something, fat, and wore husky jeans (with the label still on them). Moreover, I had to wear black corrective shoes that looked like a conservative businessman's. There was just no way I would ever look cool with these overwhelming negatives.

Still, it was much simpler growing up when you could just point to a picture on the barber's wall. If you were shy you didn't even have to speak. That was as easy as it gets.

As I grew older, haircuts became important to me because of girls. For me, that was the fifth grade. By then, I noticed that there was more to life than just playing with my Army men and sports. I started to like girls, and Gael Mosher was the girl I liked the most. Gael Mosher was one of the cutest and smartest girls at Alta Heights Elementary School.

I liked Gail as more than just as a friend. She was pretty, smart, fun and kind. She lived at 1212 Banks Avenue in the heart of the Alta Heights neighborhood.

The previous Christmas, before I liked Gael, I had been given my first bicycle. It was a full-sized men's bike with the cross bar so high that I couldn't easily get on the bike. It had balloon tires and was simply way too big for me to ride. Actually, I could ride it if I could get on it. I had to stand on the exterior staircase at our house to climb on. To dismount, I had to lean over drastically and fall over with one foot landing on the curb or street and the rest of me dangling precariously on what had become a very tilted bike. It was the only way I could get on or off my bike without the assistance of another person.

Also, if I wanted to take books or my binder home from school, I couldn't do it alone. I needed both hands. Eventually I added a basket to the front to transport my stuff, but before I got my basket, Gael used to help me get on my bike at school, before I departed for home. She would hold my books or binder and let me get on my bike. Then I would circle around and ride over to her and she would hand me my stuff as I slowly rode by. This worked well. I know it was an imposition on her, but she did it and never made me feel like I was putting her out. She was a very kind friend.

Gael Mosher, my first crush

We seemed to have a lot in common. We both tied for the reading contest (by reading the most books over the summer) and were both awarded with bookmarks. I don't know about Gael, but I would have preferred a burger and shake. Also, we both were winners at different times in the spelling contests conducted in our class. She had a great sense of humor and liked to have fun. We made each other laugh, and because we had known each other since the first grade, we were comfortable with each other.

I wanted to ask her to go to the skating rink together or maybe buy her a gift, but I didn't want to be rejected. I was not too comfortable with my weight or looks. For the first time I wanted to lose weight. This was a real problem because I loved eating more than anything. I became careful about what I ate and refused seconds.

Still, there was a bigger problem for me if I had any hope to win Gael's affections. She liked someone else. I had learned in my usual role of "big brother" that she was absolutely crazy about Stanley Hart. I knew this because when I was looking at Gael, she was looking at Stanley. After a while she started showing everyone how she felt about Stanley, putting tin foil cut-outs in the shape of hearts all over her binder and sometimes on her arms. I guess that was to symbolize her feelings for Stanley Hart (heart).

Gael was also in love with Elvis with his pompadour, but he didn't live in Napa so I only had Stanley (and his pompadour) to worry about. Unbelievably, Stanley didn't return Gael's affections. What was *wrong* with Stanley? I figured I still had a chance.

My plan to get Gael to like me was to change my looks drastically. I had to lose weight and I needed to change my hairstyle. My usual butch haircut was not going to cut it. I noticed that guys with pompadour hairstyles really had luck with the girls. These are what my buddies and I referred to as greaser hairstyles. They seemed to go hand-in-hand with rock and roll. I didn't dislike these hairstyles, but I was pretty sure I would be less than comfortable with one of the greaser looks.

I was no expert on the Ricky Nelson pompadour hairstyle, but it seemed to involve combing the top forward and flipping it up and back without a part. I really didn't know how to comb and shape the pompadour, but I do know that girls loved Ricky Nelson. This style was seen on rock stars and musicians of the times and all of them had many girls who adored them.

Elvis Presley had a Rockabilly hairdo, which was really just a pompadour hairdo only with the front of the top hair being left longer than the back. This type of pompadour allowed Elvis to create exaggerated height in the front when flipping the hair back. I am sure that lots of cream or wax was used with this hairstyle. No one could dispute that millions of girls loved Elvis. I am sure they loved his music and the way he swung his hips, too, but it was universally agreed by girls that he had a great hairdo. Besides, I know his look worked with Gael. She loved Elvis.

I was convinced that a pompadour hairdo would be my ticket to happiness and romance with Gael. What clinched this belief was when I saw how popular the boys were at Alta Heights who wore these hairdos. I only knew two guys at Alta Heights who wore the pompadour. They were Stanley Hart and Wesley Woolery. Both of these guys were well liked by the girls.

At a birthday party in the third grade at Christine Anderson's house, Wesley brought a Chuck Berry album to her for a present. I didn't even know who Chuck Berry was, but Christine seemed delighted and seemed to really like Wesley. Stanley may not have had a true pompadour but it was a version that was close to it. I am sure it didn't hurt that he was tall, dark, and handsome with a full head of long black wavy hair that was combed beautifully.

I planned to grow out my hair to comb it in a pompadour, and find a barber who really knew what a pompadour was and how to style it.

I went to Bun the Barber and asked him about a pompadour. He looked at me and said, "Look at the poster. Do you see a pompadour hairstyle on the poster?"

"No."

"Those are the only hairstyles I do. Also, I am not sure you would really want this hairstyle. It takes a lot of time to style it, along with a ton of butch wax."

Undeterred, I went to Benny the Filipino barber, located next to the Western Union Office on Second Street. Benny said he didn't know what I was talking about.

I went to Gene of Gene and Shirley's and asked him about a pompadour hairdo.

"You need to have long hair," said Gene. "If you want, we can start letting your hair grow out, but this will take a little while before your hair is long enough to comb your hair in this style."

Finally, I had a barber who listened and would work with me. So I started to let my hair grow out. It got longer and longer and started to get wavy to the point where I didn't know how to comb it. I didn't even know I had wavy hair because my hair was always kept so short. I hated curly hair. This seemed like a nasty trick that nature played on me. This is when I purchased my first jar of Dixie Peach hair wax. I plastered my hair down so it wouldn't wave at all.

I wanted straight hair. I wanted hair that obeyed me—not hair that had its own independent mind and went any which way it so desired. But if I used butch wax, I was required to use so much on my longer wavy, curly hair that I looked like a greased down, slicked down, hairy dog after a bath. Not a great look.

I soon realized that most of the barbers really didn't know how to comb the pompadour. They were all older men who were either bald or had very short hairdos. I was going to need expert help.

My next plan was to have Wesley assist me in growing a pompadour like his. Wesley's was the real deal. He really looked like a rock star. He wore tight Levi's (which I later learned were "pegged"—meaning they were sewn very tightly along the leg seams; nowadays they would be called "skinny jeans"). He wore the hippest shirts that were completely current with the latest fashions of rock stars and he was tall and lean. He was the ideal I was trying to reach. We all thought he was cool, and this universally acknowledged cool guy, Wesley Woolery, could teach me to grow and comb a pompadour.

Besides, how I could I ask Stanley for help when my whole plot was to steal his girl? Further, Wesley was in the same classroom. Even though he was so cool and popular, he treated kids kindly, even me.

But, alas, the mysterious workings of God eliminated my plan to persuade Wesley to help me accomplish the pompadour and succeed with Gael.

Divine intervention came during the fifth grade talent show in our class (thank God it was only our class). I played my accordion to the delight of my classmates. Some of the girls tap-danced or played violins.

Wesley had the guts to get up and do an a capella Do-Wop song. He started off by just snapping his fingers to get his timing right and then started with the introduction which consisted of something to the effect of "Yip, yip, yip, yip, booma, booma, booma, rama, lama, do-wop, do-wop," etc.

Actually, Wesley never got as far as the rama lama part because several of us started to laugh and then all of us were laughing. Mrs. Allen was mortified and told us to be quiet and then told Wesley to start over. Wesley, with balls of steel, started snapping his fingers again and then went as far as yip, yip, yip, before I was on the floor howling, followed quickly by the rest of the class.

This time Mrs. Allen noticed which student began laughing first, stopped the class again, and came directly over to me.

"Raymond, no one laughed at you when you played the accordion," she said in a not-so-low tone of voice. "How would you have liked it if they laughed at you? You are being rude and I don't want you laughing at Wesley again. If you do, you will be sent to the principal's office. Do you understand me?"

Well, I might as well have immediately risen from my seat and marched directly to the principal's office. I really didn't want to laugh at Wesley. I liked him and he had never made fun of me (or my weight) nor did he ever act like he was cooler than me (which he clearly was). It is just that the pressure was unbearable. I knew in my heart that I was going to do it, but I thought I might be able to stifle what I knew might be a gigantic urge to laugh. Well, hope may spring eternal, but in this case as soon as Wesley started snapping his fingers (he didn't even start singing) I burst out laughing all by myself.

"That's it, Raymond, go to the principal's office right now!" commanded Mrs. Allen. That was the first time I was banished from the classroom. I was so afraid because our principal was the spitting image of Margaret Hamilton, the Wicked Witch of the West in *The Wizard of Oz*. She even had green skin. I figured I would be tortured by her "O-E-O" guards, uniformed like doormen, or even worse, taken by the flying monkeys to some jungle and eaten alive.

It wasn't that bad at the principal's office, but I cried and felt alone and scared. I don't know if Wesley ever tried a subsequent fourth attempt at singing his crappy rock song, and if so, whether or not he made it through the song without laughter from the rest of the class. I was doing hard time with the Wicked Witch.

I admit to being a hypocrite. I would have hated anyone who even chuckled at my virtuoso accordion stylings. And, I would have probably still hated those kids to this day. But I hope Wesley doesn't bear the psychic scars from my apparent rudeness. I found it impossible not to laugh in such a situation. One should never tell an already giggling, immature fifth grader not to laugh for the third time or banishment will occur. This made it a certainty I would laugh. It is like telling a flower not to bloom, or telling the sun not to rise, or gasoline not to burn, or the wind not to blow, or a baby not to poop. It is simply contrary to the natural order of things. No matter how ill advised the laugh was, it was not intentional. It was involuntary. I felt like I was the victim.

But whether I was victim, hypocrite, or rude—one thing was certain: I was no longer popular with Wesley Woolery. I was too immature to apologize to him and just hoped he wouldn't pound me. I never approached him about the pompadour hairdo. I still regret not trying the hairstyle. Who knows—maybe it would have won over the alluring Gael Mosher.

CHAPTER 13

The Fly League

I love baseball, and my earliest memories of that great game were in the Fly League for boys eight to twelve years old. The teams were split into an A team, analogous to a varsity team, and the B team.

The fly league ball is in the middle,
flanked by a regulation softball and hardball.

The ball used by the Fly League was neither a true hardball nor a softball. This ten-inch softball was known, fittingly enough, as a fly league ball. It was white, and had molded seams rather than stitching. Some of the better players, especially the good pitchers, hated the fly league ball. They wanted to use a real hardball. In fact, Mike McLaughlin, a star pitcher in the Fly League (and a teammate of mine on the Yellowjackets) hated the fly league ball so much that he only played on our team for one year. After that, his mother lied about his age so he could play in the older kids' league with a real baseball.

I liked the Fly League because of all the strange and wonderful things that happened to us on the field. This league was truly organized, regulated by the Napa Recreation Commission (unlike all of our pickup games) and even had its own Fly League parade before the season started. The previous year's champions earned the right to lead the parade with the other teams lined up behind the champs. My brother was on the 1955 Yellowjackets team that won the league championship and earned the right to lead the 1956 parade as the defending champs.

The things that happened in Fly League practices or games helped some of us figure out that baseball was not for us. Some found out that when nature calls, it must be answered, even if you are out in the field. Others (not me) discovered that we had a real aptitude for the national pastime. Some learned the value of teamwork. And, some of us learned that baseball parallels life itself.

I don't know who came up with the idea of the Fly League, or why the teams were named after insects, but that was our league. Each team was named after a creature that had a head, thorax, and abdomen with six legs. As long as they had three body parts and six legs, they qualified to be in our league.

The only exception to the league's hard and firm rule was the Spiders, which have eight legs and are not insects. There were so many other insects to pick from before resorting to a non-insect like a spider. For example, Cockroaches, Bed Bugs, Aphids, Praying Mantises, Stink Bugs, Grasshoppers, Mites, and Ticks (*Mighty Mites or Terrible Ticks?*) would all have struck fear into an opponent. At the very least, some of these names would have had an ancillary, educational benefit. I am sure some of the kids would have been sent to the dictionary to learn all about the particular insect whose jersey they were going to wear.

I was not privy to the unpleasant, heated, and quarrelsome arguments that must have ensued between the Fly League board of directors that led them to allow a non-insect to be an authorized team name in this league. Ultimately, however, that is exactly what happened. Oh, if only I could have been a fly on the wall. (Excuse the pun).

The girls had a softball league, but it was named after birds like the Larks, Bluebirds, and so on.

The Fly League had the Northern Yankees Conference, and the Southern Rebels Conference, with the champions of each playing a best-of-three-game playoff for the league championship.

Our ball caps were all the same color—blue, and they came in very limited sizes to fit us all—small, medium, and large. There was no adjusting strap on the back of the cap and, as a result, some kids wore caps over their ears and some had caps sitting on top of their heads.

Fly League 1957 champs—The 1957 champion Locusts,
led by Tommy and Jerry Davis, Ellwin Jobe, and Bill Monroe.

The names, conferences and colors of our T-shirts were:

NORTHERN YANKEES

Termites—Brown T-shirts with white lettering
Ants—Yellow T-shirts with black lettering
Crickets –Blue T-shirts with white lettering
Locusts—Blue-purple T-shirts, white lettering
Bumblebees—Light Brown T-shirts, white lettering
Hornets—Orange T-shirts with white lettering
Dragonflies—Light Green T-shirt, white lettering
Flies—White T-shirts with black lettering

SOUTHERN REBELS

Spiders—Gray T-shirts with red Lettering
Beetles—Blue T-shirts with white lettering
Fireflies—White T-shirts with black lettering
Mosquitoes –Black T-shirts—with white lettering
Gnats—Gray T-shirts with black lettering
Yellowjackets– Dark green T-shirts with white lettering
Scorpions—Scarlet red T-shirts with white lettering
Wasps—Maroon T-shirts with white lettering

After several years, certainly by 1958, the Town of Yountville was allowed to enter a team in the Fly League. They were assigned, appropriately enough, to the Northern Yankees Conference based on geography. However, their team name was known only as Yountville. No insect was assigned to them that I ever found in my research of the newspaper articles of the day.

On the back of each Fly League jersey was a felt applique of the specific insect for a particular team. On the front, each shirt featured a baseball player in a batting stance and the words, *Napa Recreation Commission*.

Fly League Bumblebees jersey—Each insect was scary in its own way.

Fly League Locusts jersey—I didn't know what a locust was, but the team was so good that I figured it was a lethally carnivorous insect.

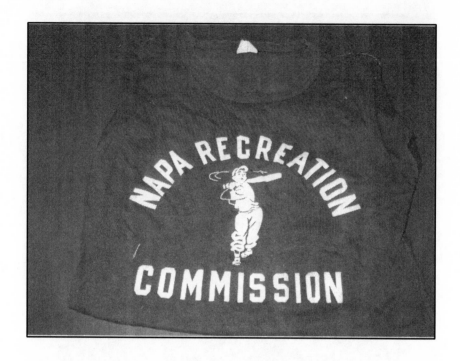

Fly League Napa Rec jersey
The league was organized by the Napa Recreation Commission.

After the first practice of the season, coaches handed out the jerseys, which were wrapped in tissue paper and enclosed in a cardboard box. They came in small, medium, and large sizes.

The significance of the jersey was deeply, even intensely, felt by some of the kids. Terry Simpkins, for example, says he still remembers inhaling the strong smell of the felt appliques. The smell was not very pleasing, but it was a welcome sign that baseball season had officially begun. Today, some former Fly League players who get a whiff of felt will also get a sensory memory of the Fly League and those jerseys.

My favorite Fly League stories are about my friends who experienced real-life incidents that young children have, some of which are humbling or downright embarrassing.

Doug Murray, who became a Fulbright Scholar and twice a McArthur Grant award recipient, had an inauspicious Fly League debut and, for that matter, baseball career. Doug was not a bad athlete by any stretch. He was coordinated, but baseball was not for him. Maybe that is attributable to what happened to Doug in this incident at practice with his team, the Bumblebees. If someone starts out bad, and then has a terrible experience, that person may have his spirit dampened and perhaps profoundly damaged. If you combine that with not really having an aptitude or passion for the game, then the bad experience may be just enough to end a career before it really starts. I believe such was the case of Doug Murray.

The Bumblebees practiced at Vichy Elementary School. Because teams were formed based on geography, the Bumblebees included the Vichy School neighborhood. It had players such as Robbie Clark (later becoming captain on the 1964 Napa High School championship football team, and still later serving his country honorably in Vietnam), and all-stars Chuck Svenson, Barry Shaw, and Jackie Schlumberger.

During the first practice game of the season, and the first of Doug's Fly League life, the coach divided his Bumblebee team into two competing squads. The pitcher on the other squad was Schlumberger, who pitched very, very fast but very, very erratically.

When it was Doug's turn to bat, Jackie's first pitch hit him right in the head. Next time up, Jackie threw the first two pitches five feet over Doug's head. The next pitch went into the ground half way to the plate. Finally, the fourth pitch hit Doug in the head again. On his third time up to the plate, Doug was so scared that he started bailing out of the batter's box before Jackie had even let go of the pitch. Doug was a good three feet out of the batter's box when Jackie's next pitch hit Doug right between the shoulder blades.

In subsequent games and subsequent at-bats, that initial experience was so stressful that Doug found that just standing in the batter's box made his knees wobble. He says he was not made for baseball, and maybe he wasn't, but these first-time batting experiences could not have been a quality foundation for Doug on which to build a confident and successful baseball career.

Even star players could have dubious starts to their baseball careers. Paul Vallerga became an all-star first baseman on every team he played on, including his first team, the Termites. But, as a young B team player, he had his troubles. In an early evening game at Lincoln School, the Termites were playing the Lincoln Hornets. Paul, who was eight, was in center field when nature called, big time. That is, Paul started to wet his pants. Knowing that he didn't want to keep wetting his pants, Paul turned his back to the infield and peed during the game while the opposing team was at bat. This was not the alternative Paul would have normally chosen, but he had no choice. It was pretty dark out in deep center field so he didn't believe anyone saw him.

In another bad experience, Paul walked right into a teammate swinging a bat and got hit right in the gut.

In the 1958 championship-deciding game against the Spiders, Termite Paul was hit by a fastball and went down with the wind knocked out of him. Before he knew it his father, Stan Vallerga, was next to Paul. Up to that point Paul didn't know how much his father cared for him because Stan was such a quiet man. This was a mixed experience, because as bad as it was to get the wind knocked out of him, the realization that his father cared about him was priceless.

The Termites of the Alta Heights neighborhood became the champions of the 1958 Fly League season without my services. I went to Alta Heights, but for some reason I was not in the Termites district. Once again I felt victimized by living in Little Italy, down on Fourth and Burnell Streets. But, in life, sometimes the thing you think is so terrible turns out to be a lucky break. Had I been allowed to play for the Termites, I wouldn't have played very much. I started on the Yellowjackets. As a starter (albeit in right field) I felt like a real ballplayer, leading me to dreams of becoming a major leaguer one day.

My Yellowjacket team was really mediocre. The Yellowjackets finished five and eight in 1958. We had some good players, like Mike McLaughlin for one year, who was good at pitching and playing shortstop. He even made the All-Stars. We had Fred Teeters, who was an excellent catcher with a very good arm. He could throw out most players trying to steal second. We also had Bill Forsythe, a backup catcher who was big and strong, batted left-handed, and could also play first base. He would have been first string on many other teams.

We also had pitcher Larry Tronstad, a year younger than the rest of us, but he was a super big kid. He grew to be 6' 5" as an adult, but even in the Fly League he threw a high-velocity fastball and was an all-star pitcher.

One game we had a shortage of catchers. Both catchers, Fred and Bill, were gone. We had no one to catch Larry, our extremely fast pitcher. The coach asked for volunteers; there were none. No one untrained as a catcher wanted to attempt to catch Larry. You could get hurt, either by a super-fast pitch or the batter's bat striking you. If you didn't know what you were doing it would be foolish to volunteer.

However, the prototypical catcher is a stout, heavy, slow person. Even the catcher's tools, the mask, the chest protector, and the shin guards are called the "tools of ignorance." That should tell you something. I did NOT volunteer to catch Larry. However, the coach must have observed that I had the type of body that cried out to be a catcher. Besides, years later when I thought about this experience, I figured that the coach probably figured that I was the one player he could most afford to spare if injury did occur. So what if the fat little kid gets hurt?

So there I was, all dressed up in my tools of ignorance, squatting behind home plate to catch Larry Tronstad, one of the fastest pitchers in the league. I didn't even get a chance to warm up with Larry before the first batter came to the plate.

Larry's first pitch was so fast that I didn't even move as it sailed high over my head. The next pitch was right down the middle and it still got by me. I did catch several of Larry's pitches, but they badly hurt my hand. Before long I was dodging Larry's pitches. I must have looked more like a matador than a baseball player. Even the umpire (my neighbor, Jess Pittore, who was a great football player) called me an "umpire's nightmare." I deserved that appellation and all the criticism that was heaped on me.

Larry was disappointed in me. His father wanted to kill me, and I was getting severely bruised by the pitches that I couldn't slow down on their way to Jess's body, some parts of which were unprotected by padding. I have no excuse, except that I was put in to play under real game conditions with absolutely no experience. I blinked every time a batter swung his bat, which didn't help me track the ball, and, finally, even without a bat waving in front of me, the pitches were so incredibly fast that I had an extremely difficult time getting my glove on them. After being hit a few times by Larry's fastball, I was less than eager to hang in there.

Also, I didn't have a catcher's mitt. The regular catchers had their cushioned mitts with them. All I had was my fielder's glove, enhancing the pain in my hand on those very few occasions that I did catch the ball.

That was how my catching career ended. There are umpires alive today who do not know how lucky they are not to have called that game that evening. My neighbor Jess never spoke to me again.

I kept track of my batting average. I had a very small strike zone, so I drew a lot of walks. I was slow afoot, but I was on base a fair amount of the time. I loved it when I got more than one hit in a game. If you got three hits, you usually got your name in the Napa Register. If you were on the losing team and you were the only one who got two hits for your team, you might get your name in the paper. I loved this. Mom would cut out the box score and the article with my name in it. I have a pretty thin scrapbook when it comes to my baseball career, but the few times I made the press, Mom added it to my book. It is amazing to me now that I could have thought of myself as a good ball player. I was awful.

The right fielder is traditionally the least skilled fielder on the team, because the ball is rarely hit to right; and even when it is hit to right, it is usually hit by a right-handed batter without much power behind it. Putting your worst athlete out to pasture in right field minimizes the damage the kid can cause your team. I played right field.

Right field was boring and terrifying. It was boring because the vast majority of the time nothing at all happened. I was either standing directly in the sun burning to a crisp, or standing in the dark where it was cold and lonely. It was terrifying because when a fly ball did go to right, it was unexpected. This happened maybe once every other game. It caught me off guard on more than one occasion.

My mind would wander. I noticed all the weeds in right field. Some were very tall and some had stickers that could hurt if you landed on them. I looked for chuckholes or divots in the dirt so I wouldn't fall when I was running after a ball. I noticed gnats, fireflies, or other bugs flying around right field. Sometimes, during night games, I would stare at some young couple that had meandered out to the deep outskirts of the ballpark, blind to the game being played, glued hip to hip, making out. Then I would start thinking about someday having a girlfriend.

Then, without warning, a fly ball was hit into right field. It was terrifying, with the ball sailing into my field of vision as I was running after the fly. It was as if there were several balls dancing in the air. I wasn't really sure which ball was real. Most of the time

I was off at the crack of the bat but usually in the wrong direction. If I came in on the fly it went over my head. If I went back on the fly it would drop in front of me. The pressure I felt to catch the ball was immense. When I retrieved the ball I usually threw it in a huge arc toward the infield. The trajectory went high but came down only a few feet away. The coach screamed at me. Often, when I threw the ball I would grab my arm as if I had hurt it. It was obvious that I was faking, but I felt it covered me in case the throw was bad.

If it was a grounder, it would get by me because I was so slow and it was so painful as I waddled after the ball, knowing that everyone was looking at me and judging how slow I was and how much I had messed up. As I tried to track down the ball I could hear the other side's fans screaming as the bases cleared and the batter hit an inside-the-park home run.

Among my friends who also played right field was Bob Benning, who played on the Dragonflies, representing Bel Aire. Bob reached the zenith of his career during his first year of play, before the season even started, when the Fly League Parade started with the Dragonflies marching at the head of the parade, based on the fact that the team had won the championship the previous year (before Bob became a member of the Dragonflies). Bob walked proudly and waved to the sidewalks packed with people, even though he had made absolutely no contribution to winning the league title.

The Dragonflies won the championship because of their pitcher, Rich Robertson, who was no longer on their team. After college, Rich began an eight-year professional career, including four years with the San Francisco Giants.

Bob says that Fly League Parade was the closest to fame that he has ever achieved, but he is wrong, as he is another of our unsung heroes who served in the United States Marine Corps, as his father did before him. Both men served their country honorably during times of war. That Fly League parade was the height of Bob's fame in baseball; but in life, he was a success as a husband, father, and citizen.

As for playing right field, Bob and I have discussed the common issues out in no man's land. One of Bob's fondest memories was contemplating the amount of tall clover that grew out in the fields. As a fellow right fielder, Bob's mind wandered as well. The great degree of inaction in right field made it impossible to concentrate on the game. Also, because of the threat of action, no matter how rare, a kid could become neurotic worrying about the possibility of a fly ball to right.

Many times when there was a fly ball in right field, the stakes were huge. There were usually other kids on base, and if the ball got by you it would be a home run. This pressure on youngsters who played right field was unfairly intense. And this situation was exacerbated when you consider that the kid in right field was usually under-equipped physically and devoid of confidence, thus adding to the stress and pressure he had to endure.

If therapists of the '50s could have recognized the grave consequences of placing a less-than-skilled kid in right field, they might have labeled the condition. Fly League right fielders could have received special treatment in school, like getting more time to take tests or extra treats, or getting out of school early to rest. Things could have been done to help alleviate our situation and reduce our anxiety. The combination of long periods of nothingness, followed by the sudden violence of cannonballs (fly balls) raining down, coupled with the pressure of knowing that the outcome of the ball game is on the line could have been called "Right Field Syndrome," or simply, RFS. I know that the condition existed, because I had it; and I know it warrants being labeled and treated, because many right field Fly Leaguers suffered from the affliction.

Parents could add to the pressure, although many were wonderful supporters of our team. Dad could be very supportive of other teammates of mine. Mike McLaughlin was pitching when the umpire kept calling balls on pitches that were over the plate. The umpire agreed that the balls were in the strike zone, but thought that Mike was throwing curve balls, which were illegal in the Fly League. The ball may have been curving (ever so slightly), but Mike was not doing it on purpose. This was very upsetting to a youngster who found himself being falsely accused by a grown-up who had complete authority. Mike was on the verge of tears.

After the game, Dad came up to Mike with words of encouragement. He told Mike to pay no attention to the umpire and continue what he was doing. A lot of kids had movement on their pitches and Mike had a natural curve. This was not Mike's fault and Mike should not worry about it at all. Mike really appreciated these words from my dad, and this conversation remains a strong memory for Mike. I was proud of Dad for helping a teammate.

Big Al's comments while he stood behind the backstop when I was at bat were less helpful.

"Are you afraid to swing?"

"That was way over your head; you shouldn't have swung at that one!"

His commentary could have waited until after the game instead of while I was facing some pitcher throwing fastballs. I could have done without that kind of "support," but I know his heart was in the right place.

Lest someone thinks that I didn't enjoy my baseball career (such as it was), I loved it despite the intense pressure of playing right field. I loved it because I was a teammate with friends— Teeters, McLaughlin, Dale Smith, Tronstad, Forsythe, and all the others. They all treated me well. They were great guys. I loved it because of Fairview Field, where we practiced, the home of the Yellowjackets. We had our own ballpark.

I loved it because of Fairview Market. It was a very short walk from Fairview Field. Walking into the store seemed so dark, coming in from the sunlight. The temperature in the store was very cool, and it was so comfortable after playing outside in the hot sun. The market was stocked with Coca Cola and other cold drinks, and tons of treats like ice cream sandwiches, Eskimo pies, fudge bars, popsicles, chocolate bars, hard candy, and red rope. I usually didn't have much money, but McLaughlin always did, and he let me bum some. A true friend.

I was so sad to see Mike leave after only one year on the Yellowjackets. He was not only a great baseball player, but he was my personal banker, who made loans to me without any red tape. Where else can you have fun, eat well, and get no strings-attached-loans that were really charitable gifts?

Nowhere else, except with the Yellowjackets in the '50s, have I ever found such a sweet deal again.

CHAPTER 14

Hardball Is Life

My post-Fly League hardball career started on an inauspicious note. In the 1950s you absolutely had to make the team. There were cuts after try-outs, and if the coaches didn't think you could help the team, you did not make the roster.

In the summer after seventh grade, after previously starting in right field for the Fly League Yellowjackets (bearing in mind that I suffered from delusions of competency), I tried out with my Alta Heights and Yellowjacket friends for the Rotary Club team of the Twilight League. This was a lower-level hardball league for twelve- to fifteen-year-olds. Most of us were only twelve, which meant that we would be among the younger players in the Twilight League, competing with older, more experienced kids who had played for the team the year before. I knew it was going to be an uphill battle for me to make the team, but I wanted to be with my friends. I did not realize that, unlike the Fly League, there was no "A" or "B" team. There was only one Rotary Club team with its fourteen roster spots.

Rotary had try-outs and practices several times over the period of two weeks. At the end of the second week, the team roster would be announced. For each practice, one of our moms would drive us. It was a carpool system that our moms set up. It was my mom's turn to drive on the day of the cuts. I didn't see this coming, but it meant, of course, that if I didn't make the team, Mom would be driving me home in the same car with my friends who did make the team.

The Alta Heights team was full of very fine athletes. They included Paul Vallerga (an all-star first basemen wherever he played hardball); Mike Kerns (eventually a starting pitcher on advanced league baseball teams); and Steve Ceriani (later a starting third baseman on much higher caliber baseball leagues). These were the boys Mom had to drive that fateful day. I was not above crying if things went badly for me.

Looking back, if one of my three buddies hadn't made the team, I might not have felt as badly as I ultimately felt. But if I thought about how athletically gifted my buddies were, I would have known that they were all going to make the team. Also, looking back, if I had thought this out, I would not have allowed Mom to drive that day. I wasn't that smart. I didn't see this coming.

Not only did Paul, Mike, and Steve make the team, they were named starters. This meant that they beat out all the older kids for starting positions from Rotary's previous clubs who were still on the current year's team. I was cut.

An older player, John Nemes, walked away after the announcement. He was not only beaten out by my buddies for a starting position, he didn't even make the team, despite the fact that he was a returning player from the previous year. John was a big guy, and a pretty good athlete, but Vallerga, Kerns, and Ceriani were really high-caliber competition. John was nowhere near their skill level. John was upset, but unlike me he was not on the verge of tears. He was angry. I felt so upset about my own fate that I walked away where I didn't think anyone could see me and started to cry.

Unfortunately, John saw me and said, in an indignant tone of voice, "What are you crying for, Guadagni? You were never going to make this team."

I didn't say anything in response to his charming comments, but I knew he was right, and on some level, I knew he was hurting too, although my brotherly love for him at the moment was pretty abstract. His comments, while true, were hurtful.

I had more important and immediate things to worry about, however, than the bitter comments of another kid who didn't make the team. It was important that I get myself under control quickly, because Mom had already arrived and was waiting in the parking lot to pick us up. Pulling myself together as best I could, I got into the car with my buddies. There was no hiding my emotions. I couldn't talk because I knew I would cry. The best thing about Mom driving was that I would get to sit in the front seat with her and my buddies would be in the back seat. At least, I wouldn't have to look at them. Talk about a silent ride home.

The guys were great and didn't say a word. I knew they were all sympathetic. Mom was always a sweet person and knew enough not to probe or cross-examine me. That wasn't her style, anyway. She just took the guys home and then we went home. When Mom and I were in the car alone I really started bawling. It must have upset her badly to see her boy so upset. She consoled me and told me that I must not lose faith, to keep trying, and not to give up. It didn't help much at that time, but at least I knew she loved me.

When I got home I sat on my couch and turned on the television. What came on was a rerun of the movie *Invasion of the Body Snatchers*, starring Kevin McCarthy and Dana Wynter. It was a film that had Communist implications. This horror film about aliens infiltrating our communities, right under our noses, was seen as a metaphor for the Red Menace with Communists infiltrating our government and becoming our neighbors, and then taking over our society. I didn't put that together as a kid. All I knew was that it was a really frightening movie that made me afraid to go to sleep at night, for fear of there being a seed pod in my house with a little "Raymond" being formed to replace my body and soul.

I will always be grateful to the *Body Snatchers* for taking my mind off one of the most miserable days of my life up to that point in time. However, the movie actually went overboard and messed me up for days.

After a few days of moping around over not making the team, as well as being afraid to sleep because of the scary movie, I was really a mess. Then, as if God, from heaven above, came to Earth to remove the two big problems in my life, I got an answer to my woes. God picked a strange messenger—in the form of a phone call from Bill Forsythe. Yes, Forsythe—the same guy who ran across the stage of the Uptown Theatre and got me kicked out because I was sitting next to him before he went up on the stage, the same guy who got me fired from the San Francisco Examiner for building a fire to keep us warm. That Bill Forsythe. He was probably the funniest guy I knew, and perhaps the most fun-loving guy there ever was—a real cut-up. In other words, he was a wise-ass. I loved him. He could make me belly laugh, and I loved to belly laugh.

Bill had remedies for both of my problems, as if he knew exactly what ailed me. I didn't think anyone but my three buddies from the car-pool ride knew how upset I was. Could it be that they had been talking to other kids about me crying? I doubt it. They really liked me as a friend. No, those guys would never do that. No one knew, except Mom, about the residual effects I suffered from watching *The Body Snatchers*. Yet Bill spoke to both of my issues.

First and foremost, he told me that he heard about a brand new team being formed, and because there were no older kids who had already been on the team from the previous year, it should be easier to make the roster.

I was more excited than I realized I would be when I heard this news. I figured if I couldn't play with my Alta Heights buddies I wasn't going to play at all. I didn't even think about playing for another team. Besides, I figured that all teams were set by now anyway, and that time had run out for making any other roster this season. Moreover, I was a little low on self-confidence at this time. I really wasn't sure that I wanted to put myself through another possible rejection.

But the more I talked to Bill Forsythe, the more he encouraged me to play, and he convinced me it would be fun. Who knows, maybe I would even be able to start on the team. I would actually get playing time. By the time our phone conservation was over, I had already taken down the information about the tryouts, and had consented to give baseball another chance. At least I would know one other person on the team, and he was a real fun guy.

My other problem was how scared I was about *The Body Snatchers*. When Bill finished the discussion on baseball, he told me about a prank he played on his two beautiful older sisters, Carol and Shirley. He and his two sisters had also seen the *The Body Snatchers* as I had. All three thought the movie was frightening.

In revenge for some of the stuff his older sisters had played on him over the course of his young life, Bill decided to get back at them. The day after the movie aired, he carefully assembled papier-mâché and vanilla cake mix, whereupon he created and crafted a "seed pod," sculpting out a very rough and vague shape of a human being in the pod itself-- just like in the movie. Both of his older sisters shared a room, and that evening both were out at the same party. When they got home and opened their closet, the screams were heard throughout the Mount George countryside where they lived. Bill describes the experience to this day as "a beautiful thing." Neither sister needed to ask who put it there. However, Bill denied having knowledge.

This put the movie in perspective. Clearly, I knew the movie was fiction. I thought about playing the prank on my brother. I abandoned the idea because I didn't have any papier-mâché, and I would never waste a vanilla cake mix. Besides, I was dealing with an older brother (not sister) who was almost four years older than me, and much stronger. I would have paid too high a price. Any revenge on my brother would have to wait.

I tried out for the new team, sponsored by the Napa Register. The coaches were Obie and Oakie. Mr. O'Brien was Obie and Mr. O'Connor was Oakie. They were really nice men, and were very kind and supportive of us. I made the team, fortunately, and became the starting second baseman. This was a perfect position for me, because second base had the shortest throw to first of any other infield position. This was so important, because I possessed both a weak and inaccurate arm. A short throw I might get away with, but not a throw from the left side of the infield like third base or shortstop.

To explain just how bad this team was, let's start with the second baseman. I was short, fat, and slow, and I was one of the better players. The team was made up of some very under-skilled baseball players, except for a few guys. We had a competent shortstop in Mike Soon (the kid I boxed in the Police Athletic League when we were five). Mike was a smooth fielder, and shortstop is perhaps the most important position in the infield. Forsythe played catcher, and he was more than adequate. An older kid named Jim O'Brien played first base, and he was fine.

The rest of us stunk. The worst part of the team was our pitching staff. We didn't have one. If you have a mediocre fielding team, and a not very good hitting team, but you have a super-fast, accurate pitcher, along with a competent backup pitcher, you can still win some ball games. We had no pitchers. Yes, we had some guys who went to the pitcher's mound and threw the ball to Forsythe, but our team did not have a real pitcher. Our best pitcher was Dave Bastien. Dave was a strong kid and a pretty good athlete, but he was no pitcher.

Think of the movie *Bad News Bears*. Remember how terrible that team was at the beginning of the season? Then the team improved over time, after adding a couple of great ball players to the roster, and ended up playing for the championship. We were just like the Bad News Bears, except that we didn't improve as the season went on. We were bad from the beginning and we stayed bad. We didn't win a game. I don't think we were ever ahead during a game and we suffered more shutouts than any other team in the league. It wasn't even close. We were a perfect 0 in the win column with everything else in the loss column. We may have been the worst team in the history of Napa, or maybe anywhere.

The great thing for me, personally, was that I was on a team, started at second base, and got plenty of at-bats. Of course, I kept track of my batting average and I did pretty well, I thought. I got on base a lot because I had a small strike zone. The strike zone then was defined as being between the shoulder blades and the knees. If you are a little guy and you crouch over as I did you have a very small zone. This means it was difficult (but not impossible) for the pitcher to put the ball in my strike zone, which meant I got a lot of free passes to first base. A walk did not hurt my batting average at all because it did not count as an at-bat. Because I got on base so much, I must have thought I was a pretty valuable player for my team. At this point in my career I thought I still was improving and had a realistic chance of making the big leagues—not the Napa big leagues but the professional major leagues.

I knew I would never be a pitcher, because I had a slow, inaccurate arm. However, our coach was so desperate to get a pitcher who could get batters out that, out of an almost hopeless despair, he made a rash and reckless decision and named me to relieve Dave Bastien in the middle of a game. Dave was being hammered by the opposing team as usual, and I guess the coach had tried everyone else, so he must have thought, why not Guadagni? I came in with the bases loaded and no one out. I was pitching to Mike Sunnafrank, of all people. Sunnafrank was a big guy and a power hitter.

I threw a couple of balls that Sunnafrank fouled off down the left field line. He had no problem getting around on me. Catcher Forsythe was throwing the ball back to me harder than I was pitching to him. This was nuts. Finally, I decided to throw Sunnafrank a curve ball. There was one big problem. I didn't know how to throw a curve. I went into my stretch and threw a soft curve ball that didn't curve, but went right down the middle of the plate. Talk about low hanging fruit. Sunnafrank hit a towering shot into deep, deep left field. The ball may still be in orbit today. No one ever saw the ball come back to Earth. Our left fielder did not even move. He just stood there in admiration of the ferocious hit. It was a thing of beauty. The first batter I faced hit a grand slam.

The coach finally came out of his trance, and immediately pulled me from the game. That was the end of my pitching career. However, in my own very warped mind, that made me the ace of the staff. Here's how I argued it to my teammates at the end of the year party: I didn't get the loss for the game, because the bases had been loaded by Bastien and we were already way behind in the score. All the base runners were Bastien's responsibility and therefore counted against his record. As a result, Bastien took the official loss on his record. My record remained a perfect 0-0. Besides Bastien, all the other pitchers on our team had also suffered at least one loss on their record. Because I never lost a game I figured I must be the best pitcher on our staff. Following my explanation, with its impeccable logic, I was severely pelted with party favors by my teammates, at least those who weren't already uncontrollably laughing at me.

The next season I once again tried out for the team that cut me—Rotary. I was determined to make that team. I went to every practice and hustled all the time. When the coach announced the final roster, I had made the team. At last, I would get to play with my close friends. The coach told me after the announcement, in a private meeting, that the reason I was selected for the team is because he liked that I hustled all the time. He had noted that even when grounding out I still ran back to the dugout. I never forgot that, and never forgot that the coaches are observing you all the time.

The Rotary team was a solid contender in the league, filled with stars like Vallerga, Ceriani, Kerns, Keller, McLaughlin, Teeters, Jack Luntey, Joe Pruitt, Ron Weien, Don Accomando, and Larry Tronstad. Kerns, Keller, McLaughlin, Teeters, and Tronstad could all pitch. Tronstad was the ace of the staff. The infield was set with

Vallerga at first, Accomando at second, Pruitt or Luntey at third, and McLaughlin or Keller at shortstop. When Teeters wasn't pitching, he was the starting catcher with a great arm. All these players could hit and Vallerga, Ceriani, Kerns, and McLaughlin were outstanding. This was a dream team. I was a backup right fielder, just happy to be on this team of great players and beloved friends. That was my lot in life. My good buddies were all great jocks and I wasn't.

I loved sports and was coordinated, but I was short and slow. That is not fair. If you are short you can still be good if you are fast—like Donnie Accomando, who was short but blessed with blazing speed. He commonly would bunt for a hit. Speedsters are in great demand in baseball.

When I felt sorry for myself, I used to think that someone in God's assembly line of Angels who made humans had made a big mistake. I was coordinated so God must have told his Angels to make me small but fast. But someone down the line must have heard "fat" instead of "fast." That screw-up cost me a sports career. You can't make it if you are small and run like a slug.

Our team had great success the year I was on the club, in spite of me. I had improved my playing skills every inning on the winless Napa Register team the previous year, but I was still slow, with a bad arm. Our team, however, was so successful that we made it to the championship game against the feared 20-30 Club. They had Jerry Davis pitching for them, and he scared the crap out of me. He even scared some of our good players, but they managed to hit him sometimes. Jerry Davis and his 20-30 team beat us in the championship.

Like all losers we had our excuses. Tronstad's family took him on vacation at the most inopportune time. He was the ace of the staff and we needed him to shutdown 20-30 until we could get to Jerry Davis. Without Larry we did not fare well, although it was a close game. Our team was good and we played every inning to the best of our ability.

One of the best things I got out of baseball was learning what my strength is in life. It happened on that Rotary team in a very important regular season game. We needed this game to ensure that we would lock up the first half conference. We were the home team and we were at bat. The score was tied. It was the last half of the last inning, so we would win the game if we scored. The bases were loaded, but the problem was that we had two outs. Unless we could get a run, we would have to go to extra innings. The coach wanted us to win the game right then and there. The next batter for our team was not one of our stars, but was certainly better than me. He had earned a starting position on the team. I was a bench warmer. The coach called time-out and said, "Guadagni, get a bat, you're hitting."

I couldn't believe my ears. No one in the dugout could believe his ears. I could hear the buzz from my teammates, and even some groaning. I was trying to process this information. It just didn't make sense. Why would any coach in his right mind (and we had a very bright coach) substitute me for the other batter? He was a superior player in every sense—bigger, stronger, faster, and more experienced. And, one more thing—he was a better hitter.

But as I was trying to sort it out the coach yelled again more hastily than ever, "Guadagni, get a bat and come over here, you are batting."

I did get a bat and started to limber up. I used two bats when I warmed up, so that when I did bat with one bat, it would feel lighter. I always felt like I could swing faster because of this. The coach was waiting for me impatiently in the on-deck circle and what he said next stayed with me forever.

"Guadagni, go to your strength." He then repeated it again and again. The same thing, "Go to your strength."

Initially, I didn't know what he meant. I didn't have a strength, as far as I knew. After the third time he repeated this, I had come up with the fact that I was so slow getting my bat around that when I did hit the ball, it usually went to right field. I figured he wanted me to go to right field with my natural swing. That was my strength, I guessed, and it made me feel good to think the coach wanted me because of some perceived proficiency in batting skills.

"You mean hit to right field, Coach?"

The coach kept his voice low.

"No, no. Don't swing. You have a small strike zone, and if you crouch over, you will probably get a walk, and we will win the game."

"Okay, Coach, but if the ball is right over the plate may I swing at that pitch?"

"Absolutely not. I do not want you swinging at all, not even once. This pitcher is getting tired. It is the last inning, he has pitched too long, and he has lost his control. He is not going to get three strikes in your strike zone before he gives you four balls. We will win if you do not swing your bat. Getting a walk is your strength. Don't swing, just stand there with your bat in your hands and do nothing. Do you understand?"'

I understood.

Normally, with the bases loaded, two outs, and the game on the line, I would have been a nervous wreck. But not this time: I had no pressure at all. I had instructions from Coach to do nothing. I knew I could do that. I took some practice swings like I would regularly do before the pitcher went into his windup. I wanted the pitcher to think that everything was normal. I didn't want him to know that I was not a threat to swinging the bat. I wanted him to think I was looking to hit the ball. Pitchers are naturally more careful with a batter if he is swinging away. I didn't want to give it away that I was looking for a walk by just standing there. Then I crouched as low as I felt would not be too obvious and just did nothing.

The first pitch was clearly a ball. It sailed a foot above my small strike zone. The second pitch was also a ball. The third pitch was a called strike.

The fourth pitch was another ball. Now the count was three balls and one strike. One more ball and we win the first half championship.

At this point the other team's coach called time out and walked out to the pitcher's mound. Was he going to bring in a relief pitcher, someone who was fresh and not tired out from pitching all those previous innings? The coach did not pull his starter but instead just talked to his pitcher trying to calm him down. After what seemed like an eternity the coach let his pitcher stay in the game and he returned to the dugout. The pitcher stared at his catcher and fired a called strike right down the middle of the plate.

Now the count was three balls and two strikes. The next pitch would determine if our team would win the first half championship or if we would go into extra innings.

Now my coach came out of our dugout to talk to me. "Guadagni, remember do not swing."

I said, "Ok, Coach, but I think they figured out that I am trying for a walk. That last pitch was slower than usual. I think he is letting up on the speed and trying to improve his control. If the next pitch is slow again, I can hit him. May I swing if the pitch is slow and over the plate?"

Coach kept his voice low but stated emphatically, "Absolutely not! You are not to swing. Is that clear Guadagni? I don't care if he throws it underhand, do not swing, ok?"

"Yeah, sure Coach, I was just checking."

While we were talking I was glancing over to the pitcher's mound. I could see the pitcher had taken off his cap and was wiping his brow. He walked off the mound and started to pace. He seemed to be talking to himself but I wasn't sure because the first baseman had come over to confer with him. At our home plate conference, Coach said, "Let's stay here talking until the umpire breaks us up. The wait is killing that pitcher."

As soon as Coach uttered those words the umpire came over to us and said—"Alright, break it up, Coach." Then the umpire yelled, "Batter up!!!"

I stepped back in the batter's box and took some phony-baloney batting swings—as if I might actually swing. The pitcher wound up and delivered his next pitch, which was a shade high near my neck. I didn't even wait for the call. I dropped my bat and ran to first base. The umpire called "Ball Four" and that was the ball game. We won. I got my walk, my run batted in, and best of all, we won the first half of the league championship.

I felt pretty good about myself for a few days until it dawned on me what my strength actually was. It was doing absolutely nothing at all. Looking back on my entire life, I have to admit with all humility that I am very good at doing nothing at all. Always was and always will be, I guess.

My dream of playing professional major league baseball was a real one, even if it sounds like a delusion. After all, I loved the game and had a real passion for it. I knew by heart everything about every ball player on the Brooklyn Dodgers, including their dates of birth, batting averages, and years in the league. I knew that I had no formal training, but that is why I thought there would be so much room for improvement. I really thought I would develop and get better and better, and soon would have the skills and abilities to play at a major league level. In my view, no one loved the game more than me, and that is why I was sure I would make it to the majors one day.

Dad was too busy to work with me, and no one ever gave me any private instructions on how to field, throw, or bat. So, I figured my potential was unlimited. The truth was, no matter how much private mentoring or teaching I might have received, it wouldn't have made much of a difference to someone so slow and short. As a batter, I also wasn't one to hang in there. No coach had to worry about me getting beaned by a baseball because I bailed out of the box based on a pitcher's reputation.

"Guadagni, I coached your brother and I always worried that he was going to get hit by a bad pitch because he hung in the batter's box too long, even when the pitcher was wild. I see I don't have to worry about that with you," said one coach. That really helped my self-esteem.

Finally, two brothers brought a swift and humane end to my baseball career, killing all hopes, dreams, and fantasies that I ever had about playing professional baseball. Jerry and Tommy Davis brought reality to me in no uncertain terms. My unrealistic dreams were dashed when I started playing hardball and pitchers started throwing curve balls. Specifically, batting against Jerry Davis after he mastered the curve ball, got me to thinking that I had a lot to learn before I could become a major league player, and that I might have to start drinking before going to the plate.

The cruel experience occurred the first time I stepped up to the plate against Jerry in the Twilight League. It was an awful experience for a young teenage boy with my limited athletic abilities. In Fly League ball, I didn't have to bat against Jerry Davis because he was in the Northern Conference and I was in the Southern Conference (this was an unforeseen blessing of living near the fairgrounds). But in the Twilight League I had to face Jerry Davis, who was fast and had a wicked curve ball.

The first time I ever faced his curve was terrifying. The ball came right at me so I hit the deck but the umpire said the ball broke over the plate for a called strike. I couldn't believe the call. I thought the umpire had been bribed. But it seemed even my teammates thought it was the correct call. No one yelled, "You're blind, ump!" The second pitch was also a curve and started coming right at me. Again, I hit the deck to avoid being hit by the ball, and again it curved over the plate for a called strike two. This time I knew it was the correct call because I watched the ball curve over the plate by looking up from my backside view as I lay in the dirt of the batter's box. I decided to swing at the ball on the next pitch, no matter if it was coming at me or not. I did swing and hit nothing. Strike three. It was so embarrassing.

At that point, I figured I would just have to learn to hit a curve or become a switch hitter. I was so out to lunch. I still entertained thoughts that I could possibly become a major league ball player. I just had to add "hitting the curve ball" to my list of things to improve on. Still, after my experience batting against Jerry Davis, I was starting to have doubts about a career in baseball.

Enter older brother Tommy Davis. Tommy was also a pitcher, and also fast, but unlike Jerry, Tommy was wild. Coaches, in our time, taught pitchers to never take their eye off of the catcher's mitt. They must stare at it the entire time through their wind-up and delivery. Apparently, this would increase accuracy. There was some sensory brain explanation that I never understood. I don't know if this was another myth, or if pitchers are still taught this today. Well, no one told this to Tommy Davis. When Tommy pitched his left leg would go up in the air (in the style of San Francisco Giant Juan Marichal) and his head would tilt back, so he was looking at the sky, not the catcher's mitt. He was not even looking at home plate. This was very unnerving to a batter. All I could see was the underside of Tommy's left shoe as he reared back to fire his pitch at the speed of sound.

That was enough for me. I just bailed out. I couldn't hang in there with a guy who was supremely fast, somewhat wild, and wasn't even looking in my direction.

I was on the hardball diamond in the southern part of the fairgrounds when I realized I would never be a major league ballplayer. It was a night game, and the lights were on. Tommy Davis was pitching his usual style: rearing back with his head looking straight up at the sky and then unloading the fastest pitch I ever saw. He was wild, but not so wild that he walked everyone. But he was wild enough to be hitting several ballplayers with his pitches every game. I was slow at everything, including getting out of the way of a pitch. I wasn't a starter in the hardball leagues (except on the winless Register team), so I didn't have to bat against Tommy very often. But in this game, in the late innings, I was put in the game and was going to get up the next inning.

When it was our turn to bat, I was in the dugout watching Tommy Davis pitching to my teammates. At some point I realized that I was hoping that my teammates would make outs. This was strange, but it was clear that I was hoping that they would make three outs before I had to bat against Tommy Davis. I didn't like these thoughts, because I was rooting for my team to fail. This wasn't right.

Finally, I was on deck, preparing to bat next. The batter at the plate, with two outs, was Mike Kerns. Mike had a very good eye for the strike zone, and was able to draw a lot of walks. I thought it was too bad Mike was at bat before me, because he probably would draw a walk or get a hit, and then I would have to bat against Tommy Davis. Luckily for me, Mike grounded out for the third and final out, and I was spared.

The fact remained, however, that I did not want to go to bat. I had not really ever had that experience before. There were a lot of pitchers of whom I was afraid, but that, to me, was natural. I still wanted to have my chance to swing a bat and see if I could get a hit. But this was different. I did not want to even go up to the plate and face Tommy Davis.

It was like a light bulb went on over my head. It was over. I could not be a major league ball player if I didn't want to bat. Where Jerry Davis set me up to have some serious doubts that I could ever hit a curve ball, Tommy Davis finished me off by making me so scared that I didn't want to even go up to the plate. Like in boxing, a jab sets up the right cross, which is the power punch that finishes the opponent. Jerry was the jab and Tommy was the right cross. Baseball career: over and done.

Years later I told Jerry about this, and he told Tommy, who said that I was right. Tommy said he was indeed wild and he didn't care who he hit; he just threw the ball as hard as he could.

My baseball career may have been over, but I love the game because it is so much like life itself. In life sometimes you miss an opportunity by not being ready when the opportunity arises. Conversely, you sometimes can take advantage of an opportunity by being in the right place at the right time. Baseball is like that. It is a game of inches. If you play a batter by shading to the left and he hits the ball directly to you, then you can make the play. If, on the other hand, you lean to the left, but the batter hits to your right, you may not be able to make the play. Being ready and not missing opportunities is a similarity between life and baseball.

In life, you may get multiple chances to succeed. You may not mature as quickly as others, and, as a result, you may bum around for a while or work in go-nowhere jobs. Then, at some point, you are ready to settle into a more permanent vocation. You can still go to school and obtain the education necessary to achieve the job you desire. In life, you get other chances many times.

In baseball it is the same. During an entire game you usually get to bat four times. Also, you get four balls and three strikes, and as many foul balls as you can hit. Truthfully, if you fail to hit successfully seventy percent of the time, you can still be a success in baseball. In fact, you would probably be in the Hall of Fame as a .300 hitter. This is true in life as well. One usually has more failures than successes. And in both life and baseball, it is the failures that we usually learn from. It is the negatives that stick with people and motivate them to compete further.

Many times in life we are asked to make sacrifices for the good of the group. It is very common that parents do without for the sake of their children. Their sacrifice is out of love, but it is a sacrifice nonetheless. Parents save for their children's education or for music lessons, etc. The same can be said about baseball. A ballplayer will lay down a sacrifice bunt to advance a runner. A ballplayer may hit a sacrifice fly ball with less than two outs so that a runner can score from third base. And that runner may be scoring the winning run. Just as in life, sometimes you do the work and someone else gets the glory.

In baseball, as in life, you can excel individually as well as succeeding as part of a team. An individual ballplayer may hit a home run and succeed individually, but teamwork is required in other situations. A common double play in baseball is a play from the shortstop to the second baseman to the first baseman. This requires complete teamwork. It is practiced over and over by the infielders until they can turn a double play like a well-oiled machine.

There is also the ebb and flow of hardball that coincides with the ebb and flow of life. You can have a bad inning where you miss the fly ball and then when you come to bat you strike out. Or, you can redeem yourself by getting a hit after missing the fly ball. You can have a good game. You can have a bad game. You can even have a good season or a bad season overall. Life is also like that. You can have good days or bad days. After a bad day, you can make a comeback and rectify whatever caused the bad day and then have a good day. People even have bad years and good years. The similarities are seemingly endless.

Life parallels hardball and vice versa. I think that is why baseball contests can be frustrating, disappointing, strange, bizarre, and yet wonderful, satisfying and even exhilarating.

That is hardball and that is life. All you can do is "play ball."

CHAPTER 15

Free Spirits and Crispy Critters

The 1950s was an era before political correctness.

It was also a time of limited knowledge about diagnosis and treatment of mental illnesses.

For example, frontal lobotomies had been performed on people such as Rosemary Kennedy, the daughter of Joe Kennedy, in order to calm her down. This was in 1941, when it was an approved medical procedure thought to help a patient with mental problems. Rosemary's procedure resulted in her being robbed of any quality of life. This was not done maliciously. To the contrary, a loving father was attempting to give his daughter a better life. The point, however, is that not much was known about treating mental illness. There were disorders that doctors apparently did not understand.

I don't believe that autism was recognized or understood, nor were the more common mental illnesses of today, such as bipolar disorder, schizophrenia, post traumatic stress, and others.

The Diagnostic and Statistical Manual of Mental Disorders (DSM), widely known as the bible of psychiatry and psychology, was first published in 1952. As it evolved, revisions have incrementally added to the total number of mental disorders, and removed those no longer considered to be mental disorders. For example, in 1952 the DSM listed homosexuality as a sociopathic personality disturbance and therefore a mental illness. This diagnosis of homosexuality remained in the DSM until May 1974, when it was removed as a mental illness.

The evolution of the DSM occurred slowly over the years, with the DSM-II coming out in 1968 and DSM-III published in 1980. DSM IV was published in 1994, listing 297 disorders over 886 pages. In this categorical classification system qualifiers are sometimes used, such as "mild," "moderate," or "severe" forms of disorders. DSM-V was approved on Dec. 1, 2012, and published on May 18, 2013. It contains extensively revised diagnoses, broadening some diagnostic definitions while narrowing others.

Clearly, the field of mental and personality disorders and other disabilities has changed radically since the 1950s. Some conditions considered mental disorders in the 1950s are no longer listed. Other illnesses recognized today were not listed earlier, and may have been improperly classified with other mental disorders. As Sir Isaac Newton said, "I can calculate the motions of the heavens, but not the madness of men."

Moreover, in the '50s whatever was known about mental illness (accurate or not) was not widely known among the kids of this era.

In the '50s, if a kid acted strangely or even just differently, he was invariably labeled by other kids as a "weirdo" or "retarded." Developmental disability, kids with special needs, Attention Deficit Disorder, Autism, Asperger's, Disruptive Mood Dysregulation Disorder (temper tantrums), Depressive Disorder (grief), Binge Eating Disorder, Anxiety Disorder, and Post Traumatic Stress Disorder, were not terms used to describe people in those days.

In Napa we had our share of kids and grown-ups who were afflicted with various types of mental maladies. I do not know what the official, current label would be for these people, but they had issues. Some were seemingly crazy or violent or just plain weird (a term I still use because of my lack of knowledge of the true diagnosis of these people).

I would tell Mom about some of these kids who seemed so strange, and she would tell me that they may actually be nice kids, but had bad upbringings or didn't have parents who were able to teach them good manners. I would tell Mom that I was talking about kids who exhibited more than just bad manners. After hearing some of the descriptions and conduct I had observed, Mom told me that they were "free spirits," and for me to stay completely away from all of the crazy or violent ones.

Easier said than done.

I didn't bother to tell Mom that the only way to stay completely away from Lonnie Hunter was to drop out of school because I couldn't get to school or return home without crossing his path. Lonnie scared the crap out of me.

Let me put it this way: Lonnie was really into intimidation and he was the best at this game. He could frighten people. You might even say that Lonnie was an artist who dabbled in the field of intimidation the way other artists worked in oils or clay. He was the Leonardo de Vinci of intimidation.

He carried with him a bike chain that he would menacingly twirl around like a badass David taking on Goliath. He also brandished a big and scary homemade switchblade knife made mostly of wood, spring loaded so the blade would come out automatically.

Even the place where he lived was intimidating and gave him an advantage over us mere mortals. He lived on Coombsville Road, high above road level, and would come barreling down his hilly driveway on his bike, gaining speed as he went downhill. You could hear his bike tires crunching the pebbles and rocks of his dirt driveway as he pedaled toward his victim (the sound of rubber meeting a rocky dirt road still scares me). Added to this sound was his frighteningly high-pitched Confederate rebel-yell war cry as he traveled to the end of his driveway. After the first time that happened, I never again waited for Lonnie to start coming down the hill before I ran. I just took off as soon as I got anywhere near his driveway.

Why was Lonnie so intimidating? I have often thought of this question because of how scared I was back then. This is the answer I came up with:

For starters, his looks were the stuff of nightmares. Lonnie had a wide, accentuated jaw that made him look somewhat deformed and oddly ferocious. He also had jet-black whispery thin facial hair that made his appearance look like a big-jawed Genghis Khan.

Also, he looked so much older than us, like a man riding a bicycle. I estimated his age to be forty-two but that may have been exaggerated in my mind because of how scared I was of him. I think he was about four years older than me.

More than age and appearance, he had brute strength. I was sure he could beat up anybody's parents easily, and probably could handle more than one adult at a time.

Another thing: none of us could remember him ever attending school. Although the law required it, none of us remember him in class. Maybe he was Napa's first home-schooled student. That was not a term heard back then, however.

Finally, he just seemed mad and angry all the time. He was intent on scaring kids. It was his purpose in life—or so it seemed. Heredity? Environment? Or just plain scary weird? I don't know.

Lonnie bicycled, from time to time, to Alta Heights Elementary after school was out, when no teachers were around to protect us. There was a big oak tree on the lower field, next to wooden picnic tables. It was the same field that the Fly League Termites used for practice.

One day, Lonnie rode over on his bike to Alta Heights and chased my best buddy Paul with his infamous bike chain. Paul was a super athlete and could run faster than Lonnie could pedal, so Lonnie, out of frustration, wacked his chain on the wooden table top repeatedly with such force that it left big scars on the table that remained there for the rest of the poor, scarred table's existence. No amount of sanding would ever smooth out that table.

As to the kids he did catch, Lonnie mistreated them. He liked to take his handlebars and cross them over a victim's body, trapping them in his bike clutches. I don't know why we never told anyone about him. We just ran.

With most tough guys, I could suck up or make them laugh, and soon they would like me and wouldn't pound me. Besides, I was too little to improve their tough-guy reputation, anyway, so they left me alone. But with Lonnie, I couldn't get close to him. He was aggressive and would be chasing me with his bike chain and switchblade before I could introduce myself properly. It is hard to suck up when you are waddling as fast as possible away from a perpetrator.

"Free spirits" were not what all of my friends called them. The term most often used by guys my age was "Crispy Critters." That term conjured up a variety of people and it painted a broad brush of different characters, not all of them violent. Some were just slow, while others were just weird. Some were adults; some were kids; some were nice, and some were jerks. All of them were different.

For example:

Junior Prescott worked for the garbage company. He was built like a condominium. He was about 6'2" tall, raw-boned, solid muscle and out-of-this-world strong. My friends thought he was very slow-witted, but that assessment was likely influenced by the strange attire that Junior chose to wear. He wore a large belt buckle on his pants and a cowboy hat with big horns on it.

Some of the tricks played on him by jokesters were to fill a garbage can with water to see if he could lift the can. Junior lifted water-filled cans easily. Someone dared him to fill a can with bricks to see if he could lift it. He took the dare and lifted the can without breaking a sweat. My personal favorite story was when several guys placed an engine block in a garbage can. Junior grunted and strained, but succeeded in lifting the can. No one who knew Junior Prescott would ever forget him or his feats of strength. In fact, he was used as a point of reference for strength among my friends from childhood through high school. It was the highest form of praise to hear a kid say something like: "That defensive tackle had Junior Prescott strength!" or "That girl almost hit the softball over the fence at Kiwanis Park. She is Prescott strong."

Jerome Starr rode his bike all over town. Not all of what he said could be taken as gospel.

Jerome once came into Stan's Hardware Store and saw Stan's daughter, Stana Lee, working there. Stana was a pretty and popular high school girl. After staring at Stana for about two hours Jerome finally said something.

"You are almost as cute as my girlfriend, Mei Ling."

Jerome was referring to Mei Ling Fong, who was Stana's age and the daughter of Peter and Yipee Fong, the owners and operators of Alta Heights Market (also known as Yipee's Bait Shop). Alta Heights Market was a restaurant, general store, and bait shop, all combined. It was the last place to go for bait as you headed up to Berryessa or Conn Dam to fish. They had a pool table, as well as the dirtiest postcards to purchase while paying for bait. Later, as an adult, I saw a lawyer buy twelve of the nastiest cards he could find at Yipee's to send along with his alimony check to his ex-wife each month.

Jerome created a credibility gap with his statement about his girlfriend Mei Ling, because she was not his girlfriend. Jerome had no girlfriend. No one remembers Jerome ever having a girlfriend.

Another noteworthy incident involving Jerome: he was riding his bicycle around town, crossed a road, and was hit by a car. Luckily, it only clipped him. No insurance information was exchanged, and because Jerome was not really hurt, no ambulance was called. However, there was damage to the driver's car. How is that possible, one might ask? Well, Jerome, feeling embarrassed or angry, tore off the driver's bumper. This settled the case. No lawsuit, no police involvement, no insurance company contacted. Case closed.

The next few examples were not crispy critters, or free spirits, or even weird. They were just regular kids, but they had things tragically happen to them and were labeled by other kids because of their abnormalities. These nicknames became normal in the vernacular and were therefore used openly. I don't believe that would happen today. Sure, nicknames are used today and kids will talk behind each other's backs, but in a small town in the '50s, there was a normalcy and openness to it that is absent today. Almost everyone seemed to have nicknames. Not nicknames that your parents gave you like Skippy, Chip, Butch or Scooter. These were nicknames that kids gave to each other.

In the '50s names were fairly common. Many kids were named John, James, Steve, Billy, Joe, and Michael. Hence, there was a real need for nicknames to keep everybody identified properly. Therefore, we had Curly Bill, Big Mike, Freckles, Crazy Legs, Shorty, and Butterball (me).

As to the regular kids struck by tragedy, there was a young boy who was called "Flipper Boy" because of an accident in which he got his arm caught in a wringer washing machine. A little boy's arm was never intended to be inserted into such a wringer. The result was that it flattened out his arm. It was cruel for kids to refer to him like that, but some kids could be very hurtful.

There seemed to be several kids around town who had experienced serious mishaps. It didn't seem abnormal.

One kid had swallowed lye and consequently had a tracheotomy. His voice squealed when he talked. His nickname was Squeaky (I do not claim these nicknames were creative).

The next example was a kid in junior high school who became known as "the boy with a tail." He came from Wooden Valley. There weren't too many students from that rural part of the county. In the shower after P.E., some of the guys noticed that his tailbone stuck out and he had a little tail. I think his tailbone went longer than normal and it was furry. In any event, he was the boy with a tail.

Then there was the tragic case of two boys who were playing with their cap guns in a garage with the door shut. They were very young. After shooting their cap guns for a while they just took the rolls of caps out of their guns and started to hammer them on the cement floor. This procedure would explode the cap louder than by just the little hammer on their cap guns. Depending how much force was used with the hammer the cap would make a loud popping sound and occasionally a spark would be emitted from the minor explosion. Unfortunately, on one of the hammer-induced cap explosions, a spark ignited a can of paint stored in the garage and started a fire that led to catastrophic consequences. The young boys were unable to open the garage door and thus were trapped in the garage. One of the boys lost his life, and the other suffered major burns over his face and body. He was known as Third Degree by kids who had no sense of decency.

I didn't even know what third degree meant. These names, along with other kids' nicknames, became so common in conversations that it seemed to kids that no disrespect was meant or intended. They were just their names.

Medical procedures were not as advanced in the '50s as they are today. As a result, there were people around town who had injuries or disfigurements that may very well have been preventable in current times.-

A prime example was the main employee at Dad's junkyard. George had the use of only one hand (he had to use a suicide knob on his steering wheel). George's other hand was very deformed. His fingers were permanently bent and he could not straighten them out. His hand was paralyzed in that manner. Dad bragged that George could do more work with one hand than most men could accomplish with two. George had a great work ethic and his production was better than most men. His determination was admirable.

George said that when he was a teenager he was in the bed of a pickup, and when the truck made a quick turn, he was thrown off the truck and broke his hand. That was it. Just a broken hand. I didn't ask him which doctor set the hand, but I should have. I never wanted to go to that doctor. That had to be malpractice.

Donny Accamondo also had a fairly routine injury that went awry. Donny, one of my best friends at Silverado Junior High School, was not very tall, but he was strong and ran incredibly fast. When he was very young, he was holding onto his older brother's hand and looked out between two parked cars to see if it was safe to cross the street. As soon as he looked out, he was clipped by a moving vehicle and somehow Donny's foot was dragged by the rear tire of the vehicle for a short distance. The medical procedure used by Donny's doctor was to set the break and graft skin from Donny's back to his ankle. The result was a huge lump of skin for an ankle.

Donny was barred from playing school sports because of the potential for further injury, and thus liability to the school if they permitted him to play. This was a terrible blow to Donny, because he loved sports and was a good athlete. He was still very fast afoot and probably would have been a champion sprinter without the injury. His brother had record speed and there is no reason to believe that Donny wouldn't have followed in his brother's footsteps. Donny's brother was a witness to the accident and ended up with a permanent stutter as a result.

Many years later, after reaching adulthood, Donny had a fairly simple procedure performed in which some bones were fused and he was as good as new. His only comment was that he wished he had the repair procedure performed years earlier.

The next free spirit was an old Italian man who everyone called High Pockets because he wore his pants so high up above his waist. The strange thing about him, besides his fashion sense, was that he talked to himself constantly. It didn't matter if other people were around him or not, he carried on his own personal conversation. I sort of envied him because he was never alone. He always seemed to keep his own company wherever he went.

One of the conversations carried on between High Pockets and High Pockets was about a car engine he repaired. It was a Model T engine and High Pockets was going on and on about the fact that he was able to rebuild it.

"I didn't know what I was doing, but look, I rebuilt it and I got all these parts left over. . ."

He seemed so proud and so surprised at his accomplishment. Maybe nothing was wrong with High Pockets, and maybe he did rebuild a Model T Ford engine, but no one ever saw it. Talking to oneself is not, in and of itself, cause for concern or that uncommon. He was broadcasting his own life as he lived it. Nothing wrong with that, I guess, but it was unique.

I don't know if poor hygiene is a sign of weirdness, but there was an older man who had greasy, unwashed hair, body odor, and whose toenails were so long that they extended far beyond the sandals that he wore. Because of the length and sharpness of his toenails, it was said that he had the ability to swoop down on the river and stab a catfish.

Then there was John Massa, Paul and John Vallerga's great-uncle. He was a funny character. Not ha-ha funny but weird funny. First of all, he never had a Social Security number. Apparently, he got jilted and never worked again. When you saw him around town he would commonly be wearing a pea coat and stocking cap. He owned a wiener dog named Carbino, who was always with him. He survived by fishing, bartering vegetables, and hunting mushrooms.

As to the jilting incident, that was also weird. Weird not because of how John got jilted but, rather, his response to this reality. First, the jilting: when he was an up-and-coming young man and gainfully employed, he met a woman and fell in love. The relationship evolved and eventually John and his girl became engaged to be married. He bought and gave her a beautiful engagement ring.

One evening John's girl, for some reason, was unable to see him. Without a date for the evening, he went to Syd's Union Station at the corner of Soscol Avenue and Highway 29. What his intent was that evening is unknown for sure, but it is clear that at one point in the evening he went to the nearby dance hall and peeked in the window to see what was going on. There, he saw his fiancé dancing cheek to cheek with some other guy. Massa did nothing but go home.

The next day he arranged to take his girlfriend for a ride on the streetcar. While on the streetcar he asked her if he could see the ring he gave her. Unaware of anything unusual, she took off the ring and gave it to him to presumably examine. However, John just took the ring and jumped off the streetcar. John never saw the girl again and never worked again.

The jilting is something that happens to people from time to time. Having your feelings hurt and even your heart broken happens in life. It was John's reaction and response to this betrayal that seemed extreme and unusual. The following is what he did for the rest of his life because of this failed relationship.

John Massa lived on the Vallerga family ranch and stayed in a converted room in a portion of the barn that he equipped with a heater and a light. There was no plumbing and the room was the size of a tool shed. He used an abalone shell for a soap dish. He shaved with cold water, using a mirror hanging from a tree.

He caught catfish from the Napa River and put them in a wine barrel. He cooked and bartered them. He also bartered vegetables grown on the ranch and the mushrooms he hunted. But he never had gainful employment again. He sort of dropped out of life. He got drunk a lot.

John never had a driver's license, but he drove, nonetheless. Some kids at St. John's remember seeing him driving by the school going the wrong way. He may very well have been under the influence of alcohol.

As a great-uncle he would give both his great-nephews, John and Paul Vallerga, advice from time to time. As to women, Uncle John once told nephew John that he should get himself a Russian woman. Why? Because she would be strong and could work hard and would know the demands of a hard life. She would have a peasant mentality, and most of all she would be dedicated, devoted, and loyal. These were not his exact words, but it was his sentiment. His actual words were laced with profanity and slurred from the consumption of alcohol.

Uncle John had a drinking problem. He routinely slept in front of Stan's Hardware, but the truth was that he wasn't really sleeping, but passed out drunk.

One time he staggered his way onto the football field at Napa High's Memorial Stadium and stood right next to coach Pete Rivers. He was dressed in his pea coat and his stocking cap and had his wiener dog Carbino with him. He was escorted off the field.

At Cathy Vallerga's wedding in the 1960s (Cathy was a first cousin of Stana Lee, Paul, and John), Great Uncle John Massa wore his 1920s pinstripe suit with wide lapels and vest. He also wore a wide Hawaiian tie with palm trees. The tie clasp was a Meyer's Jewelers seventy-fifth anniversary tie tack from a Napa jewelry store prominent in the 1950s. He also brought a six-pack of ABC beer to the reception to make sure there would be beer there.

When John Massa was found dead, he had a shopping list that said "garlic, onions, booze." He drank himself into oblivion. He seemed to just quit on life after his relationship with his fiancé failed. Does that make him weird? Does that make him a crispy critter? Does that make him a free spirit? The priest who presided over his funeral service may have summed it up best when he said, "Who are we to judge this man?" -

This next weird thing was neither rumor nor speculation. It really happened. I have friends who witnessed it. Helen Razzler was a very religious young girl. Her dad, who was also very spiritual, started to build a boat. Soon, it became clear that he was attempting to build a big boat. Then it became clear that he was building an ark. In fact, he announced to anyone who would listen that another flood was coming and that we were welcome to go on his boat if there was enough room after all the animals boarded.

Another odd person to me was my friend's dad who was a building contractor. When he wasn't working on a job site, he was building extensions to his house. There was always a room he was adding on. Apparently, building regulations were not strict in the '50s in Napa, at least by the looks of this mystery house. I don't think this would pass muster under today's permit requirements. But in the '50s, in Napa, you could add on to your existing house without bureaucratic red tape or adhering to setback requirements (if there were any). You could also carve up a tract of land like a Christmas turkey.

The bizarre behavior of some of these people is difficult to classify. As of yet, the DSM V has not acknowledged some of these afflictions. Certainly, the first DSM did not, either. But these characters definitely existed in 1950s Napa, although I don't seem to see these types of people today.

Perhaps these people—the weird ones, the injured, the maimed, or the seemingly abnormal—were more noticeable because Napa was such a small town in the 1950s. Maybe these same types of people exist today in our community but do not stand out because there is a greater understanding, acceptance, and treatment options for free spirits who are different, for whatever reason.

CHAPTER 16

Napa's Color

I was five or six, walking down First Street, holding Mom's hand. She was shopping. I was going along for the ride, because after shopping we were going to lunch, my favorite event during her sprees.

Across the street to the right, walking in the same direction, was a very dark-skinned man dressed in what looked to me like a full-length bathrobe, wearing a turban. His attire had a lot to do with my fascination, but the color of his skin made him stand out to me as well. Had he been white, I might have thought he was just a man in a costume, but I knew he was different. He was the real deal. He was a foreigner. I don't recall any visceral negative feelings when I saw him, but I was wondering why he was in town. No one lived here who looked like him. No one.

I was completely riveted to this man. I couldn't take my eyes off him. He looked like the natives I had seen on television from far-off places like India or Africa. I wasn't really scared, because I was following him from across the street and he hadn't looked at us. I couldn't see a weapon, although I looked for a spear or sword. Mom hadn't said anything unusual, although I probably was tuning her out due to my fixation on this man.

Mom was on the inside of the sidewalk with me on the outside, closest to the curb. My eyes never left him, and as I continued to stare at him and watch his every movement, I ran full on into a parking meter. I never saw it, so I hadn't slowed my walk or put up my hands. The immovable object won this battle, as the left side of my face took the full brunt of the blow. I went down in a heap.

I cried so hard that my voice left me and I thought I would pass out. I couldn't breathe for a moment, and then suddenly my voice came back louder than ever. I was wailing. Poor Mom had no idea that I wasn't paying attention to where I was walking, so she was unable to prevent the accident from happening. She first consoled me, but then lovingly lectured me on the importance of watching where I was going. After regaining some semblance of normality, I looked across the street; the stranger was gone. It was as if he had disappeared into thin air.

Later, we went to my favorite place, Burrell's Fountain Shop on First Street near where I first saw the strange man. I had my usual egg salad sandwich, and engaged Mom in conversation. The topic that day was the stranger.

"Who was he and why was he here?"

Mom said that she didn't know him, but was sure he didn't live here. She said there was nothing to fear about this man. He just didn't look like us because he had different colored skin. Except for this difference, he was a human being, like us.

I wanted to know why he didn't have skin like ours.

Poor Mom struggled to answer all of my questions, and maybe that is why she quickly allowed me to have a milkshake—a treat that I didn't usually get. She knew if she bought me food, it would divert my attention immediately and indefinitely. She may have also wanted to buy me a treat to make up for the fact that my face was red and swollen from the impact of the parking meter. I had this very unattractive lobster-colored, partial-helium-head look.

I ordered a vanilla shake—my favorite. It came with a full tall fountain glass of shake plus a large round metal container with the rest of the batch that the soda clerk had prepared. I loved this because it was like having almost two full milkshakes. I am not sure the bribery of a milkshake was enough to silence me, but I never forgot that incident. It is as vivid today as it was when it happened.

Racial diversity was not prevalent in Napa County in the '50s. The City Directory of 1950 states Napa was ninety-nine percent white. The only thing I noticed was that there were Italians and non-Italians. In my East Napa neighborhood, Little Italy, my neighbors were mostly Italian. I am sure there was bigotry among the Italians and non-Italians, in both directions, but I didn't experience it. Even this observation seemed to diminish as I got older. What was clear, however, was that I lived in an almost completely Caucasian community.

Not having much intellectual curiosity, I never gave much thought as to why there weren't any other races in Napa. There were some Mexicans and other Latinos who worked in the vineyards and orchards, but not many in school that I recall. They were mainly seasonal workers.

In my world, there were no blacks. None. One seventh grader who was of mixed race may have been part African-American, but he was not here for more than a year.

Rare were the instances when race was involved; usually it was some story told to me by people other than my relatives or friends. For example, the biggest story I remember between the races that affected our town was the fight following the Vallejo High/Napa High football game in Vallejo on Friday, October 21, 1955, which resulted in several people being injured. The Napa Register Saturday edition was headlined, **"GRID RIVALRY EXPLODES INTO RIOT."**

The Register article reads:

> The traditional football rivalry between Napa and Vallejo High Schools exploded into mob violence last night, sending one Napa lineman to the hospital and injuring three other Napans less seriously. Hundreds of students of both schools milled around the parking lot and practice fields at

Vallejo High for more than half an hour before reinforced police squads could clear the area.

> Most seriously injured was Cliff Stocking, 17, senior guard on the Indian team. He was treated at Parks Victory Hospital for severe cuts on the right ear and forehead sustained when a hurled rock shattered a window of the bus carrying the team out of Vallejo.

Other Napa football players were less seriously injured, according to the Register. Ross Franco, a seventeen-year-old halfback on the team, was hit in the mouth with a helmet swung by a Vallejo player as the game ended, and seventeen-year-old center Ken Squier was hit in the back by a rock. Halfback Wilbur Tallman, eighteen, was slugged in the head as he headed for the dressing room.

"As long as I am coach of Napa High School's football team we'll never play Vallejo again," Napa coach Bob Covey was quoted as saying. "I'll resign my coaching post before I'll ever take another team of mine into Vallejo. I'd rather see Napa withdraw from the North Bay League than play there again."

According to the Register:

> Buses carrying the Napa football players and band members were stoned by jeering youths as they pushed their way through a human barrier strung out across the entrance to the parking lot. Several band members were stung by flying glass when one Negro youth broke two windows with a piece of lead pipe.

The Register reported that a game between these two schools "invariably generates a good deal of tension due to the rivalry of the two schools." But in this case it exploded. The police on duty to patrol the playing field because of this tense rivalry were overwhelmed and "swept up in the maelstrom of more than a dozen incipient brawls, and radioed headquarters frantically for more men." Apparently, three squad cars filled with patrolmen "converged on the scene and cooled things off before the area could turn into one huge donnybrook."

Was race at the root of this brawl? I certainly didn't know, as I didn't attend the game; I was only nine at the time. I only knew what I read and heard. The Napa Register had this to say about what started the incident:

> Cause of the brawl could not be pinpointed by police. It apparently started on the playing field in what Covey termed an "overly rough" game, and spread to the parking lot and practice fields adjacent to Corbus Field.

> The majority of the Vallejo youths involved were Negroes, but a spokesman for the police department's juvenile detail discounted reports that the disturbance was primarily a race matter. "There were plenty of white kids involved, on both sides," he said. "Most of our (Vallejo) boys were Negroes, however."

Later in the Register's article, however, it is speculated that the incident may have been planned:

> Members of the Napa band said they felt certain the incident was premeditated far ahead of last night's game, which Vallejo won by a score of 19-0 (see Sports).

> "One of these colored kids came up to the bandstand at half-time and said to me, 'You're from Napa, huh? Well, we're gonna get you when the game's over!'" one bandsman said.

While the article says it was undetermined whether race caused the incident, I inferred that race may have been at the root of the problem and that the blacks instigated the brawl. Was this the local paper reflecting the racial views of its constituents? Or, was this factual reporting based on what the reporter uncovered?

For me, this was the most infamous incident between blacks and whites during my childhood, and the cause of it is somewhat equivocal. Napa-Vallejo football games were suspended and not reinstituted until 1962, when we played Vallejo at Napa Memorial Stadium, winning 13-12.

Other incidents involving racial issues in Napa during the '50s came from credible friends or their parents. A friend of mine from American Canyon, Larry Hamilton, was a little guy with good speed, so he participated in track, running sprints. When you get to be a teenager, you start playing other teams in other counties. Larry participated in a track meet with Vallejo High hosted by Napa High School. Because Larry was one of our star sprinters, the other schools quite naturally knew of him. Likewise, Larry knew some of the better athletes from Vallejo.

As he was warming up, someone posed a question.

"Hamilton...ain't you got no birds?" The question came from a young black athlete, who was also one of the league's top sprinters. "You know," he continued, "black birds."

Larry turned around and looked at the crowd, and there was not one black face in the crowd. The Vallejo kid was amazed.

As a junior in high school, Larry, probably because of his proficiency as a sprinter, started to bump up against black culture. This may have been due to the fact that he had won a couple of races against Armijo and Hogan High. These were sprint events where black athletes were expected to dominate. Larry's name was circulating among young black sprinters, around the league. Not only was Larry white, he didn't even look like a sprinter. Maybe he resembled a miler, but not a sprinter. Stereotypes were flying, and the black athletes were very curious about him. As such, Larry was approached by some of them at each meet.

Larry had some great personal conversations with them. In all probability, Larry was one of the few kids at Napa High who'd been exposed to the lives and attitudes of black kids. According to Larry, this was not a fact that he shared with other people, due to the racial climate of Napa at the time.

One day, after he won against Armijo at Napa, the team manager for Napa, who was standing at the finish line shouted, "He beat the nigger, he beat the nigger!" to the approving grins of many in the crowd. At this moment, Larry was staring into the eyes of the kid with whom he had a great conversation with just moments before, and his "welcome to my world" expression put Larry on a road to looking at things with an altered perspective.

Conversely, things were a mirror image when Larry won at Vallejo. There was stunned silence, and the predominately black crowd was looking at Larry like he had stolen something from them. Larry's visceral feelings were that the crowd seemed really hostile.

Larry's recollections were not the norm for kids in Napa, to my knowledge. So, while most kids did not have to consider it, Larry was forced to realize that race mattered. Unfortunately, as a sixteen-year-old kid from Napa, he had the unique and disquieting experience of staring into the face of racism from both sides of the aisle. For me, I was oblivious to these realities. Napa was that kind of sheltering place for me, and most kids, at that time.

The kid of mixed race in our seventh grade class at Silverado Junior High stood out because it was so rare to see any person of color in Napa. Paul Vallerga said this kid was the only black person he knew, until he became involved in high school athletics. Paul was a great athlete, but in middle school we never played other schools outside of our county.

However, in high school we not only played schools outside our county, we also traveled to those schools. Paul spoke with a black athlete during a track meet against Santa Rosa High School. Paul got to know him, and wondered what the big deal was with race relations. He said that the guy was a really nice person and he really liked him. Paul believes that those talks with this kid helped form his early racial views.

I was no great shakes as an athlete, so I never met black kids through sports. I did, however, play the accordion, and my view of blacks was somewhat influenced by my personal musical experiences. I met a black kid while playing the accordion in talent contests around the Bay Area. I guess you could say that John was one of my competitors. His talent was playing the piano and trumpet at the same time. He was really talented.

Reconnecting with John Turk at his birthday party in Oakland in 2015.

A young John Turk and me in 1954, jamming at his home in Vallejo.

My talent was that I was so young and small, yet still played a full size accordion. I had to sit on a stool to hold it; the accordion covered most of my body. You could only see a little pudgy head sticking out on top and a couple of shoes at the bottom of the accordion. It wasn't my talent so much as it was how cute or ridiculous I must have looked to the audience.

After John and I met, we started playing music together outside of the music contests. I respected him greatly because he was older, genuinely talented, and very kind to me. Mom would take me to his house in Vallejo where she would visit with his mom, Rose, while we played music together. His name was John F. Turk Jr.

John went on to play with his classmate Sylvester Stone in the band Sly and the Family Stone, and recorded or performed with such luminaries as Etta James, John Lee Hooker, Charlie Musselwhite, and BB King. As Director of Music at Glide Memorial Church, he leads the church band and its world-renowned eighty-voice Glide Ensemble.

Playing music with John Turk was my sole childhood experience with African-Americans. If you asked me, I would have said I was not racist, and my parents probably would have said the same. It just wasn't an issue that was on our radar.

There was a television show in the early '50s called *The Amos and Andy Show*. The star of the show, Kingfish, was played by Tim Moore, who I believe was a comedic genius. Kingfish was the lodge leader of the "Mystic Knights of the Sea." His catchphrase, "Holy Mackerel," soon entered my vocabulary. He was always trying to lure the naïve Andy into get-rich-quick schemes like raising chinchillas (actually rabbits) in the basement of the lodge. The way they said "chinchilla" was enough to make me laugh until tears ran down my face.

I watched the show when reruns were aired nightly during the week, in 1962 on Channel 2 at 6:00 PM. The next day at school I would seminar on the previous nights episode with Paul. We would review our favorite jokes and lines and help each other when the other guy missed something. We enjoyed tons of laughs over the show. Paul and I never once talked about the program in terms of race. Neither of us thought of it that way. It was pure comedy and pure joy to us. It was just one more thing that bonded Paul and me together as friends.

The Amos and Andy Show is universally viewed today as a racist show and, in fact, was banned from television due to pressure from the NAACP and other organizations. That view, however, was outside of my realm. There had been nothing in my childhood that happened that was overtly racist that involved me. My experience with African-Americans was very limited. My friendship with John Turk was an entirely positive contact. To me, *The Amos and Andy Show* was just good comedy. If anything, the show enhanced my feelings toward African-Americans because I thought the actors (almost all black) were comedic geniuses. I was such a fan that I wrote an appreciative, get-well letter to Tim Moore when it was announced on television that he was in the hospital suffering from tuberculosis. I remember praying for him. I wanted him to recover. Mom supported me in this endeavor. I loved his work so much that, in college, I named my dog Kingfish out of respect for the best comedic actor ever.

Napa had two drive-in theaters, one near the KVON radio station called the KVON Drive-in Theatre; the other was the Crescent Drive-in theatre, located at the Napa-Solano county line in Vallejo. Right across the county line was an all-black neighborhood. I knew that some blacks worked at Imola (also known as Napa State Hospital), but did not live in Napa County. I was pretty sure that some of them might like to live in Napa. The only other black people that I ever saw in Napa growing up in the '50s were fishing off the bridges or on the banks of the Napa River. It was very clear to me that blacks lived in Vallejo and whites lived in Napa.

While most of us were sheltered from race confrontations and overt racism in Napa, there were instances when I would hear a friend's father, or even some kids I knew, use the "N" word. I assume many kids picked up some of their attitudes about people of color at the dinner table. Some white fathers were probably out-and-out racists, but many white dads were contradictions of their generation—they had any number of friends of color, but held fairly common prejudices about ethnic groups. For the most part, however, I don't remember the "N" word being used except very infrequently. Mom referred to blacks as Negroes or Negras. My father would use the term colored. The former was considered proper at the time and the latter was not improper but more colloquial. Even the NAACP used the word colored in its name.

Some of the most bigoted responses in my life had nothing to do with blacks. My Italian Auntie, Inez Guadagni and her non-Italian, Caucasian boyfriend wanted to marry. Ironically, it was our family that objected as much as his family.

I also had a good friend in elementary school, Mike Soon, who was Chinese-American. Our friendship carried over to Silverado Junior High and Napa High School. I had known Mike since I was five when we boxed against each other at the Police Athletic League. We were not best friends, but we played baseball together and liked each other. One day, Mike was teased by his best friend, Doug Murray, regarding his ethnicity (something about Chinese rickshaw drivers). Mike's reaction was to chase and tackle Doug, sit on him with clenched fists and tell him to never say that again. Later, Doug said he had picked up this joke from his father and thought it was funny. He used the expression on Mike jokingly, assuming—as we all did in those days—that if you were friends with someone you surely had license to joke about anything.

Unfortunately, Mike's time in Napa was full of much worse treatment. At one point he was dating a Caucasian woman and they both wanted to get married. Both families objected to the marriage. It wasn't long after that experience that Mike disappeared from Napa. I lost all contact with him.

Native Americans had been run out of the valley by the turn of the twentieth century. I was told that if Native Americans were seen around here at that time they were shot on sight. When the Chinese laborers were no longer necessary, there was a fire in Chinatown (on Main Street at Second) and that part of Napa history was gone.

What happened to the Native Americans and the Chinese indicates that there is a lot more to the story of race relations in Napa. These experiences have nothing to do with blacks in Napa but they are worth contemplating when thinking of racism, which affects much more than black-white relations. It is an attitude born from the fear of the unknown.

Some of my friends regularly went at lunchtime to a barbershop that was right across from Foster's Freeze on Lincoln Avenue near Napa High School. The two barbers would regale the guys with a running commentary about blacks, Jews, and others. Most of the guys found it hilarious, but at times the barbers were quite serious in that suppressed, angry way that the most bigoted of that generation could be. I suspect my friends learned a lot of prejudicial attitudes and language amid the camaraderie found in that local barbershop.

As I grew up I heard rumors that real estate brokers and their agents conspired to not sell to African-Americans. In addition, the landlords and real estate property managers would not rent to African-Americans. I didn't know if these rumors were true. If they were, it seemed to me unfair; but I didn't think about this much and did not necessarily believe these rumors, at least as a young kid. I had not yet met a real estate broker or agent. My father didn't do business with real estate agents. We rented all of my life growing up in Napa until 1963. So, we had no occasion to deal with realtors nor did it concern a boy in grammar school, middle school, or even high school. I just didn't think about the subject.

Larry Hamilton's father, Jack, was a real estate broker with the firm of Conger and Hamilton. Jack was a realtor with an excellent reputation. I learned this as a young lawyer in the '70s when my law firm, as well as most firms, would only use certain appraisers whom we believed were considered credible by the local judges. Jack Hamilton was one of them. I used his expert services on more than one occasion if the other side had not already retained him. I knew that whatever figure Jack determined to be the fair market value would be reasonable and fair and likely adopted by the judges.

Jack discussed with his son the racial issue of selling or renting to blacks. Larry's impressions from these conversations were that the attempts to keep blacks out of Napa were not driven by the real estate community, but by their perception of community attitudes, and what would happen to them if they cooperated with black buyers. They were, after all, independent businessmen, who worried that the community would no longer do business with them.

Young Larry didn't know why they thought that, except that there was something in the adult world in which they interacted that convinced them of this. Larry assumes that it was the underlying attitude that prevailed in the community. Jack affirmed to Larry many times that this was the case.

Larry said that one time his dad, a John Kennedy man, did represent black buyers. Jack did so in a very open manner. The sellers balked at this and life became very stressful for Jack for a number of months. Jack never shared the details with his son, but at one point Jack thought he was losing his business due to rumors being floated around about his willingness to sell to blacks and thus hurting the resale value of Napa's neighborhoods. He genuinely feared a boycott of his firm.

My friend Scott Sedgley, a Napa City Councilman, grew up in Napa and was aware of the discrimination in sales and renting to blacks in the '50s. He said that was just the way it was. Old timers told him that Rancho Del Mar in American Canyon was developed just north of the Napa-Solano county line in order to establish white-only neighborhoods to prevent the spread of African American neighborhoods into Napa.

In 1963 the Rumford Act became law in an attempt to end the practice of discrimination in sales and renting to different races. According to Scott, realtors and developers in California rallied together and placed Proposition 14 on the ballot, nullifying the Rumford Act. Proposition 14 narrowly passed and discrimination in real estate continued. More houses were built in Rancho Del Mar. In 1966 the United States Supreme Court ruled that Proposition 14 was unconstitutional.

It was not uncommon to have deed restrictions based on race contained in older Napa deeds, which is probably true in many other places in California. With little difficulty I found two such deed restrictions in Napa County—one made August 19, 1940, and another on January 26, 1950.

The 1940 deed restriction stated in pertinent part:

3. Limitation of ownership: no person of any race, other than the Caucasian race shall use or occupy any buildings or any lot except that this covenant shall not prevent occupancy by domestic servants of a different race domiciled with an owner or tenant.

The 1950 deed restriction stated in pertinent part:

2. No persons other than those wholly of the white Caucasian Race, shall use, occupy or reside upon any part of, or within any building located in the above described subdivision, except servants or domestics of another race employed by the occupants of any of said lots.

These deed restrictions and those of a similar nature are illegal today, but did exist during this time period and were not uncommon.

There was a minister at the First Methodist Church in Napa named Andrew Juvenal. I knew his son, Ralph Juvenal, from school. He was a few years older than me. In the early '60s, the Rev. Juvenal's house was reportedly firebombed.

His daughter, Jaqui Juvenal, clarified the incident:

> A doctor and his wife, both from Africa, arrived in Napa after the doctor was offered employment at Napa State Hospital. Apparently, the doctor contacted Dad because he and his wife could find no one who would rent them a place to live. Dad was surprised. He, along with an attorney in the church, decided to start a campaign in the Napa Register with a form that people could sign saying they would sell or rent their home to anyone regardless of race or religion. Then the rumors started that he was busing in black people from the South. This was totally false. This was, however, during the civil rights movement led by Dr. Martin Luther King, Jr., and Dad had gone down to Selma to march with Dr. King himself.
>
> Anyhow, people started leaving the church. Mom and Dad would get hate calls in the middle of the night, and a white cross was placed on our front lawn (not burned). This happened around '63 or '64. Dad had been at the Napa church for seven years. The first five were very successful and the church thrived. However, after the incident, the

Methodist bishop moved him to a church in the Haight-Ashbury.

Joel Tranmer, a longtime Napa resident who was a member of the youth group at the Methodist Church when Rev. Juvenal was in Napa, said that when he was about eleven years old, around 1955, Rev. Juvenal held a Bay Area Methodist youth retreat in Napa. He recalls:

> There were several black teenagers who attended and when the parishioners found out that they were black they would not house them. My parents took in four or five of them and they slept at our house for the weekend.

Kristin Bush (McMillan), also a classmate of mine from Napa, shared an experience that she had with a substitute teacher. The teacher was a black woman who had been hired as a long-term substitute by the school district to teach a class in speed-reading. The regular teacher, Mrs. Prichard, had died in December 1963, after teaching the first semester. In January 1964, the long-term substitute began teaching the class.

Kristin said she was a very classy woman who was very kind to the students, very eloquent, and obviously very intelligent. After acclimating to her class and becoming comfortable, she eventually shared with her students her experience of not being able to rent a place in Napa. Her beliefs were that it was rooted in racism. The owner would not rent to her because of her race and for no other reason. The teacher said she and her husband had no choice but to live on the Napa State Hospital grounds, where her husband was employed as a doctor. Kristin was appalled to hear this was happening in her hometown.

Years after I became a lawyer, I had a conversation with Judge Thomas Kongsgaard, a Napa Superior Court Judge revered by lawyers as one of the best judges this county has ever known. In this informal conversation, which was off the bench, the judge indicated to me that in the early 1970s he had heard a black psychiatrist testify in his court at a mental illness hearing. Judge

Kongsgaard was impressed that the psychiatrist was so knowledgeable in the subject matter of his testimony. He seemed so bright and intelligent, the judge felt he would make a great contribution to the Napa County Grand Jury.

After the hearing, Judge Kongsgaard asked to talk with him in his chambers. The judge asked if the doctor would consider serving on the grand jury, as the judge felt that he would be able to make a significant contribution, and the judge was looking for diversity. The doctor told Judge Kongsgaard that, while he did work at Napa State Hospital, he did not live in Napa. When Judge Kongsgaard pressed the issue and inquired if the doctor might consider moving to Napa sometime in the future, seeing how the doctor's place of employment was in Napa, the doctor replied that he had already attempted to purchase a place in Napa and was unable to do so. Judge Kongsgaard was embarrassed to learn of this; he expressed his great disappointment to me in our casual conversation.

The belief that local realtors wouldn't sell or rent to blacks was widely held by kids in Napa. Almost all of my classmates who I have talked to believed that to be the case. Others I have spoken with who were in other classes before and after my class have also confirmed this belief.

Redlining was a common and probably a predominant practice by realtors and banks across America during the time we were kids in the '50s and early '60s. It was the practice of not renting or selling to a particular group by realtors, or denying or charging more for services by banks on loans. It was often racially determined. An example of redlining would be where a bank would loan to lower-income whites but not to middle- or upper-income blacks.

Another friend and my former law partner, Joe Flax, recalls an incident in the late '70s when a neighbor of his apologized to Joe and his wife because he sold his home to a black family. Joe and his wife later went to their new neighbor's house and welcomed them to the neighborhood. The family thanked them and told them that they were the only family to do so.

In the early 70's, the Napa Police Department ran a sting operation in which a black couple tried to rent a house in Napa and then a white couple would attempt to rent the same place. There was no criminal prosecution, but a civil lawsuit ensued when the black couple was denied housing and the white couple was successful.

The question of racism in Napa is an intriguing one that I have pondered more than once since reaching adulthood. What was our community attitude toward blacks? What may have led to de facto segregation? How did we get to where we were, racially speaking, in the '50s?

While I am not writing a history of race in Napa, I have often speculated about this question and believe that several factors may have impacted our racial climate in that decade.

A newspaper reflects its subscribers and advertisers. I have heard that the Napa papers that existed at the time of the Civil War mostly supported the South and the Confederacy. One of the junior high schools in the '50s was Ridgeview Junior High School, whose student body was known as the Rebels. The school colors were red and gray, the colors of the Southern Confederates' military uniform. The band members wore the hats of the Southern Confederate Army when they marched. The Pom-Pom girls wore school sweaters in school colors and a picture of Johnny Reb on the front.

The Ridgeview Rebels Junior High Pom-Pom sweater with Johnny Rebel's face in the middle of the sweater.

319

There was a presence of the KKK in Napa County documented in the 1920s. In her book, *"Prohibition in the Napa Valley,"* Lin Weber wrote about a KKK presence in Napa as follows:

> In 1923, some two thousand people gathered under the moonlight in a field near Napa State Hospital to watch one hundred men in hoods and robes be initiated into the group. Many of the newly minted Klansmen were sailors from Mare Island. The KKK identified the Napa Valley as an untapped reservoir for new initiates.

> The Klan wooed this new resource with a fire-and-night extravaganza held in a field south of St. Helena in August 1924. They chartered a special train on the electric line that ran parallel to Highway 29 and provided parking for more than two thousand cars packed with the curious as well as the convinced. Only sixty new members were embraced into the white-sheeted bosom of the brotherhood but between and eight and ten thousand watched the ceremony, which ended with words of warning from a leading Klansman. If there were any bootleggers in the audience, the hooded knight promised, 'The Klan will get you!'

Weber concluded:

> The Klan maintained a small but occasionally menacing membership in the Napa Valley that endured long after Prohibition was over.

If there were 160 new KKK members initiated in Napa between 1923 and 1924, and if there were thousands of people in attendance that Weber reported were mixed with the curious as well as the convinced, how would that translate into the number of people in Napa who shared those views in the 1950s? In 1950 in Napa, there were 13,000-plus people in the city; approximately double that for the entire county. How many of them might have been KKK-minded people? The answer is difficult to say.

The Little Rock Nine in 1957 saw the developing power of television on the civil rights movement and future movements. Many people in the know saw that television was tremendously powerful—being in everyone's living room every night.

Paul and I, watching television, saw white people attacking black people, using fire hoses and attack dogs. We witnessed, on television, white women spitting on little black girls trying to go to school. It had a profound effect on anyone who watched these visual images on the screen. But that was television, and this was Napa, where there were no black families to my knowledge. These cruel and sometimes savagely brutal acts were happening in faraway places across the country from where we lived. It just wasn't an issue for most people locally. None of the local papers were creating much of their own content on national or international issues back then, and since there were no local crises, the civil rights movement received little or no local coverage.

Napa wasn't overtly racist because there were no blacks in town (and very few in the entire county) and therefore no confrontations. Some friends of mine from Napa in the '50s told me that they were naïve enough to think that black families must not have wanted to live in the valley, because there were none. Segregation was very quiet and very smooth. Except for a few extreme instances, like the Reverend Juvenal firebombing incident, there were very few signs of it, other than the absence of minorities, especially blacks. It was only as I grew older that I became aware of the unwritten rules regarding renting or selling to blacks, which helped open my eyes to the viewpoint that blacks may have wanted to live in the valley but were not permitted to do so.

My speculation about what may have contributed to racially prejudiced views toward black people in Napa and why we lived in a de facto segregated town is just that: pure speculation based on hearsay recollections of people. The fact is, we lived in a racially bigoted area that was devoid of obvious racial conflict because it was segregated.

Racism existed as a strong undercurrent when I was growing up in Napa; it was not as overt as it was in the South, but anecdotal evidence indicates that many Napans were supportive of a separation of the races.

In a Napa Register article on April 8, 1968, just days after the assassination of Dr. Martin Luther King, Jr., a Napa minister summed it up.

"As long as there are communities that subtly restrict civil rights, who subtly note that the problem must be somewhere else, the problem will not be solved," said the Reverend Norman Redeker, pastor of St. John's Lutheran Church.

CHAPTER 17

My Magic Moments At The Fair

I didn't like living so far from Alta Heights Elementary School. All my buddies lived up on the hill near the school grounds so they always played together, while I was alone. It was too far from Fourth Street where I lived for Mom to trust me to travel alone up East Avenue safely, where she feared I might encounter people in cars who needed help finding their dogs, or those who knew where the chocolate bars were, or men in heavy overcoats on warm days.

Also hazardous to life was the intersection of what everyone called "Jumbo Corners," the world's most dangerous intersection, where five roads converged in a frenzy of traffic. Adults were baffled by this intersection, and eight-year-old boys like me were completely confounded.

On the east side of this maze was the Napa Marble and Granite Mill that specialized in tombstones, so that relatives of those entering the intersection didn't have far to go. Backing up to the Marble and Granite mill from the east was Tulocay Cemetery, which also spared mourners a long commute.

Mom was right. No child should try to join his friends on this route. As I got older I was allowed to ride my bike to the school grounds to play with my buddies, but I didn't do it often enough to really become part of the Alta Heights inner circle.

But when the Napa Town and Country Fair arrived, my place across the street from the Fairgrounds entrance was the premier location on earth. From opening day on Wednesday (Kid's Day with a parade) to closing on Sunday, we could experience each day's theme.

They not only had the parade each year in which I could be found with my neighbors (all the Italian girls) on a float, playing the accordion, but also nightly talent shows, which I occasionally won—including the year Dad and his pals (none very obedient to the laws of fairness) crowded around the applause machine and clapped and bellowed and screamed so that the exhausted machine had to proclaim me the winner. I really admired his devotion to my success. I was so proud of this that later on in the evening, while my family was visiting with another family and they were congratulating me about winning the entire talent show at the fair, I informed them of Dad's fervent acclaim that caused me to win. Dad instantly rebuked me with his usual, "That's enough, Raymond," then shot me one of those Joan Crawford-Mommy Dearest looks that communicated, "You dumb shit, wait until I get you home."

The wondrous scents at the fair were unforgettable. Upon entering, to the immediate left, was the Napa City Fire Department's booth, where corn-on-the-cob, dripping in thick salt and melted butter, was sold. It was simply scrumptious. The many food booths and their smells blended into a rapture of good times. I was swept up into a state of bliss by the experiences and the smells.

The Sons of Italy had a spaghetti-and-meatballs booth that was identical to Italian home cooking. Every year there was also a fried chicken booth sponsored by some organization (Moose Lodge, Napa High School, Druids, Job's Daughters, Elks, etc.) And, of course, the hamburger booths were wondrous. Salvador's hamburger stand had special sauce and finely chopped onions. The Browns Valley School hamburger booth had big, luscious patties with all the trimmings, dripping with flavor.

The fair was so entrancing that I even admired the livestock with their pungent smells located in the buildings far back in the remotest part of the fairgrounds. Those buildings housed pigs, cows, sheep, chickens, roosters, rabbits, ducks, and goats. The 4-H club was very active at the fair and contests were held for the top-prize animal. Auctions were held and animals sold to the highest bidders, raising money for the kids who raised them. Other buildings contained produce, with ribbons awarded for the finest vegetables.

Paul's brother John entered vegetables at the fair and came home with many a ribbon. He grew his produce at his grandparents' ranch on First Street, and some of the vegetables were astonishingly huge, resembling mutants resulting from a nuclear disaster. I was given permission to bring some of the remaining vegetables home in my red wagon, and proudly thought I was contributing to our household until Mom realized the giant vegetables were not edible due to too many seeds and too much rot.

These outlying buildings were also a contest venue for baked goods. I craved these pies and brownies, but even I never brought these goods home because anything remaining by Sunday looked very sad.

The biggest building was known as the pavilion, at the center of the fairgrounds. Town events were held there when the fair was not in session, such as fundraisers for schools, bingo games, and dances. It was where Dad would take my brother and me to watch tag-team wrestling matches between the Sharpe Brothers (Ben and Mike), and Leo "the Lion" Nomellini and another wrestler. Nomellini, born in Lucca, Italy, was a player with the San Francisco 49ers and wrestled in the off-season. The wrestling was scary but thrilling.

During the fair, exhibitors demonstrated their magical cleaners and shiny jewelry and amazing appliances. Anything you can think of was sold there. I once bought a tiny can of miraculous cleaner that cleaned your car, kitchen floor, even your eyeglasses, and anything else that you owned. A little can of this magical substance would last many years because it could be diluted with water to make gallons and gallons of extraordinary cleaning solvent. I used it to clean my pennies and, while I can't vouch for it as a floor cleaner or a car polisher, I did possess the bragging rights to the shiniest pennies of anyone I knew.

My favorite exhibitor was Stornetta's Dairy. Who cared about the milk? They had a tank of helium and would blow up balloons for kids. My brother and I would bring the balloons home and let them go inside, where they floated immediately to the tallest ceilings of our old house. There they stayed for days. A balloon released outside would seemingly float to the heavens. My brother and I would also inhale the helium so we could talk funny. Our voices became like little cartoon creatures, high and excited. We still crack up when we reminisce about those times.

As I got older I also found perverse pleasure sitting in my basement watching the adults exit the fairgrounds with young kids. Quite often a little tyke, with his helium balloon tied to his little wrist, would walk under our big pine tree and his balloon would pop when it hit a needle on an overhanging branch. The kid would burst into tears, causing distress and chaos in the family. You could almost see the parents evaluating the options: Should we go back to get another helium balloon? How do we distract him? Few parents chose the first option.

Helium balloons were wonderful, but the finest attraction at the Stornetta Dairy booth was the Mechanical Man. He was a mime, dressed in black except for a white shirt sticking out of his black coat. He had thick make-up on and stood utterly still for hours. He was frozen in position. Once in a while he would stir and change his stance like a mechanical robot so we could see that he was not a statue. It was riveting. I could not imagine how a living human could be so still for so long. I don't even remember seeing him blink. My brother and I concluded that he was super human. It wasn't something that I formed an ambition to become, but it was still astonishing. The super powers I desired included flying, invisibility or super strength, and only Mom wished that I could be the Mechanical Man. "Why can't you be still and quiet like the Mechanical Man?" she used to ask.

Law enforcement always had a presence at the fair. The CHP had a booth where you could sit in a simulated car with your foot on the gas pedal with a green light on. When the light turned red you were to take your foot off of the accelerator and put your foot on the brake pedal as fast as you could. Reflexes were tested by the speed of your reaction. The day's winner was announced. Try as I did, I never came close to winning. My snail-like reaction time was the same as it was in sports.

In the evenings there were various exciting things going on, including a talent show, and a rodeo, located on the eastern side of the fairgrounds. Also on the eastern side of the fairgrounds were stock-car races. This was riveting to me because Dad would sometimes enter one of the cars resurrected from his wrecking yard and sponsor both the car and the driver. My brother and I screamed for our entry to win. The excitement was intense because many times there would be crashes and accidents when drivers miscalculated turns and spun out of control. A catastrophe always seemed possible.

People enjoyed the crashes so much that a different exhibition evolved called the Destruction Derby, where drivers were required to destroy each other's beat-up vehicles. The Destruction Derby was by far the loudest event of all aside from rock and roll groups. Derby cars were once American made-standard automobiles—Buicks, Oldsmobiles, Fords, sedans, coupes and station wagons. These old cars were modified so that only the seats with special safety cages were left. The glass in these vehicles was removed as well as anything else to make the cars lighter and/or safer. Only the most aggressive drivers participated. Drivers scored points by the number of hits on other vehicles and by showing the most aggression. They would whack their cars into each other and the tires in the purposefully muddied track would hurl chunks of dirt into the stands giving the fans a mud bath. It was exhilarating.

There was so much to see, do, and love at the fair. I loved all of it: the food, exhibitors, stage acts, bands, animals and livestock; baked goods and produce; art exhibits; games; rodeo, stock car races, Destruction Derby, and carnival. During the five days of the fair I only hated leaving, and wished I could live every hour at the fair. My dream was to come home only to change clothes, eat something for free, get more money, and immediately return. Thanks to the wonderful fair manager my dream came true. I was able to live at the fair each and every day, and, as I got older, every night.

The fair manager always gave the closest neighbors an unlimited five-day entrance pass for two. Fair management felt that the closest neighbors should be rewarded for having to put up with the crowds and chaos that resulted during this five-day and four-night extravaganza. It never made sense to me as a kid that someone could possibly object to such a wonderful fair and carnival right across the street. I never questioned it, and was overwhelmed with gratitude for the free admission. This was not just a bunch of tickets, it was a special laminated, large unlimited pass for two people. I guarded it with my life. My popularity at fair time depended on letting my buddies and girls in for free.

The pass was an unsurpassed benefit to a kid, and even to his parents. For example, it was not uncommon for my parents to give me some money and send me across the street with my unlimited pass to purchase hamburgers for our dinner. Most of the time this worked out well. Dad, tired from a dirty day's work at the wrecking yard, could wash up and my mom wouldn't have to cook while I was purchasing delicious hamburgers from the hometown booths at the fair.

Once, Dad stuffed my pockets with money and told me to get four hamburgers for us and to come right back. I promptly went to the nearest burger booth I came to and ordered four hamburgers. I do recall the man looking at me a little strangely but I didn't think anything of it. After he filled my order, I raced home with our dinner and was ready for a great meal.

Dad was never one to stand on ceremony, and before I could even sit down, he had unwrapped his burger and taken a huge bite. The next thing I heard was a sound that always struck a nerve in me. It was my father in his loud booming voice yelling, "What is this shit?" I had no idea what was wrong. Dad then cross-examined me with questions: "Where did you get these shit burgers from? What was the name of the booth? Where was it located?" After this grilling he was able to determine that I had purchased the burgers from the Seventh-day Adventist Booth. They were not burgers at all—they were made from some kind of mystery veggie. No bigger sin or larger waste of money could have been committed by Al's son, than to purchase vegetable burgers when he thought he had paid for real hamburgers. My father loved beef. You could dehorn a steer, wipe its ass, and send it from the kitchen directly to him and he would eat it, but do NOT give him a veggie burger (especially veggie burgers in the '50s, which were awful). The mistake never happened again.

Mostly, however, nothing but good things came from that unlimited fair pass, especially when I became interested in girls during my adolescence. With that pass I was an instant celebrity with my female classmates. Word spread that Guadagni had an unlimited pass that included one guest, and that he could come and go as he pleased, making multiple trips, bringing friend after friend into the fairgrounds for free. Yes, word spread because I spread it. I was no longer a Nobody. I was important. I was a girl's ticket to free entrance, thus sparing them this expense, so they would have the money to spend on all the other important items at the fair.

I got to escort the most popular and prettiest girls from school. During non-fair times, some of these girls just ignored me. But during the fair, they all waited in our basement while I walked each one over separately. Therefore, as I walked each girl over she would sort of have to talk with me. Wow. This was great, just being seen with them one-on-one. I figured that this was not a one-time experience either. After all, the girls would remember that the fair was an annual event and would maybe be nice to me the rest of the year—who knows, maybe even acknowledge my existence beyond the five days of the fair.

Unfortunately, I was still nothing but plate glass to girls. For example, I was walking downtown with Mike Kerns and Don McConnell, two buddies of mine. We were about fourteen years old, and Mike and Don had not reached their full height, but they were already both tall and lean. I had not reached my full 5' 5" adult height, either. The three of us were walking on the sidewalk with me in the middle. Girls passing by would invariably say "hi" to Don and Mike, but not even look in my direction.

I realize that the three of us were quite an unusual combination, as Mike became 6' 3" tall and was a strapping young buck as a young adult. He became a star football player and boxer. He was good looking and reminded all of us of Wally Cleaver, the good-looking athletic older brother of Theodore on the *Leave it to Beaver* television show. Don, likewise, was a tall dude. He became 6' 4" in height, a star basketball player and was tall, dark, and very handsome.

After a while, I started to bitch about this phenomenon.

"What's up?" I would say. "I am a human being, too. Can't they even say 'hi' to me? Can't they acknowledge my existence? Am I just invisible to girls?"

Mike and Don were great guys, and they would try to get me to laugh it off, but I was very sensitive to this problem and completely positive that none of these girls would even spit on me. That would require that they had some feelings about me, but there was no emotion toward me at all. They were completely indifferent toward me. It wasn't fair. It was my parents' fault for both being so short and stout. I was a victim of circumstance. Lesson learned—life isn't fair.

The truth is, girls liked me, except they didn't like me in "that way." I was more of a brother to them. In fact, so much so that girls would often come to me to ask if I knew whether another boy liked them or if I could find out if he liked anyone. I did not like this role, but I played it to the hilt. It got me face time with plenty of girls and I figured sooner or later (much later in my particular case) some girl might like me in the way I so desperately desired.

In any event, an ancillary benefit of being like a brother to these girls was that I got pretty good at delivering bad news. For instance, if a girl wanted me to make an inquiry about a boy and let the guy know she was interested in him, and, if it turned out, he didn't reciprocate these feelings, I started finding diplomatic ways to let the girls down. I didn't have the heart, wit, or guts to be completely candid, so I would fudge a bit. I might say, "Gee, Sally, Bob doesn't want a girlfriend right now. He wants to play the field. But he did say he likes you very much and if he ever was interested in dating someone exclusively you would probably be the one he would be interested in." This let Sally down easily and perhaps gave her some hope. It also was usually pure bullshit.

Bob might actually have said, "Sally? That pig? I would rather poke my eyes out than be with her!" My approach seemed more humane than the brutal truth and it usually worked well, unless Bob started going steady the next week with some other girl. In such an event, I would tell Sally the next time we met that she must always remember that men are scum. Most of the time, however, this awkward situation almost never happened and all went well with my little white lies intended to protect a hopeful, lovesick girl.

Unfortunately, the unlimited pass only got us inside the fairgrounds. Once inside, it was up to me to impress the girls that I walked in with, but things didn't always go as I had hoped.

One evening, I had walked in Gael Mosher and Lana Bisson. Both were nice girls who already liked me as a friend, independently of the benefit of an unlimited entrance pass. After I walked them into the fair, I had to leave them to get back to my house so I could walk in other girls waiting in my basement. Gael and Lana both agreed to meet me at the carnival in about one hour. Super—I had a date with not just one girl, but two, and they were both beautiful and popular. My evening was set.

We met at the carnival after I had just eaten two cheeseburgers, an order of fries, and a Coke at the Salvador School booth. I chose Salvador because I loved their special sauce and it was the closest of the great hamburger booths. I didn't have time to go to the Browns Valley Booth because it was too far away and I had places to go and girls to see. I was in the ninth grade at Silverado Junior High School and was feeling sort of grown up.

When I met up with Gael and Lana, they were ready to go on a few rides. The first ride, known as the Octopus, went around in a circle, but continually tilted or slanted as it went around. As they circled, riders sometimes rode high and sometimes traveled low to the ground. Additionally, each individual car was able to spin in circles as well, while traveling faster than the speed of sound. The carnie controlled the speed and time of the ride, so it could go very fast and very long, depending on his whim.

I was experiencing internal anguish. I needed relief in the worst way. And that is exactly what I got. After the first circle around, Gael started spinning our car. Now I really didn't feel well. I leaned over to Gael and told her that I felt sick. Gael replied in a very serious tone that convinced me that she knew what she was talking about.

"Just close your eyes, Ray, and that will really help you to feel better."

Trusting Gael implicitly, I closed my eyes as if it were a wise old remedy for people getting sick on carnival rides. Moments after closing my eyes, my head began to spin, and soon I was throwing up. Always the gallant gentleman, I didn't dare puke to my left or right as I sat in the middle of Lana and Gael. I puked straight over the middle of our car. I still remember hearing Gael's evil laugh and some groaning from Lana. I knew I had been had, but it was too late. I was unloading chunks of puke faster than a howitzer.

I learned later that Cindy Alonzi, another fun girl I went to school with, was on the same ride that evening, and caught some shrapnel from my bombs. Typical Cindy, however, thought I was spitting on her so she just started spitting back. Little did she realize how outgunned she was.

Finally, if puking in front of two cute girls is not shame enough, the cherry on the parfait was still to come. I suspect that the carnie may have left his post for a while, because this ride's duration must have been close to a world record. When the ride finally ended and the carnie opened the bar to allow us out, I realized I still had some ammo left. Again, I couldn't go to my left or right because of the girls, so I went straight over the middle with another load. Unfortunately for the carnie, he was right in the line of fire in front of me. He jumped like a matador and was able to miss most of the lethal spewing. But, oh, how it pissed him off. He yelled at me that I should stick to the kiddie rides. I still can see his dirty sandy colored hair, greasy clothes, and four not-very-pearly-white teeth as he screamed at me.

I agreed with the carnie, but I was too sick to express my affirmation. Lana and Gael and I split up at that point and, for once, it was my idea. I had to go home, clean myself off, and go to bed. The number one lesson I learned was not to consume two cheeseburgers, fries, and a Coke, and then immediately go on the Octopus. I might have made it on the Ferris wheel, but never the Octopus. A secondary lesson I learned was to never trust Gael Mosher.

Most of the time the carnival was just plain fun. I would meet up with friends and we would take loops around the carnival to see who was there in the never-ending tireless search for girls. We all tried to look our best. I had my finest (and only) Levis with the Husky label torn off of it, and we all had our hair styled with ample quantities of Butch Wax or Dixie Peach. Who could resist us?

About a year after the Octopus fiasco, I was taking loops around the carnival grounds with Mike Kerns and Frank Davidson, looking to see if there were girls to meet and trying to look as cool as possible. However, this was an unusual night, because the perfect storm was brewing: a fight!

Mike had just been dumped by his girlfriend, Geneva Bennett, and was in a foul mood. Mike, like me, came from a broken home and already had a well of anger from this. He didn't live with either parent, but with a very elderly great-aunt. Mike's hot temper got him into lots of fights. So, with the mood he was in, even if he was perhaps not actually seeking a fight this evening, he was not going to duck one.

Three guys stood off to the side of the carnival near a rear entrance of the fairgrounds. These guys apparently were also looking for trouble. The three fellows were strangers to us, and they were an odd combination. One was sort of a regular looking white guy who seemed maybe our age or a little older (we were about fifteen). The other guy was a much bigger and much older-looking white guy. He had receding hair all butch-waxed up, and wore a white T-shirt with the short sleeves rolled up on each arm and a pack of cigarettes in one of the sleeves. He had two large plastic cups and was pouring a beer from one cup to the other as if he was mixing a drink—only it was beer. The third guy was of Latin descent, and someone in the group decided that this guy was Puerto Rican. He was the shortest of their group and apparently the one most looking for trouble.

The Puerto Rican called out to his buddies as we walked by, "Look at the little prick in the middle."

Apparently, I was the little prick. I am sure I did look extra short next to buddies who were much taller. Further, there was no doubt that I was in the middle. But, regardless of the accuracy of his statement, the challenge could not go unanswered. Mike immediately went over to the Puerto Rican guy and made inquiry of him.

"Did you say something about my buddy?"

Of course, to me Mr. Macho Camacho Puerto Rican guy was tough—he was clearly much bigger than me and looked to be in good shape. However, as soon as Mike Kerns stepped in, the Puerto Rican guy folded like a cheap tent. Not a word of bravado came from him, and, in fact, not a word at all left his lips except to respond to Mike that he had no beef with him. What a chicken-shit jerk. Certainly, I had no beef with him either. I had never laid eyes on him before. Bullies usually go after the little guy and fold when someone their size or bigger stands up to them.

In any event, that was not a response that was going to placate Kerns. In fact, it was an invitation for Mike to educate the Puerto Rican by explaining to him that if, indeed, he had a beef with Mike's friend then he had a beef with him.

Enter big older white guy (who must have been at least twenty-one, based on the fact he was blatantly drinking a beer in public, and clearly looked much older than any of us). Stepping to the aid of his Latino friend, the older white guy told Mike that he now had a problem with him. No problem for Mike, because now he had a beef with someone his size. It was quite a sight, seeing these two guys jawing at each other—the older white guy constantly mixing his beer from one cup to the other, and Mike eating from a very small plastic package of shelled peanuts.

After very little discussion, the big older white guy attempted to throw his beer on Mike. Mike, of course, could see this coming a mile off, and sidestepped the beer while throwing a punch. He knocked the big older white guy down with one punch. He started to crawl away so he could get to his feet, but Mike was on him like a hawk. These guys were not fighting by the Marquis of Queensberry Rules. Mike immediately started to pummel the guy, and within seconds someone yelled, "Police!" and everybody scattered. Mike had the older white guy's blood all over his shirt, but he was unscathed.

The big guy didn't anticipate that Mike was a southpaw who threw his punch from a different direction than the older white guy would have expected. Also, Mike was tougher, knew more about boxing, and had plenty of experience in fighting.

Years later, Mike became the Golden Gloves heavyweight champion of the novice division out of San Francisco. He was actually supposed to fight George Foreman (a future two-time world heavyweight champion and Olympic gold medalist), who at the time was the Police Athletic League champion out of Oakland. This would have been an exciting fight—a black amateur heavyweight champion against a white amateur heavyweight champion. However, Foreman was injured in training and the fight was called off. They never rescheduled.

I am so glad of that. Mike is one of my all-time best friends, and I fear that if he and Foreman had fought, Mike might have had to take all future meals from a straw. Besides, now we can always say that Foreman pulled out of their fight.

To girls, it was as though I wasn't there. They looked right through me. But this was not so for bullies. Being short and stout is an invitation to bullies to notice you. I was a poster boy, the guy to pick on. I would have loved to be noticed by girls, but not by bullies. But the ironic, nasty trick that nature played on me had the opposite result.

Fair time to me meant strange and embarrassing times, but also wonderful times and great memories. Notwithstanding the vomit and being the bully-target, I was the guy who had a basement full of eager girls and that alone gave me my moments to shine and made me forever thankful to have been the next-door neighbor to the Napa Fair.

CHAPTER 18

Napa Legends Of The '50s And '60s

To me, a legend is a famous or notorious person, especially in a particular field. My legends of the '50s and early '60s—noted celebrities, along with their great accomplishments and fame—are limited to the Napa County area. They were almost all older than me by several years and their reputations and feats made them legends in my eyes.

DICK BASS

The first person I can remember being famous to me was a high school football player from nearby Vallejo High School. The year was 1954 and I was seven years old. I was a guest of my best friend, Paul, and his father Stanley Vallerga. They took me to Memorial Stadium at Napa High to watch the football game pitting the Napa High School Indian football squad versus the Vallejo High School Apache football team.

I recall seeing lots of adults in trench coats and hats. I remember seeing people's breath because it was a night game and was very cold. Being short and the field being sunken, I could only see the top half of uniforms. I was on the west side of the stadium and I could hear the roar of the crowd on the opening kickoff. I saw a white uniform (Vallejo was wearing their visiting white uniforms) racing by everybody. The referees and all the players on both teams were trying to catch up. It was like a man against boys. It was no match at all. It seemed so unfair. On one particular play this Vallejo player took the ball 102 yards for a touchdown zigzagging and darting in and out of opposing players. Again, the referees and players were all following this player trying in vain to catch up. This time, however, instead of silence from the Napa crowd they were roaring like it was a good thing. I didn't understand. Paul's dad explained to Paul and me that a penalty flag was thrown and the play was nullified. Apparently, there was a clip by one of the opposing players and there would be no touchdown this time.

That exciting play was not needed by the Vallejo team because this player went on to score four touchdowns that did count, until the coach took him out of the game. It was an act of charity by Vallejo's team. It seemed like every time this kid touched the ball it was even money he would score a touchdown. I couldn't see that well but Paul's father would occasionally hold me up as we were in between the bleachers. My view was enough so that I had a lasting impression that I was watching Superman playing against mere mortals.

Needless to say, the game was no contest from the beginning to the end. The headline in Saturday's Napa Register Sports page, on October 23, 1954, was **"5,500 HORRIFIED FANS SEE INDIAN MASSACRE."** The sub headline was **"Vallejo Butchers Timid Napa Squad 53-0."**

The reason for the mismatch, of course, was that the Vallejo team was a much superior team, due in no small part to their main weapon: running back Dick Bass.

Paul and I talked that Saturday afternoon as we got our haircuts from Bun the barber about how great Dick Bass was and how Napa would never win another game against Vallejo until he graduated. The barbers and other adults in the shop begrudgingly agreed with us.

Graduate he did, and Bass went from being an all-state running back at the high school level to becoming an All-American at the College of the Pacific (now University of the Pacific) in Stockton, California. He still seemed like a man against boys even at this level to me, and I remember hoping that my favorite professional team, the San Francisco 49ers, would draft him when his college career was over.

To my large disappointment the 49ers biggest rival, the Los Angeles Rams, drafted Dick Bass with the second pick of the first round and, again, he was a star. Maybe he was not an adult against children at the professional level, but he was talented enough to become an All-Pro three times and had a wonderful professional career.

I will never forget the greatness of this young running back. I had never seen anything like it and never, at the high school level, did I ever witness such total dominance again.

ARLIE LLOYD

Later in the '50s, it became Napa's turn for football greatness. Arlie Lloyd was a Napa legend to all young boys in the '50s who loved football. He anchored the defense of the revered 1959 Napa High Indians' first-ever undefeated, untied season. He was the foundation of that team's defense as a standout tackle. One San Francisco newspaper selected Arlie as one of Northern California's top defensive high school linemen.

To boys five to fifteen years old, Arlie was a real star. He was all we heard about. During Friday-night games, there was Arlie on the Indians' defensive team, wreaking havoc on the opponent's offense. The next morning, at my dad's wrecking yard (Al's Auto Wreckers), I was waiting to go to lunch with my dad—who always worked on Saturdays—while the adult customers and my father would be talking about this "man among boys" being a one-man wrecking crew. You didn't have to see him play to be in awe of him. He is all you heard about if the subject was football. There was only one high school football team in Napa at the time, and there was only one undisputed star linebacker.

The Napa Register's sports pages were filled with Indian football articles featuring Arlie, with action shots of him tackling some opposing running back, or holding some award. I would have asked for his autograph if I could have made myself talk around him. I would just gawk.

On the field Arlie dominated and I could not take my eyes off of him. At home in street football games I used to pretend that I was Arlie Lloyd but only in my dreams did I play like him.

My friend, Joe Flax, himself a star football player for Napa High several years later, walked from his home at Linda Vista and Pueblo Avenue to Memorial Stadium on Friday evenings just to watch the Napa Indians. He said Arlie always stood out.

Wayne Davidson, also a star Napa High defensive end, called Arlie, "A defensive gem. I doubt we would have been undefeated without Arlie."

His coach, Bob Covey, said:

> Arlie Lloyd was an outstanding Napa High School football player. If I were to select a dream team, Arlie would be on it. He is one of the two best tackles that I have ever coached. He had the desire and determination to be the best that he could be. With that, he was also physically tough, strong, and fast; a great combination for a superb lineman. Besides the above, Arlie was a quiet leader, who others looked up to. He made better players out of his teammates, who aspired to reach the level of Arlie's abilities. He is a good example for others to follow.

Arlie was named the Most Valuable Defensive Player on his Napa High team as a senior. He started all games in his two years at Napa High and was distinguished by his coaches as "playing the most minutes," "best tackler on the team," "sack leader," and "sets an example for rest of the team." In one game, he had five sacks for total losses of seventy-five yards.

Arlie Lloyd will never be forgotten by those of us who loved the game and grew up in Napa in the wake of his great football achievements. He was inducted into the Napa High School Hall of Fame on the first ballot at the first inauguration of Napa's Hall of Fame.

JO JO BISSON

It seemed like every Friday evening since I was in kindergarten my parents played pinochle with the Bissons, Frank and Louise. The

Bissons had two children, a boy named Joe and a daughter, Lana. My brother was Joe's age and they were about four years older than Lana and me. Lana and I were exactly the same age both being born on the very same month, day, and year.

Our parents would alternate hosting these card-playing evenings. The Bisson's son was nicknamed Jo Jo, and he was a close family friend who became a legend in my eyes.

Jo Jo was extremely quick. I remember watching Jo Jo at Silverado Junior High School running the 50-yard dash. I was a seventh grader and Jo Jo was in the tenth grade (junior high went

Varsity Basketball

from the seventh to the tenth grade in those days). It appeared to me that Jo Jo was churning up the ground. In fact, to me, it seemed that he had blinding speed. Jo Jo matured early, and by the time he reached his junior year in high school, his height stopped at 5' 8".

I would have loved to have seen Jo Jo play football because he was very muscular. However, Jo Jo's father would not allow him to play that game; as a result, Jo Jo became a basketball star. He was a starting point guard on the Napa High Indians basketball team and a leader on the floor directing his team's offense. He was such a great free throw shooter that he set the Napa High School's record for most consecutive free throws.

He made thirty-five shots in a row without a miss. It was a Napa High record that stood for many, many years.

His combination of skill, determination, muscular build (without lifting weights) and good looks were unbeatable. He had a great Wally Cleaver haircut (Beaver's handsome older brother from the television show *Leave It To Beaver*)—a cool looking flat-top.

On top of all of his qualities was his kindness. My brother told me that Jo Jo, at school dances, made it a point to dance with the girls who weren't usually asked to dance by the boys. My brother could not believe that this big man on campus who was adored by all of the popular girls, cared about the happiness of all of his fellow students. There was no ulterior motive on Jo Jo's part. He was just a caring soul. Years later my brother was still impressed by Jo Jo's gesture. He told me, "Who else would have done that? No one I knew. Certainly not me."

POPIN MILLER

Though I had heard of him for years, it wasn't until the fall of 1962 when I was a junior in high school that I finally actually saw "Popin" Miller in person. It was at Mel's Diner (now Nation's Giant Burgers). It was a Saturday evening and I was engaging in the ever-so-common practice of going to a diner with my friends after spending an empty evening of bombing around in our cars.

Our usual order was a Coke and fries, unless you could afford a burger. As we approached the joint, we observed about twenty people in the parking lot. They were mainly guys that I knew. There was also a small but much older group of guys. The guys I knew from school and hanging around town were all about seventeen or eighteen. This group of adult men were older, in their early twenties. What was clear to me, though, and is still clear to me to this day, was the way most of the kids in the parking lot were acting. It wasn't the same as they usually did on a Saturday evening out on the town. First, the crowd of guys was bigger than normal. Second, no one was being boisterous or loud. The kids my age were quiet and just standing around, looking at their feet. The small group of young men were looking us over.

One of the young adults started addressing us in a way that sounded like a challenge. He was saying something about his buddy was tougher than any two or three of our guys and did any of us want to find out. In our group were some of the toughest guys of our junior and senior classes. I specifically remember Mike "Kid" Kerns, who had been in his share of street fights and always prevailed in those battles. There was Dennis Pallet, who was a real tough kid who could kick the heck out of most opponents. There was a senior class kid who was tough as nails, named Mike Sunnafrank. But none of these guys stepped forward.

I didn't really understand why until another of my friends, Frank Davidson, nudged me and said, "Guadagni, see the guy in the middle? That's Popin Miller!"

I looked at the guy being pointed out and I shuddered. This was the person I had heard about for years who had a reputation as the toughest guy in Napa. He was bigger than life in my mind, but in person he looked like a regular guy in his early 20's. He was not tall or real big, though he was not small either. He was not heavy or hefty, but he was somewhat broad shouldered. He looked like he may be strong but in a boney, sinewy way. He was dressed in Levis with brown buck shoes, and a white T-shirt with a black jacket. His face was serious and stern looking. His hair was dark and short in accord with the times. This was a look I won't forget because it didn't match the look in my imagination, but it still struck fear in me. I remember thinking that one of my tough buddies could have easily underestimated Popin Miller because, if you didn't know his reputation, he probably didn't look that tough. But all of us knew who he was that night, as word spread quickly. We all just stood around as the challenges that Popin's friend laid in front of us went unaccepted. Most of us were just waiting for this to be over. No one was leaving, so as not to look too much like a chicken, but no one was giving eye contact to the older guys either. Most of us just stood there with our heads hanging down. Before long, but what seemed like an hour, the older guys left and our group dispersed as well. I don't remember anyone saying that they were about to stand up to Miller and pound him. It wouldn't have been believed anyway.

Duayne "Popin" Miller was born in 1939 and raised in Shipyard Acres. His family was from Oklahoma. He had several brothers, including a fraternal twin, Wayne "Blackie" Miller. Blackie was taller and more outgoing. He was instinctively friendly, but was tough in his own right. Both Blackie and Popin used to babysit two other friends of mine who came from Shipyard Acres: Tommy and Jerry Davis. Tommy and Jerry were, of course, much younger than the Millers, but that was so impressive to me because both Tommy and Jerry were nice but tough guys in their own right, when we were in high school. By that I mean that bullies didn't mess with the Davis boys because they would stand up to them.

Popin Miller attended Napa schools and graduated high school in 1957. Popin Miller is a legend to me because he was known around Napa as the toughest guy in town, "tougher than a two dollar steak." He was shorter than Blackie, but much more broadly built, with very fast hands and farm-boy strength; some said he was as strong as an ox.

Popin was not a bully. He was very reserved and quiet. This manner had its own way of provoking guys who had heard about him and wanted to take him on. Popin's mom said he ran with the wrong crowd. He was known to run with a wild bunch—Hell's Angels types.

According to Blackie, Popin's reputation had grown so large that a man from Vallejo came to Napa to see just how tough Popin was. It reminds me of the Old West, when a gunslinger with a reputation always had someone itching to knock him off and become the fastest gun in the West. As in the Old West, the Vallejo man came looking for Popin Miller. Popin had never seen the man and had no grudge against him. The man thought he was tough by Vallejo standards, and wanted to see for himself just how tough Miller was.

He found Popin drinking in a bar with his friends. The man introduced himself to Popin and said he wanted to fight. Popin smiled and invited the man to sit down and have a beer. Popin said he did not want to fight. The man sensed Popin might have been afraid of him so he pressed on.

In recalling the incident years later to Blackie, the man said he was amazed by how friendly and polite Popin was. He couldn't believe that Popin was taking his provocative barbs. The man realized that he would have to make Popin mad to get the fight on, so he continued to needle and antagonize Popin until he was finally willing to fight. Even the way the fight started surprised the man. When Popin was ready, he simply said, "Outside."

They went outside, and again, Popin declined to throw the first punch. He simply told the man, "Let's go." The man threw the first punch, but before he could land it, Popin had struck one blow into the face of the man and the fight was over. Popin then picked the man up.

"*Now* will you let me buy you a beer?" Popin asked.

The man told Blackie that he had never been hit with such a strong blow. He had been in lots of fights in Vallejo, and thought of himself, until that night, as the toughest guy around. Not anymore. He spoke of Popin with the kind of reverence reserved for rock stars.

BOB MOUNT

I attended a million (give or take a few) baseball games as a kid in Napa, as a player in the Fly League and in the hardball leagues, and as a fan watching from the stands. I watched many pitchers, good and bad.

Of all the pitchers, two stood out as legends.

Robert "Bob" Mount was the complete package. He had blinding speed, and was a feisty competitor. His control was good enough to strike out most batters. It was also wild enough to prevent batters from digging in at the plate. Most kids found it difficult to hit a ball when they were flat on their back. He struck fear in the hearts of all the kids of his era, especially those who had to bat against him.

I had the opportunity to see Mount pitch at the Fly League level because my brother was on his team. The 1955 Yellowjackets won the Fly League Championship because of two pitchers: Bob Mount and Roger Wilson. Alternating those two pitchers was enough to dominate the league. I attended all of my brother's games, and could not believe my eyes watching Mount's speed. It was blazing to me. My brother told me that the pitchers who scared him the most were on his team. It was much easier to face other pitchers around the league after batting against Mount and Wilson in practice. Watching him in hardball games was equally exciting. He was a superior caliber pitcher.

My group was several years younger than Bob, and in awe of him. Several of the gifted pitchers of our group, including Tommy Davis, Jerry Davis, Mike Kerns, Mike McLaughlin, Wally Keller, and Larry Tronstad, thought he was the best pitcher of our time. That view was unanimous among those players who caught Bob, and the poor guys who had to bat against him. He was regarded as simply the pinnacle of pitchers.

RICH ROBERTSON

Rich Robertson also stands out, not just because he made it to the major leagues, but also because he made a lasting impression whenever he pitched. The buzz around town about this guy was remarkable. Rich was a big, physical presence on the pitching mound. Even as a kid, he looked incredibly comfortable and supremely confident when he pitched. At a very early age, he clearly stood out among the rest of the players in the league. There were other excellent ballplayers around the league when he played, but Rich Robertson was the cream of the crop.

Rich was a basketball and baseball star at Napa High School. As a senior, Rich led the Indians' basketball team in scoring, rebounds, shooting percentage, and free-throw percentages. He was team captain and Most Valuable Player.

But it was on the baseball diamond where this gifted athlete really shone. Rich's talent was so obvious that he lettered at Napa

High School while attending Redwood Junior High School. He was a three-year starter at Napa High, earning All-League honors as a senior. He was the captain of the baseball team.

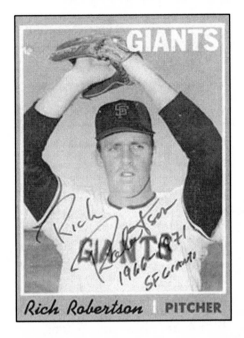

Rich Robertson | PITCHER

Rich earned a baseball scholarship to the University of Santa Clara, where he was an outstanding pitcher. He was second team All-League in a very strong league.

After college, Rich began an eight-year professional career, including four years with the San Francisco Giants. He was a Pacific Coast League All Star with Phoenix in 1968 with an 18-9 record and landed a spot on the Giants' 1971 division championship team. The highlight of his career was a complete-game shutout of the Pittsburgh Pirates on May 23, 1969, during which he struck out Willie Stargell and Roberto Clemente in succession.

Bill Buckner and Warren Brusstar were also former major league baseball players from Napa, but they came after Bob Mount and Rich Robertson. In the '50s and early '60s, Mount and Robertson were the stuff of legends to those of us who lived in the Napa community.

PAUL VALLERGA

Paul Vallerga was my classmate from kindergarten through my high school years. More importantly, he is a lifelong friend.

Legends are usually people from an earlier time. They were older and had well-known reputations, some of which may have been embellished or exaggerated. But the legend was usually established.

This was not the case with Paul. He was a contemporary of mine, yet he became a legend before my very eyes as we grew up together.

Paul was the star athlete of our class, our school, and our town. He was a three-sport star at Napa High School in track, basketball, and football. He was a starter for one of the best basketball teams in Napa High's history in 1964 when it won the league championship and lost in the finals of the Tournament of Champions.

In 1963 and 1964 Paul was two-time league high-jump champion, two time Hollister Tourney high-jump champion, and set the Napa High high-jump record in 1964. He finished third in the North Coast Section high-jump competition.

He was a two-year starter for the Indian football team, and was named in 1963 co-outstanding back, All-League flanker back, and player of the game against Hogan and Vallejo. He helped lead Napa to a league championship and was named All North Coast

Section Flanker. He was also named the 1964 Athlete of the Year. Paul was inducted into the Napa High School Hall of Fame in the very first year of the Foundation's existence.

Paul went on to excel at the college level, twice earning All-American honors in football at the University of California at Santa Barbara.

Paul signed a professional contract to play with the San Francisco 49ers in 1968, but an early injury ended his dream of playing professional football.

Because Paul was a contemporary of mine, I was familiar with more than his sports accomplishments and feats. I knew Paul as a regular guy. He was not perfect.

There was the time when nine-year-old Paul knocked out his five-year-old brother John with a punch to his face. The boys were at home goofing off with an inebriated babysitter sleeping on the couch. Paul covered his tracks by dragging unconscious John to their bedroom and hiding him under the bed. John still remembers waking up and staring up at the box springs. There was the time when twelve-year-old Paul threw a lighted match at eight-year-old brother John and it burnt his cheek. Paul made his brother tell their parents that John got the reddish mark by attempting to shave. Their parents thought it was funny and told the story many times. Poor John was teased about this event each time his mom told it to her friends.

There was the time at Wally Keller's house, when we were still in elementary school, and everyone started throwing rocks at each other. Paul was throwing rocks with the rest of us. Unfortunately, Steve Ceriani accidentally hit Paul in the eye and he had to get two stitches. He didn't tell his mother but she, of course, noticed and took him to the doctor.

Paul, as a seventh grader, was one of the managers of the Silverado Junior High football team. Paul and another co-manager, Mike McLaughlin, "borrowed" some of the varsity football jerseys so they could wear them during the summer. They proudly wore the jerseys during the summer and were spotted wearing them by one of the coaches. They were required to bring them back to the school. During traveling basketball games, some of the guys (Paul included) were known, at times, to lift some things out of the lockers.

Both Paul and I would compare our 45 record collections with each other. In our piles of records that we each claimed, there would be records with names of other kids on them. Still, we claimed them as our own to each other and even traded them amongst ourselves. I remember Paul having a 45 record I wanted that had "Kerrigan" written on it. Kathy Kerrigan was a classmate of ours at Silverado Junior High. It seems that Paul borrowed it but "forgot" to bring it back. I ended up with it because I traded him for one of "my" records that had the name "Marsha Anderson" all over it.

In our early teens, we would hang out at Mike Lawler's pool house where we would listen to the raunchy humor of Red Foxx and imbibe some of Mike's dad's booze. We thought we were pretty cool.

Sometimes sitting around with the guys we would try our hand at impressions. Mike Kerns could do a pretty good Englishman. Billy Forsythe could impersonate almost any accent. Paul would give his impressions as well—Irish, English, Asian, but all of his attempts came out Swedish. Every sentence either began or ended with "Yah." Paul was not good at everything.

As good as Paul was physically in sports, he could not hear well. We would listen to records and he would ask me why the lyric didn't make sense. There was a song by Johnny Tillotson called "Poetry in Motion" recorded in the very early '60s. Paul heard the lyric as "Oh-A-Tree-in-Motion." Johnny Rivers recorded a song called "Secret Agent Man" that Paul thought was "Secret Asian Man."

Paul has always loved cars and speed. I think he peeled out of the Foster Freeze parking lot on Lincoln Avenue every time he left.

He would be in his parents' 1962 Pontiac Grand Prix. He was also known to drag race other guys taking their cars out of town to do so.

Paul would allow us to go to his grandparents' ranch and take old, rotten vegetables so we could throw them at other kids or cars on Halloween. The only thing different between regular guys and Paul was that he was way more accurate in his pitching of rotten vegetables. Also, should a car stop and attempt to pursue us on foot, Paul had the advantage of being the fastest of our group. All of us would be caught before Paul.

Paul was far from perfect. He was a regular guy who had fun with his friends and enthusiastically participated in whatever the moment would bring.

I always admired Paul, because even though he was blessed with the natural physical attributes of a gymnast and a ballet dancer that he combined to achieve greatness in sports, he never treated me or anyone else in a way that gave an impression that he thought that he was too good for us. He believed that his gifts were just that, and not an excuse to exclude others or feel superior.

The people referred to here were all legends of my generation and have remained in my memory throughout my life, due to their amazing accomplishments and reputations. They were mostly local high school kids that younger kids of my age looked up to and even idolized.

These were the youthful stars of our community. We could see them around town. We could see their pictures or read about them in the Napa Register. We could watch them live playing sports at Memorial Stadium or on the high school basketball court or the baseball fields. We couldn't have been more impressed or proud, had they been professional athletes.

They were special to me and have remained so.

CHAPTER 19

Napa's Heroes: Selfless, Brave, Humble

In his book, *The Greatest Generation*, Tom Brokaw asserts that the World War II generation consisted of people of great character. He clarified this by saying these men and women developed values of "personal responsibility, duty, honor and faith," and that these were the characteristics that allowed the United States and its allies to defeat Hitler, Mussolini, and Japan, and preserve freedom throughout the world.

Much of the freedom and affluence that we enjoy today is because of this generation.

"They have given the succeeding generations the opportunity to accumulate great economic wealth, political muscle, and the freedom from foreign oppression to make whatever choices they like," Brokaw wrote.

This was the generation I have always admired the most. As a kid in Napa in the '50s, I knew the adults in our community came from that great generation, yet I never thought of them as heroes. I think that is because of another point Brokaw makes, which is that the people of that generation were remarkably humble about what they did for us.

"It is a generation that, by and large, made no demands of homage from those who followed and prospered economically, politically, and culturally because of its sacrifices," Brokaw wrote.

Napa had its share of these men.

As a child growing up in Napa I knew many adults, but I wasn't aware whether these adults served in World War II. Later in my life I learned the heroic war stories of a few of these men. Their stories weren't told to me by any of them personally, but, rather by a third person. In some cases, a family member may have told me, and even some of these family members learned about the details of sacrifice and heroism of their fathers from others.

It has been said that the cornerstone of human civilization is human sacrifice. A hundred people die so a thousand might live. The veterans I knew made it home alive, but were not without the scars of war. All of them made great sacrifices for the greater good. All of us owe them a debt of gratitude that can never be repaid.

KENNETH CASANEGA

Kenneth Casanega was the principal of Napa High School when I attended. I was a friend and classmate of his son, Len Casanega. The strongest memory I have of Ken Casanega was that he treated me very well. He was a nice man, well liked, and a very popular principal. Beyond that, I had heard stories, not from his son, but from other adults, that he had played football for the 49ers. At the time, I had never heard anything about his military service to his country.

In later years I came to understand more about this extraordinary Napa man.

Ken finished his college career at Santa Clara University, which was then a national powerhouse in football. He played in the East-West Shrine Game, and was drafted in 1942 by the Pittsburgh Steelers with the sixteenth overall pick.

Instead of entering the NFL, Ken chose instead to enlist in the Navy, where he flew airplanes off of aircraft carriers. Years later, when his son asked him why he chose the Navy over playing professional football, he said he "got steamed up about Pearl Harbor."

Initially, Ken was deployed in the Atlantic, then later in the Pacific. On one mission, his plane was shot in one of the sea battles with the Japanese; he told his crew to prepare to jump, but then he discovered that if he held the stick all the way to the right, the plane would fly level. When he returned to his carrier, he was unable to land because the carrier had been hit by a kamikaze plane and was badly damaged. Ken then landed on another carrier. The next day he was awakened at about 2:00 AM and ordered to fly his plane back to his now-repaired carrier.

This information was derived from the Internet and books because Ken only told funny stories about himself; he never mentioned his heroism.

After coming home, Ken received a telegram from Buck Shaw, his college coach and the first coach of the San Francisco 49ers, asking if he would play for the 49ers. Ken thought, "Who the heck are the 49ers?" (1946 was the first year of the team.)

As a cornerback, Ken set several records in 1946, including interceptions (eight in a fourteen-game season).

Ken was the second-highest paid player on the team in 1946, earning $6,449 for the season. This was good money in 1946. However, Ken decided he had had enough travel, and quit playing. After he left the Niners, he taught math and coached four sports at John Swett High School in Martinez.

Coach Buck Shaw visited him and reminded him that he could do much better financially playing for San Francisco (about $7,000 as opposed to $2,400). Ken told his coach he was tired of plane trips, and missed his wife, whom he hadn't seen much over five years.

In 1948, Ken was hired to teach at Napa High and as assistant football coach for Napa Junior College. The 49ers asked him again to return, and the school district gave him a leave. He played in a couple of games, but said his heart wasn't in it. As he was one of the highest paid players on the team, they let him go. He played defensive back, halfback, and backup quarterback, though they wanted him to play quarterback (he was a single-wing quarterback at Santa Clara and his college—now 49er—coach Buck Shaw knew he could run, pass, and punt quite well). Ken wasn't interested and returned to teach in Napa.

Ken twice gave up a potentially more lucrative and exciting life in football: once to serve his country in the U.S. Navy, and then a second time to devote himself to his family, and to contribute to the youth of his community as an educator. He was a credit to Napa and to his country. His family is very proud of his accomplishments and more importantly, they admire him and love him for who he is: a very kind, brave, consistent and loving husband, father and grandfather, who is a wonderful role model and person.

I never knew anything about Ken's record of sacrifice and service to his country. He never acted as if he was an extraordinary person or a hero, but he surely was. I knew I liked him from the beginning, but I never knew of his accomplishments, because he was a classic member of the greatest generation: selfless, brave, and humble.

JUDGE WILLIAM BLANCKENBURG

William L. Blanckenburg was a Napa attorney who joined the service and was also part of the greatest generation. He became a Superior Court Judge in the late 1950s in Napa. I had known Judge Blanckenburg since 1952, because I attended Alta Heights Elementary School with his daughter, Kathy. We both started kindergarten together.

Kathy and I were usually paired together as we were the two shortest students in our class. We were folk-dancing partners and sat in the front row when class pictures were taken. She was an absolutely wonderful person, and we became great friends. I knew her father as a very big, handsome man who was always very nice to me.

What I didn't know, and never learned until after his death in 2014, was his war record.

Bill Blanckenburg was practicing law for the firm of Coombs, Dunlap, and Blanckenburg in Napa before the war broke out, having come to Napa as a result of being a fraternity brother of Frank Dunlap. They both attended Boalt Hall at the University of California at Berkeley. When war came, Bill enlisted in the Army as a private in the infantry. This fact alone seems remarkable to me. As a lawyer, he could have become a commissioned officer in the Judge Advocate Corps. He would have entered the war as an officer with the rank of second Lieutenant.

However, Bill chose not to do this, and as a private in the infantry put himself in a much more dangerous position, with the likelihood of combat duty quite probable. That, of course, is exactly what happened. Bill went ashore at Anzio and became part of one of the bloodiest battles in Europe in World War II.

He and his outfit slogged through the blood and guts of war casualties on their way to Rome. Along the way, Bill had experiences that no person should ever have to encounter. In some incidents, he witnessed some of his fellow soldiers blown apart in puffs of smoke. In another incident, he and another soldier made it into a depression on the side of a hill so that they could take cover. Another soldier died in front of them at the opening of their shelter. This dead soldier became a shield for Bill and the other soldier. Bill could feel the bullets and shrapnel hit the dead soldier's body; this unfortunate young man saved their lives.

In yet another incident, Bill was standing guard outside of his patrol's shelter, located just south of Rome. It was late at night and it was very difficult to see. There was another American soldier with a Tommy gun guarding the road across from Bill. Both of them heard a motorcycle coming; Bill didn't know if it was friendly or an enemy. The guard across the road shouted several times for the vehicle to halt, but the vehicle not only didn't halt, it seemed to speed up, instead. The guard fired upon the motorcycle, but his Tommy gun misfired.

Bill, then believing it was an enemy motorcycle, fired his M-1 Rifle and heard a crash. The next morning they learned that indeed it was carrying enemy German soldiers in a motorcycle with a sidecar. The driver was killed by the crash and the passenger was killed by Bill's rifle shot. Bill had fired upon the enemy in combat before, but this was his only confirmed kill.

Later, Bill joined what was known as the Battle Patrol. This was a group of ten men who were trained in hand-to-hand combat and other special warfare. They were also armed with automatic weapons because the Battle Patrol was tasked to go behind enemy lines to do reconnaissance and generally mess things up as much as they could while behind the lines. This was a highly skilled unit, given very dangerous orders.

In one situation, the captain of the Battle Patrol gave an instruction for two of the men to do some reconnaissance down the road and report back what they found. The first soldier assigned was a soldier that Bill usually did assignments with. It was not uncommon for two soldiers to be paired because they knew how to work with each other. However, on this particular occasion, the captain pointed to a second soldier who happened to be standing next to Bill's usual partner and told him to go.

These two soldiers proceeded to go on their assignment and were gone for a couple of hours doing reconnaissance. It was very dark when they came back, and when they were fairly close to the group, the youngest member of the Battle Patrol inexplicably did an incredibly stupid thing. He threw a hand grenade in the middle of the two returning soldiers, blowing them to pieces. One of those soldiers killed would have been Bill, had he been paired with his usual partner—a very close call for him.

June 4, 1944, marked the fall of Rome, and Bill survived with the remaining Battle Patrol members to be part of that historic victory in which the Allies defeated the Germans.

Bill was later offered a commission as a Judge Advocate Corps Officer, which he accepted. He went to Judge Advocate Corps School in Indiana, and became a major by the end of the war.

Bill came back to Napa and practiced law with Frank Dunlap and Nate Coombs. Eventually, Bill left Coombs and Dunlap to be a sole practitioner. He was appointed by Governor Goodwin Knight in the late '50s to become a Superior Court Judge, and served as such until his retirement in 1979.

In all the years I knew him, while I was a kid in the '50s and into the '60s, and in all the time I practiced in front of Judge Blanckenburg as a lawyer in the '70s, I never knew anything about his service in the war, or of the dangerous missions and combat duty he engaged in for our country.

After he died, I learned all of this by reading his memoirs of his combat experiences and from his friend, former Superior Court Judge Philip A. Champlin.

Once again, this Napa soldier did his duty, returned home, and went back to work. He was selfless, brave, and humble.

JUDGE THOMAS KONGSGAARD

Another Superior Court Judge in Napa in the '50s who also fought in World War II was Judge Thomas Kongsgaard. I did not personally know Judge Kongsgaard as a kid growing up in the '50s but I had heard of him. There were only two Superior Court Judges in Napa at that time, and in a small town people knew who they were.

Before the war, Iguald Thomas Kongsgaard (Tom) was a young Capitol page in Washington D.C. and later became a Capitol policeman there.

After the war broke out, Tom went to officer's school and became an ensign in the United States Navy. He was sent to the Pacific as a Naval gunnery officer on a minesweeper that was equipped with one gun.

This is where he was during the Battle of Okinawa. A minesweeper that was near the one that Tom was aboard hit a torpedo and blew up. Tom's minesweeper was sent to aid the other damaged minesweeper and, unfortunately, also hit a torpedo and blew up. The ship sunk, and all the men on Tom's ship were killed, except him. He was thrown overboard and his leg was shattered.

Thomas Kongsgaard, in uniform on the left, pictured here
at the Naval Hospital at Mare Island, Vallejo with a visiting friend,
Senator Henry "Scoop" Jackson.

He was loaded onto a hospital ship and eventually sent to Mare Island Naval Hospital in Vallejo, California, which was the amputee center for the Navy and Marines. Because of his severe injuries, Tom lost his leg. However, this is where Tom met a nurse named Lorraine Streblow, through Dr. Dwight Murray. Tom and Lorraine fell in love and eventually married.

Lorraine became a lawyer, and Tom finished college, getting his undergraduate degree from the University of California and his law degree from Stanford Law School. He became a member of the law firm Riggins, Rossi and Kongsgaard. In the late 1950s Governor Goodwin Knight appointed Tom to the Napa County Superior Court bench.

I personally became acquainted with Judge Kongsgaard when I was a young lawyer in the '70s, frequently appearing in his courtroom. He is still acknowledged as one of the leading judges in California during his term on the bench in Napa. He served continuously from his appointment until he retired in 1985. Even thereafter, he continued working as a private judge, conducting mediations and arbitrations. In this field he was once again acknowledged as one of the best.

After I became acquainted with Tom, we remained friends for the rest of his life. His last speaking appearance was at my swearing-in ceremony as a Superior Court Judge in 2001.

In all of my appearances in front of him in open court, and in all of the in-chambers discussions I had with him, things were informal and relaxed. However, despite all of the bar association parties we attended together, and throughout all conversations we shared, Tom never once mentioned his service to his country.

There was the visible evidence of his amputated leg, and the times when the bailiff would tell us he was in great pain on a certain day, but he never talked about it. In fact, his daughter, Martha, said that her father never ever thought of himself as a hero. He had a wonderful attitude toward life, and although it may seem strange, I found myself envious of such a great man for his courage, humility, outlook, and kindness. He was a true hero to his country, and such a credit to the community of Napa.

By virtue of my law career in Napa, I met this next group of Napa citizens. I didn't know them in my youth, although it's possible I might have met some of them through their children during that time period. Mainly, however, I became acquainted with them in the '70s when I was a young lawyer.

FRANK DUNLAP

Frank Dunlap was a Navy Lieutenant and the radio officer at Midway Island during the pivotal Pacific battle there. I vaguely knew Frank in the '50s, because I knew his daughters: Helen, who was in my class, and Mary, who was a year behind us. They were both highly intelligent people, and friendly to me. I met Frank during that time, but it wasn't until much later that I got to know him, since we both practiced law in Napa.

DAVE YORK

Dave York, who became Napa County District Attorney and a judge, was a Navy intelligence officer present on the USS Missouri when the Japanese surrendered in Tokyo Bay.

I knew Dave's two daughters, Jane and Ellen York, who also practiced law. We practiced at the same time in the '70s, before Jane became a judge in Fresno. Ellen remained here, is a former Napa County Bar Association President, and is still practicing law.

Dave was reserved on the bench, extremely intelligent, and was always kind to me. I learned of his service to his country through other sources after he passed away.

JOHN DUNLAP

John Dunlap, who became a California State Senator, was in the U.S. Army Air Corps. Again, I knew him from his practice in Napa.

ROBERT ZELLER

Robert Zeller is a long-time Napa attorney. He is in his 90's now, and still practices law. He is an expert in estate planning, wills, trusts, and probate. He still goes to the office every day.

He was only nineteen years old when he saw combat in World War II. From what I have heard, he is very lucky to have survived. He fought in France and at the Battle of the Bulge. While on the front, he was afflicted with trench foot. He was hospitalized but once recovered he elected to return to active duty.

Robert is very approachable, and he never hesitated to assist a young lawyer who always had questions (me). What a kind, intelligent, brave and humble man—another credit to the Napa community.

ROBERT BENNING

Another longtime Napa resident who contributed significantly to his country is Robert Earl Benning. He served for many years as Napa County Auditor. I knew Bob in the '50s because he was an elected official, and because his son, also Robert, was a classmate and friend of mine. Bob was another member of the Greatest Generation whom I got to know well later when I was an adult. We had many conversations, but he did not bring up the war or his sufferings, even though there were visible signs of this by the fact that his left leg was amputated above the knee.

I learned about Bob's military background from his son and one of his granddaughters, who interviewed him for a school project. At her urging, and to help his granddaughter with her schoolwork, Bob disclosed most of the following information, although his son supplemented a bit.

Robert Earl Benning enlisted as a private in the United States Marine Corps shortly after Pearl Harbor at age eighteen. He was well trained in several areas. He completed radio school, scout-sniper school, and an intensive course in intelligence and demolition. His primary classification was combat intelligence.

The years of 1944 and 1945 dramatically affected his life. In June

1944 this young Marine was on board a troop ship destined to strike, invade, and recapture the Mariana Islands (Guam, Saipan, and Tinian). These islands would afford the Allies use of a good harbor and excellent airfields, some within bombing range of Japan itself. Bob's company was part of a landing force scheduled to hit the beach on Guam three days after the invasion of Saipan.

The Marines who landed on Saipan suffered heavy losses. The battle for the island raged longer than expected. Because of this, Bob's company did not land on Guam as anticipated, but instead sailed back to the Marshall Islands and waited aboard ship for new orders. They were a floating reserve for the Marines who were on Saipan.

The new orders resulted in Bob and his company hitting the beaches of Guam on July 21, 1944, in the middle of shelling and small arms fire from machine guns and Japanese snipers. Their orders were to work their way behind lines and reconnoiter the possible location for a future command post. Instead, they were pinned down in the Agana River until the next morning. Then they slowly fought their way further into the island.

On July 25, 1944, Bob, now a sergeant, and a fellow sergeant were in a foxhole in the front lines serving as a listening post. Bob said everything was quiet—unusually quiet except for some artillery shelling that occasionally passed overhead. He described the sound of the artillery shells as the sound of freight trains. The protracted quiet was broken with the sound of a single shot. Then there were a few more shots, and then all hell broke loose.

The next morning the hillside across from Bob's position was covered with hundreds of bodies. Reports later indicated that the Japanese suicide (Banzai) attack cost the lives of more than 3,500 Japanese troops and at least 1,000 Marines.

On August 11, 1944, organized Japanese resistance ended. Throughout the island, small groups and individual Japanese soldiers held out. On August 12, Bob, now twenty years old, went out on patrol checking out the caves. He was shot through both legs. The bullet to the left leg tore off the calf. The Browning automatic rifleman with Bob was wounded in the chest. The Marines carried Bob out of the hills and transported him to a medical tent. He temporarily regained consciousness and found himself placed in a pile of dead bodies.

When he saw a red tag on his wrist Bob said, "Oh! I rate a red tag!" Bob's words caused a Navy Corpsman to shout, "This one is alive!" Indeed, Bob's dog tag had been clipped and he had been placed with the dead. He was immediately removed from this location and subsequently loaded on the hospital ship, the USS Solace.

This ship, loaded with the wounded and dying, sailed to the Marshall Islands and then to Pearl Harbor. Bob was given numerous blood transfusions, preparing him for the trip back to the States. It was at Pearl Harbor that Bob suffered one of many attacks of malaria.

Bob was then boarded onto the Army ship *Sea Star*, bound for California. On October 2, 1944, while still on the ship destined for San Francisco, one of the ship's cooks and several sailors came into Bob's compartment carrying a birthday cake and singing "Happy Birthday." Bob had turned twenty-one.

The next day, Bob landed in San Francisco. He was placed on a stretcher, loaded into an ambulance, and transported to Mare Island Naval Hospital in Vallejo, the amputee center for the Navy and Marines. It was chaotic there, so busy with patients suffering from various kinds of tropical diseases, the many wounds being dressed, ongoing surgical procedures, and, sadly, some dying.

While in the hospital with many other wounded servicemen (Bob's ward had forty beds), a bucket was kept in the middle of the floor. Every time a piece of shrapnel worked its way out, you could hear the clank as it was thrown into that bucket.

Bob's right leg was saved, but he lost his left leg. Unfortunately, the left leg was amputated above the knee.

Things had been fairly bleak for Bob, but in January 1945, he was introduced to a WAVE named Patricia Cook, who worked as a secretary in the supply building. It was Bob's lucky day. On September 6, 1945, Bob and Patricia were married in St. Peter's Chapel on Mare Island.

In March, 1946, Bob visited Napa for the first time. Bob hitched a ride from a man traveling north from Mare Island. The man warned Bob that when the stores closed, so did the town, and it would be difficult to get a ride back at that hour. Bob found the town to be small, full of a variety of shops and small businesses. He also found that the people were the friendliest he had ever met. He felt he had to return and show Napa to his wife. Both Bob and Pat fell in love with the valley and settled in Napa in 1946. Bob and Pat remained there for the rest of Bob's life.

Bob wore an artificial leg for many years, until he developed arthritis and eventually went to a wheelchair.

Bob's first job in Napa was at Hedgeside Distillery, the old stone buildings still at the corner of Monticello and Atlas Peak Road. His job was to document the liquor tax that was levied at the time of production. Charles Harney, County Treasurer, then hired Bob to work in the County Treasurer's office, where he worked as an Assistant County Treasurer. Bob ran for County Auditor in the early '50s. The race was virtually tied, but one of the last precincts counted was the California Veterans Home in Yountville, which gave Bob the election victory. Bob served twenty years as Napa County Auditor before he retired.

Bob and Pat had four children and seven grandchildren. He was married to Pat for fifty-seven years.

There is a display case that remembers Robert Earl Benning and his wife Pat at the Mare Island Museum.

JIM MAGGETTI

Another Napan from that generation and another person who put his life on hold was Jim Maggetti. He graduated from the Napa High School, class of 1942. He planned to attend U.C. Berkeley and study civil engineering.

Instead, he became a member of Gen. George Patton's Third Army, 94th Infantry Division, and fought in the Battle of the Bulge. The weather conditions were extreme and Jim developed trench foot, which is the slow freezing of the foot. He was treated for trench foot and sent back to the front lines. Only two men from Jim's original platoon of forty men survived.

Fighting on, Jim and another soldier, after their commanding officer was killed, went up on an elevated area to survey the area. They observed a unit of German soldiers trying to destroy a German machine gun battery to prevent it from falling into American control. From their position, Jim and his fellow soldier fired on the enemy and succeeded in neutralizing those German soldiers. The U.S. Army acknowledged this action by awarding Jim the Silver Star.

After his discharge and return to Napa, Jim picked up where he left off. He soon went to UC Berkeley and earned two bachelor's degrees and a master's degree. He later became a vice president at Kaiser Steel, and then served on the boards of Napa Valley Bank, Westamerica Bank, and Oregon Steel.

I had heard of Jim Maggetti for years in the community, not as a war hero, but as a respected businessman. I finally met him when I was a guest at a local Rotary club. He was friendly, kind and self-effacing.

The sacrifices these Napa citizens gave to their country are immeasurable. Some of them reached very low points in their lives and felt alone, scared and empty. All of them faced danger and life-threatening situations. Yet they did their duty, made their sacrifices and just kept going. Heroes, all of them.

Selfless, brave, and humble.

CHAPTER 20

Arrivederci

When Mom separated from my father between my eighth and ninth grade years, she asked my brother and me about the idea of moving out of town. She was going through a period of not wanting to be under his thumb nor take any of his verbal abuse again. Who could blame her? Also, by remaining in this small town she knew he would be spreading false stories about her, and she didn't want to hear about it. She said she would like a fresh start.

My initial reaction was very negative. I loved Mom with all of my heart, but I wasn't now going to lose all of my friends. I told her that I would not move. I would stay with one of my friends. Of course, this very self-centered, selfish position was just what Mom needed to hear to get her to rethink her inclination. She would do anything for her kids and when she heard such resistance she abandoned the idea. The move never happened. Fortunately, Mom ended up really quite happy in Napa where here friends were, where her children went to school, where her children were happy with their friends, and where she had settled all her life since having kids.

Though I feel bad about being so adamant about not moving from Napa without any regard for what may have been in Mom's best interests, I am glad we didn't move. I had such a strong attachment to this town. It was the only home I knew. All of my friends were from Napa. It is where I played sports, music, went to parties and dances. I had a variety of jobs growing up and all of them were in Napa. Basically, every formative experience of mine was in Napa. It is where I grew up and I knew Napa as a friendly, happy and nurturing community. Except for college and law school all of my education was in Napa.

Except for being a lawyer in Stockton for three years after law school, my entire legal career was in Napa.

When I did return home to practice law, Napa had changed. In fact, I remember thinking "What did they do to my town?" Gone were many of the gorgeous old buildings—the Behlow Building, the Migliavacca building, the old Carithers building. Brown Street no longer went all the way through from First to Third Streets. And, then there were one-way streets. The old shopping center across the freeway west of First Street was a shopping center that never seemed to thrive. The big tenant was Allen and Benedict Furniture and Purity Market, as well as West Side Pizza. Later it was replaced by new factory outlet stores. The Uptown Theatre became run down until George Altamura renovated it and gave the community something to be proud of from our past. The old Opera House was saved and renovated to once again become a beautiful theater, until it was changed to a cabaret setting with the lovely theatre seats being replaced by not-so-beautiful urban style tables. Some of the old eateries I loved where I enjoyed a warm neighborhood feeling were still there when I first returned as an adult, but eventually all of the family style Italian restaurants were replaced, as were all of the old time drive-in joints like the Wright Spot and Kenny's. Even Jonesy's Restaurant at the airport is no longer there.

The old Napa Register building was beautiful and it still exists, but it no longer houses the newspaper. The stately old library building, which housed the Goodman library on First Street is still there, but the building is now occupied by the Napa Historical Society. It has survived (barely) an earthquake. The Gordon Building on First Street where I had my very first elevator ride is still there. The majestic Post Office building, a WPA project, was still there and functioning when I returned home as an adult but has since been severely damaged by the earthquake of 2014.

Many in the community are fighting to save the building even though the United States Post Office is no longer interested in using the building for its services.

Gone also are all of the old swimming resorts where my friends and I used to love to swim during the summer months.

My old elementary school, Alta Heights, is still there. It is built on a hillside with the lower classes at the bottom and the higher classes in the upper parts of the school. This always made sense to me. As a student, I couldn't wait to get uphill so I was king of the hill as the sixth graders were then.

My old junior high school, Silverado Middle School, is still there but looks different than when I first attended seventh grade, which was the first year the school was open. The campus now contains buildings that hadn't been built yet when I attended, including an auditorium and gym. Still, I love that school and spent most of my school years there because junior high at the time went from seventh through tenth grades.

The impressive and authoritative building that housed Napa High School is still there, but the structure is no longer used as classes for the high school. Rather, it is used by school administration. Still, the beautiful building remains as a representation of when Napa High was THE only high school in town. The Napa Junior College, as it was called then, is no longer across the lawn from Napa High School, but has its own home in South Napa along the highway

The changes notwithstanding, I still felt at home upon my return. I reunited with many of my friends who either never left town, or were returning from military service, or as I was, returning from college. We settled in Napa as adults in the community we came from. I think it is a reflection on the nurturing and kindness we experienced in this community. There seemed to be lots of adults during this period that didn't hesitate to give of their time to mentor kids. We were lucky and fortunate to be raised here.

As for some of the people mentioned in this book, many of them have moved on, as they must. After all, six decades have transpired since I was a kid in Napa in the '50s. My parents have both passed and my brother is retired.

Eugene remained in Napa for many of his adult years. He married and had one daughter, Janene. To support his family, he worked for Dad in the wrecking yard business after high school and after being married. However, that did not work out because of the difficult challenges of working for an extremely demanding father who was quick to criticize him in a loud and boisterous manner with no qualms of embarrassing Eugene in front of anyone within earshot.

My brother could not do anything right in Dad's eyes and I knew it was only a matter of time before my brother would leave Dad's employ.

The scars of his abusive childhood left him with little self-confidence. He struggled with alcohol for many years. He later obtained gainful employment as a retail clerk at Lucky's Grocery Store in Napa and had a successful career there.

Eugene continued to have conflicts with our father, though his contacts with him, even when both resided in the same town, were minimal. He later remarried and had another daughter, Christina, and a son, Nicholas. Almost as soon as he retired from Lucky's, and following the death of our mother in 1984, he moved to Minden, Nevada and became completely estranged from our dad.

Eugene continues to reside in Minden with his wife, Dorothy. All three of his children have given him grandchildren, who keep him busy. Additionally, my brother evolved into an exceptionally talented pianist and his love for music has never waned. His style was honky-tonk, and he is the best at that style that I have ever heard. He continues to play with other musicians in Minden, at retirement homes or at pubs, where his honky-tonk piano is very much in demand.

I am thankful for his love of music, because it was a place where Eugene could lose himself. There, his sadness dissolved and he found only happiness, fulfillment, and confidence. He is a very loving brother who has a kind and generous heart. He didn't deserve his upbringing and he still has his demons. However, he survived his youth and had the intelligence to move away from his roots. We talk and get together and he is always very kind and loving to his little brother.

After Mom reconciled with my father after a couple of years of separation, she was very pleased to have her own home and for a while after the reconciliation with my dad, things went well. However, before long Dad started to revisit some of his old habits and was not treating her very well, heaping lots of unreasonable and abusive criticism on her.

When Dad started seeing other women, my mom decided enough was enough. This time it was not simply a legal separation but an actual dissolution of marriage. This was the best thing that could have ever happened to my mom. She missed not having a partner and friend to share things with, but Dad was neither a good partner nor a friend. He had continued to verbally and emotionally abuse her and was disloyal.

Once she was free of Dad, Mom really blossomed. Dad, after the divorce, told me that he saw Mom walking with a friend down the street once, and they were laughing. He said that Mom seemed to have lots of bounce in her step.

"If she had that kind of pep when I was with her I would have never left her," Dad told me. He had no insight that he was the cause of her not having any pep in her step when they were together.

My loving mother.

Mom was the parent I could talk to. She had a calm strength that I was attracted to. She loved talking with me as well. We helped each other. She would ask my help in composing difficult letters to people with whom she needed to communicate.

She is the parent who decorated the Christmas tree with my brother and me. She loved and cared for our pets more than my brother and I did. She would always take me Christmas shopping for my brother and then would shop with him for me. She was caring and generous to my friends and to this day, when the subject comes up, they always have a kind word about her.

She tried to give her boys everything she could, even when she couldn't afford it. She would have items put on layaway, as local stores would do, and she would pay them off regularly. There were some wonderful shop owners in this town. For Christmas, she would open up a Christmas Club bank account just so she could save for presents for us.

Despite her lack of confidence, she showed great wisdom in the way she treated people. She showed kindness to people even if they didn't deserve it. When people did nice things for her or her family it was quite often followed by a card to that person expressing thanks and appreciation for their kindness. Austin Kelly, a local educator, once showed me such a card and told me that showed real intelligence.

Her new life became one filled with babysitting her grandchildren, with whom she was patient and loving.

My wife, Ann, and I had such comfort when Mom would have our girls in her care. We both knew that she would love them and guard them with her life. In her social life, Mom lacked a lot of self-esteem after forty years of being with a man who destroyed her confidence. However, with both Ann and I nudging her (sometimes not so gently) Mom blossomed.

She started to have a social life with her lady friends. Some friends had confided in her that they weren't comfortable being around her when she was with Dad, but were so happy to see her now. Once comfortable with a new life and new friends, she really started to enjoy life. She played cards twice a week. She started to take train and bus trips with her friends to Reno, where they would gamble and dine and have wonderful times.

Ann and I took Mom with us wherever we went on vacation with our kids. In this way, Mom could vacation with us without expense and babysit for us so we could have some alone time. It was wonderful. Ann loved my mom and vice versa.

Mom didn't have any income aside from Social Security and spousal support from my dad. Unfortunately, Dad was not consistent or timely with his payments. When Dad skipped a payment, Mom could not make ends meet. It would bother me that he would be seen out to lunch paying for his friends, yet not paying his court-ordered spousal support.

I needed to help Mom. I worked a deal with attorney Joe Peatman, who loved Mom because she was like a family member to the Peatmans. She cared for the Peatman children for years. The deal was that I would do all the legal work for my mom's divorce case and Joe would sign the letters and represent Mom in court. Usually, Dad would pay up, but it would take a threatening letter or two to get the payment, and sometimes months would go by. I was always glad I could help Mom because she had always given me so much.

Because Mom needed more money but wouldn't take charity, I asked my law partners, Joe Flax and Pat McGrath, if they would let her clean the office twice a month. Mom was unskilled but she was a wonderful housekeeper. Not only did Joe and Pat agree, they consented to pay her a top wage for her cleaning services. I am forever grateful that Joe and Pat allowed Mom to save her pride. They never had any complaints when Mom did the cleaning. It was spotless.

Her last years were spent the way she wanted them to be spent: with her family, grandchildren, and friends.

She died in 1984, far too young, at the age of seventy-two.

Mom was a wonderful role model with a kind, generous and loving heart. I still miss her.

My father was a different story completely. He was a problem and burden to me until the day he died. Watching him dish out his verbal and emotional abuse to Mom and my brother was awful. Till the day he died, he continued calling Eugene a "stupid idiot" so often that it might as well have been his name. Mom was so beaten down she developed bouts of hives that her doctor said came from stress.

He abused public servants as well. He once caught a burglar in his wrecking yard and fired his pistol in the air to ensure the burglar stopped in his tracks. Then Dad held the crook at gunpoint and called the police. The burglar was arrested, but the verbal abuse Dad dished out to the arresting officers for not promptly responding, resulted in Dad being charged with unlawfully discharging a firearm in the city limits.

Guess who had to handle that case? I set it for a jury trial, figuring a jury would be sympathetic to a citizen who catches a thief and then is, himself, arrested. I knew I could never put Dad on the witness stand or he would be convicted of the charged crime based on his "charming testimony." After setting it for trial, the District Attorney ultimately dismissed the case. They were obligated to release his gun to him but I asked them to keep it during the appeal period. I didn't want Dad to get it back. He then accused me of being a poor lawyer because he won his case, but couldn't get his gun back.

He abused us financially. Without explanation, he once ordered my brother and me to come to his bank at 10:00 AM the next day. When we got there he informed us that he wanted us to co-sign for a loan for him. He would take all the proceeds and we would be responsible for the loan payments. I actually think my brother would have signed without my presence. I told Dad that I wouldn't do that because Mom had told me on her deathbed not to give him the property that she was giving us. That property was what the loan would be based upon. Mom must have anticipated such a thing, because it came true.

My dad working on a transmission at his wrecking yard.

Once Dad was turned down, he started yelling inside the bank. For about one year he didn't talk to my brother or me. I would hear from friends of mine around town about how he was badmouthing us. Steve Ceriani came up to me on the street and said, "What did you do to your father? He says you are an ungrateful son after all the things he did for you."

He even abused government inspectors. I was at the wrecking yard while the Environmental Protection Agency was serving a search warrant on Dad to see what toxic violations he may have committed. There was a white man, an Asian man, and a woman. They were dressed in what looked like outer-space suits and were looking into his metal drum barrels. Dad had them labeled in chalk as to what each barrel contained. One barrel had motor oil, one had gasoline, and one had transmission fluid. These barrels were not properly labeled. There were paper labels from the EPA that were to supposed to be used and affixed to each barrel. Not properly labeling the barrels was subject to stiff fines by the EPA.

The poor Asian man (who we later found out was on his first inspection) was so nervous he would laugh every time Dad would yell (which was every time Dad opened his mouth). Dad was under stress with the government there, and became infuriated by the man's laughter. The woman then became assertive with instructions to Dad.

"I ought to get my gun," Dad responded. Of course, he couldn't get his gun because it was still tied up in the legal system because of his previous court case. This understandably upset the woman, who later reported to the District Attorney that Dad had threatened her life and asked that a criminal complaint be filed against him for his assaultive behavior and death threat.

I knew Dad was just nervous, and I really thought the lady was overreacting. He had no gun. He didn't say he was going to shoot her ("I ought to get my gun"); she should have understood that she was dealing with a hot-tempered person about shutting down the business he had built and worked at for most of his adult life. Nevertheless, I dealt with the subsequent letter from the District Attorney's office. No charges were ever filed after sitting down with the District Attorney and reviewing what really happened. Dad did have some sympathetic facts going for him, if he would only keep his mouth shut.

He was frequently embarrassing. Once, in a bank parking lot when we both arrived at the same time, he saw my family and me exiting our vehicle, and from across the parking lot he shouted, "Hey tubby!" I think he thought he was being funny, but I failed to see the humor. Once he came to my office on my birthday and put an envelope on my desk. I said, "Well, you did remember my birthday after all!" He didn't. The envelope was just another legal problem that he had brought for me to solve.

The most disappointing thing to me was that he paid no attention to my two beautiful daughters. He didn't even know my kids' names. He called my eldest daughter, Julia, "Juliann." He called my younger daughter, Angela, "the other one."

There are many things to be angry about regarding my father. However, even though he never told me he loved me, I knew he did. He had a horrible childhood, and while that doesn't excuse everything, it does explain a lot. I would run into people around town who would tell me how he bragged about me or told them how proud he was of me. The best example of how I knew Dad was proud of me and loved me came in a most strange way.

In the mid '70s, a young police officer who knew my father from dealings with him at the wrecking yard came to my law office on Brown Street. In full uniform he asked my secretary if he could see me. When she asked what it was regarding he said it was personal. I came out to the lobby.

"I am Officer Dave Chambliss of the Napa Police Department. Are you Ray Guadagni?"

I was a little nervous even though I knew I had not broken any laws. "Yes, that's me, Officer, what can I do for you?"

"Nothing, really, I just wanted to meet you and shake your hand." With that he put out his hand and I shook it, not knowing why we were shaking hands.

He explained that for the last year his beat included the area where Dad's wrecking yard was located on McKinstry Street. He would talk to my dad from time to time about Dad's pet peeves or complaints. Dad would also tell him how bad our town was being run, but that things would change soon. Dad explained that his son, Raymond, was an attorney and was moving back to town to practice law.

"When my son gets here he is gonna clean up this town," Dad bragged. "You wait and see. He will make changes and clean up the graft and corruption we got here!"

Dave told me that he just had to meet the person who was going to clean up Napa. We both laughed.

"I hope you know, your dad is very proud of you," he said.

I was in a bit of shock. It made me feel good to hear such a compliment but it was surprising to hear that my dad said those things, which were certainly never said in my presence.

I always tried to keep the officer's comments in mind when Dad would invariably say something hurtful. He had a tough life, and he did his best to survive, without any real guidance or education. Although I can't excuse his bad behavior, I know he loved me.

He attended my judicial swearing-in ceremony in January 2001, and when I introduced him, I looked out into the audience and there he was, wiping tears from his eyes with his handkerchief and waving to me. When I talked to him later about coming to the after-party he said he wanted to rest but that the ceremony was great! There was no doubt he was happy and proud. Later that year he passed away, on August 30, 2001 at the age of eighty-four.

Dad was difficult to deal with throughout my entire life. However, in the years after he passed I have come to understand that he was a product of his own dysfunctional upbringing. That understanding has allowed me to replace some of my anger toward him with compassion.

I still see my friends. My law partners, Joe Flax and Pat McGrath, are both retired and still live in Napa. We get together often for lunch and shooting the breeze. A lot of laughing goes on at those lunches. I love those guys.

Three or four times a year, a breakfast gathering is held for all of the guys from the class of 1964. Those meetings are great opportunities for us to see each other and talk about the old times as well as our current situations (which usually includes the scintillating subject of our present ailments and our multitude of medications). The attendance varies but we usually have twelve to twenty-five guys at every gathering and we all have a lot of fun.

My buddies, Mike Kerns, Wayne Davidson, Frank Davidson, Fred Teeters, Mike Crane, and Steve Ceriani are friends that I stay in close touch with throughout the year. We get together from time to time and the laughter with, and at, each other continues and always will.

My best friend from kindergarten to this very day, Paul Vallerga, always stays in touch with me. He visits from Bend, Oregon several times a year, and I visit him there as well. At times we travel to far off places and have great adventures, but most of the time we have as much fun just watching old movies and sharing our stories. Our friendship has never wavered through sixty-five years.

I also get together with my Italian neighborhood girls on a yearly basis. That loving group is where it all started for me and I do not intend to ever lose contact with them. The roots of our friendship are deep. We are closely connected because of our shared experiences.

Me with my best friend Paul in Venice, Italy.

As for me, I remain in the town of Napa and am very happy to be here. I have the strongest of attachments to this community. My roots remain here. I am fortunate to live here with my wonderful wife, Ann. My two adult daughters, Julia and Angela, live here with their families and I get together with them on a regular, almost daily, basis. This means, of course, that Ann and I see our grandchildren almost daily and have the honor of regularly babysitting our young grandchildren.

Those grandchildren, Joey, Bella, Florentina, and Elianna, have been the most joyous, meaningful and loving experience of my retired life. Getting to see them grow up and being able to be at their games, dances, performances and recitals leaves me grateful beyond words. Knowing my grandchildren are being raised in this still nurturing and kind community gives me more comfort than I could hope for.

One of my beautiful granddaughters, Florentina.

I miss the simple times. As a kid I thought that way of life would last forever.

I miss those times where I knew the kids and their parents on a more intimate basis, when play dates didn't have to be formally arranged. I miss being able to stay out in the summer evenings until dark and all day on the weekends. It was safe and fun. Our houses and cars were left unlocked, and nothing bad happened. What a wonderful and exciting time for kids. I wish it could be that way for kids today but, of course, it cannot. The world has changed and life, as it must, has moved on.

Ray and Ann
My lovely wife Ann and me in Florence, Italy.

Bibliography

Chapter 7 (The Dreaded Virus)
http://www.cdc.gov/vaccines/vpd-vac/polio/dis-faqs.htm
http://poliovaccine.umwblogs.org/impact/
http://poliovaccine.umwblogs.org/impact/

Chapter 8 (The Best Invention of All Time)
http://www.earlytelevision.org/american_postwar.html

Chapter 9 (Bombs Away)
http://www.atomicarchive.com/History/coldwar/page04.s
    html
http://www.atomicarchive.com/History/coldwar/page06.s
    html
http://www.atomicarchive.com/History/coldwar/page08.s
    html
http://undergroundbombshelter.com/news/when-bomb-
    shelters-were-the-rage.htm
https://en.wikipedia.org/wiki/History_of_nuclear_weapons
    #Cuban_Missile_Crisis

Chapter 15 (Free Spirits and Crispy Critters)
http://psychcentral.com/blog/archives/2011/07/02/how-
    the-dsm-developed-what-you-might-not-know/

Chapter 16 (Napa's Color)

http://national.deseretnews.com/article/5361/how-
government-policy-created-ghettos-according-to-one-
historian.html

"Prohibition in the Napa Valley," Pages 108-109, Lin Weber

"Roots of the Present: Napa Valley 1900-1950," Pages 250-
252, Lin Weber.

CPSIA information can be obtained
at www.ICGtesting.com
Printed in the USA
FSOW02n0459031216
28029FS